Rev. David Burke, S.J.

THE CARDINAL'S STORY

THE MACMILLAN COMPANY
NEW YORK · BOSTON · CHICAGO · DALLAS
ATLANTA · SAN FRANCISCO

MACMILLAN AND CO., Limited
LONDON · BOMBAY · CALCUTTA · MADRAS
MELBOURNE

THE MACMILLAN COMPANY
OF CANADA, Limited
TORONTO

THE
CARDINAL'S STORY

✠

THE LIFE AND WORK
of
JOSEPH, CARDINAL MINDSZENTY
Archbishop of Esztergom
Primate of Hungary

✠

By STEPHEN K. SWIFT

NEW YORK

THE MACMILLAN COMPANY

1950

TO

ALL CHILDREN OF GOD

IN EVERY LAND

WHO HAVE SUFFERED

FOR THEIR FAITH

THESE PAGES ARE DEDICATED

FOREWORD

THE CARDINAL'S STORY was never intended as a conventional biography. It grew from a conference in Washington, on November 16, 1948, when information had become available indicating that the plans of the Communist regime in Hungary to "liquidate the Mindszenty problem" were moving toward the challenging climax: the Cardinal's elimination had become a matter of weeks, perhaps days. This gave me the first impetus to publish a record of his historic efforts in resisting the forces that threaten to engulf our civilization.

In appraising the Cardinal one must keep in mind that he had conducted his office as primate since June, 1947, when the Communists seized the power in Hungary, during one of the most difficult periods in the history of the Hungarian people, confronted by a government exercising coercion, intimidation, and force. While in the face of Communist terror voices grew fainter and fewer his incessant vigilance against all encroachments on the freedom of man forced him to the forefront of the battle between two opposing world orders. To some it may have seemed at first that his undertakings were simply phases of the world-wide struggle between Church and Antichrist; but soon it became apparent that the Cardinal was engaged in a dynamic pursuit of the right of man to his own freedom, to his own soul and creed, and that of his fellow man.

At an early time the Cardinal had recognized the real goals of the Communists, who, while groveling in villainy, aimed not only at political control but at power over the souls of the people. Measuring his time with the measure of history, the Cardinal rose to the challenge. Men are few who fought so courageously against Communist power, gave such vigorous expression to the concept of the freedom of the soul, pleaded so eloquently the cause of Christian civilization. His proud courage commanded the respect even of political and religious leaders who, at times, objected to his policy of determined resistance and, in the face of the stunning shocks of Moscow's betrayals, advised calm and deliberation as the more practical policy. Historians of coming generations may be able to determine the wisdom of the course.

While I made arrangements to receive from Hungary the original records and documents, subsequent events altered the original concept. The day after Christmas the Cardinal had been carried off; at his trial, forty-six days later, he was sentenced to spend the rest of his days in a penitentiary. To all familiar with Communist justice the outcome of the trial was a foregone conclusion; still, observers who had known him well were shocked by his demeanor. The once commanding personality, revered for his courage and outspokenness as an unyielding opponent to all that this court represented, appeared as a pathetic figure. The entire civilized world was amazed by the Cardinal's transformation; still, it was by no means without parallel in Soviet annals. Ever since the first purge trials in Moscow, in 1936, it has been my ambition to discover the methods of inverting man's spiritual personality while his outward appearance remains practically unchanged. Discrepancies in certain details of the Moscow trials gave some slight clues; reports of men who had been imprisoned by the Communists supplied additional details, but not the answer to the quest.

Before the Cardinal's trial efforts were made to enlist the services of trustworthy individuals in Hungary who had contacts by which they might secure the authentic transcript of the trial proceedings; the efforts bore ripe fruit, in that, by coincidence, the facts concerning the Cardinal's treatment in prison came to light. The report on the meetings of the "planning group" originated from a person close to a Communist minister—the very person who originally had sent abroad the word of the impending dangers to the Cardinal.

Shortly after the trial I left for Europe to collect the documentary material and the testimony of the eyewitnesses, on which these pages are based. Twenty-nine days of exhaustive investigations and interrogations ensued, and no effort was spared in scrutinizing the reports and in securing corroboration of the facts. Trustworthy persons who had fled Hungary have substantiated these accounts, and there is no reason to doubt their fidelity and sincerity.

Thus events themselves outlined the structure of this volume, which is divided into three books. "In the Footsteps of Saints" embraces the Cardinal's life from his youth till the hour he lost his freedom; here I have attempted to present clearly the rise of the humble priest Joseph to the primacy, the historical background of his time and of the people from whose midst he came. While I do not pretend to have presented every single phase of the Cardinal's life, I am convinced that no events or developments that were vitally influential in the forming of his character and convictions have been omitted. Conscious of the fact that no biography of a dramatic figure like Cardinal Mindszenty can hope to command universal assent, I nevertheless hope that it will bring its message to all men, regardless of their degree of sympathy with the Cardinal's point of view.

"The Martyrdom of a Soul" presents the Cardinal's experience in the hands of the Communist police; it contains the reports on how his elimination was planned, and the transcript of his trial. In the latter every word uttered by the Cardinal or addressed to him is reproduced; for the sake of brevity the trial of his codefendants is touched only, having had little or no bearing on his case.

The documentary material, originally in Hungarian, reached the overwhelming total of 740,000 words. Limits of space have made it necessary to choose what should be considered as of primary importance. The reader will find the Cardinal's papers divided into two groups. Embodied in his biography are all excerpts which constituted an integral part of his own personal history; grouped independently, in "No Fear but Courage," are certain papers which complete the portrayal of the shepherd and furnish the background for the developments that led to his deep tragedy.

Throughout the volume I have attempted to let the facts speak for themselves, as all who speak in these pages are living persons. Wherever I could dispense with my own conclusion, or commentary,

I have done so, letting the reader form his own judgment from the facts themselves.

For whatever virtues these pages possess, I feel privileged to share the credit, assuming the blame for any faults. I am indebted in particular to the dignitaries of the Roman Catholic Church in Europe for having enabled me to examine original documents and to gain access to the papers of Cardinal Mindszenty. Their comment and advice have been of great value.

Gratitude also is due to those Hungarian political exiles through whose cooperation I secured authentication of the reports received. The personal and political sidelights thrown upon the Cardinal by members of the Hungarian National Council, who had been in close contact with him, were of invaluable assistance.

I am profoundly grateful to the Archbishop of New York, Cardinal Spellman, for having graciously released his sermon "Rebellion to Tyrants Is Obedience to God" for this book.

I also wish to express my appreciation to the Command of the United States Forces in Austria for facilities granted, and to the Command of the British Occupation Forces and the Staff of the French High Commissioner in Austria for courtesies extended, making it possible for me to conduct on-the-spot investigations and to gather material for these pages. Finally I must acknowledge the kindness of the delegations of the United States and the United Kingdom to the United Nations in furnishing the documents contained in Appendix I.

That these pages may serve in some measure the cause of a civilized world, praying for the liberation of all mankind from the dark forces of tyranny, is my sincere wish.

STEPHEN K. SWIFT

NEW YORK CITY, September, 1949

CONTENTS

"REBELLION TO TYRANTS
IS OBEDIENCE TO GOD" *

By FRANCIS, CARDINAL SPELLMAN
Archbishop of New York

"A new god has come to you, my people. His fiery eyes do not flash through clouds of incense or from altar candles. They do not gleam from gold-framed darkened pictures of saints. This new god is not a stone statue worn smooth by the kisses of the faithful . . . he was not born in heaven. He is not far away, nor is he hidden from us. The new god is born from earth and blood. . . . He strides ahead and under the thunder of his steps the globe trembles from East to West. . . . This is the red god. The Seine shudders at his impact and tries to break its banks. Westminster trembles before him like Jericho, and across the green ocean his red shadow falls on the walls of the White House. Hosanna! New god."

My dear friends, you know these words are not mine! They are the words of an Hungarian Communist, words that echo the thoughts of men depraved and deranged—men who do not know Truth, Love, Justice or Faith—men who, as their gods, know only Satan and Stalin! Yes, these lines come from the pen of a Satan-bred man and are taught to the youth of red-enshackled lands—lands where everybody is afraid of everybody else, where even a son fears his father and fathers fear their own blood-sons, as all become serfs and victims of the relentless God of Baal!

Yes, the blasphemous lines I have just quoted to you are wild words, but they are wild words of warning and, unless we listen well and realize that we must counteract them by concerted prayer and action—then these words but foretell America's and the whole world's doom.

* A sermon of February 6, 1949, at St. Patrick's Cathedral.

May 8, 1945—VE Day! On that day I delivered from this pulpit my Prayer of Thanksgiving for the victory of the hour, begging peace with justice, beseeching that as victors we do not offend God by sinning against His Mercy. The peace that came was not God's peace, and because in the ensuing post-war years men's hearts have not been won back to God, I must this day as a protest against the crucifixion of humanity entreat your prayers for persecuted, tortured, victimized Cardinal Mindszenty.

This is Cardinal Mindszenty Day—a day of prayer and of protest! Prayer for what? Protest against what? There is no use to try to save Cardinal Mindszenty's life, for from the very hour he was taken away in the black of night from his home, his flock, his aged mother, Cardinal Mindszenty became the victim of torturings and druggings that put him beyond the reach of realm of human help! It was he himself who said to me when he was my honored guest less than two years ago—"My enemies can take from me no more than my life and that has already been given to God." No, the physical Cardinal Mindszenty can no longer be saved. It is the spiritual Cardinal Mindszenty in his martyrdom of mind and body that we can fortify by our prayers, that in his soul he may know that in another part of the world other men are holding high God's torch of justice for Hungary's anguished peoples and the enslaved peoples of every land. And in our dear land each free man and woman must protect and fight to keep his own integrity of conscience, his own God-given freedoms—and exert every effort to save America and the rest of the democratic, God-loving world from trickery, torturings, disaster and defeat. For if we fail to learn a lesson from Cardinal Mindszenty's martyrdom, we shall fail ourselves and ourselves face Communist conquest and annihilation!

When first Cardinal Mindszenty answered the call of Christ, "Come, Follow Me," to that day when, only two years ago with 30 other priests and myself, he was received into the Sacred College of Cardinals, he has lived a life full and priestly. Then we rededicated our hearts, our souls, our lives to God, the propagation of our Faith and the perpetuation of Christ's Church.

And only three days ago Cardinal Mindszenty—priest of a people

who love, honor, trust and revere him, was brought to mock-trial
for his life, even though his life had already been signed away by
the Lords of Communism—men among whom there is no honor,
love or trust, either for one another, for their neighbor or their
God. Thus has the symbolic red of his Cardinal's robes literally
become the blood red of martyrdom!

Had I a hundred tongues, a hundred mouths, a voice of iron, I
could not compass all the crimes of the "men of sin" as they wage
war against the "Man of Sorrow"; neither can I recount the miseries
perpetrated by these slave-men, crimes which it is neither in my
personal power to relieve or prevent. Nevertheless—so long as my
heart beats and breath lingers in my body, I shall never cease to
pray and labor to protect America, and warn and work against
Communism and all the evils growing from out its rotted roots, for
I believe that "Rebellion to Tyrants Is Obedience to God."

While a whole world waged war and tragically talked of peace,
I witnessed the suffering of men in a world trapped by fear, famine
and madness called COMMUNISM. It was then that I resolved to
try to pour into the minds of every American a sense of great gratitude to God for our freedom, our liberties, our opportunities, and
instill within those minds the realization of the imminent dangers
of atheistic communism to America. And I avow that unless the
whole American people, without further ostrichlike actions and pre-
tenses unite to stop the Communist floodings of our own land, our
sons, for the third and last time, shall be summoned from the comforts, tranquillity and love of their own homes and families to bear
arms against those who would desecrate and destroy them. Yea, it
is full time that a strong and vigilant America unite in prayer and
protest against wasting the youth of her own nation, and try to help
save civilization from the world's most fiendish, ghoulish men of
slaughter, lest the anguished spending of a million lives will end
again in war's beginning!

Therefore I beg you, my beloved people, let us not confuse prudence with lack of vision, unity, courage and strength as we watch
nation after nation fall victim to Communism, for prudence is often
but an excuse for silence, procrastination and compromise. Even

today as we read newspaper releases from the Communist-controlled press of Budapest that tell us contradictory stories about a Cardinal-priest who, so little time ago, we took unto our own hearts and homes, millions of Americans refuse to recognize that we ourselves are faced with these same merciless dangers!

You have all seen pictures of Cardinal Mindszenty in the newspapers at his mock-trial in his own country. And all of you saw pictures of Cardinal Mindszenty when, a free man, he sat kindly, willingly for his picture in America. Can you fail to see here a man tortured and drugged—even though the Communist press dares to print that he "denies duress"? The Communists believe the American public is still easy to fool, willing to be "drugged" into believing whatever leaves them their own comforts, their own freedoms.

But are we, the American people, the tools and the fools for which the Communists take us? Are we always to endure the insults and wounds they inflict upon our American honor and decency as they enslave countries and persecute peoples, as they inflict wounds and beatings upon decent, God-loving men and patriots like Cardinal Mindszenty? For when the Cardinal confessed to treason against the present Communist government in Hungary he but professed his loyalty to his country. If this be treason—to deny allegiance to an atheistic Communist government, then thank God Cardinal Mindszenty confessed to treason—as would I, if this free land of America were ever conquered by the demoniac people now using every foul means to overthrow our republic.

How long are we, free-minded, fair-minded, freedom-loving Americans, going to allow these same fiendish Communists to drug us with their propaganda and our own apathy? When will the American government, the American public, the leaders in all phases of American life, religious, educational, political, labor, industrial, communications, yes and in entertainment, when will all free men raise their voices as one and cry out against and work against Satan-inspired Communist crimes? How long—O my God—shall we stand by and see Thy peoples who love Thee reviled, persecuted, and murdered by atheistic Communists who deny Thee and hate Thee even as again and again they crucify Thee upon Thy Cross! Cardinal

Mindszenty's jailers gave him drugs—perhaps without his knowledge. They did not want another hero like Archbishop Stepinac. No, not another martyr would they have in Cardinal Mindszenty. They would break his will and show him to his people broken, weak and faithless. That is why they took Cardinal Mindszenty away in the night because the first time he was arrested by the Nazis, he walked through the streets with his captors, daring to bless his people with the Sign of the Cross as they lined the streets to pray for him and beg his prayers for themselves who would, they knew, also be persecuted, abused and slain.

Yet we should not grieve at the death of Cardinal Mindszenty, for man is not completely born until he dies to live in God. No, let us not be sorrowful nor tearful for him—but rather for one whom I pray God to take unto Himself ere her heart be more deeply pierced by anguish for her saintly son. I speak of Cardinal Mindszenty's 85-year-old mother! Like unto Mary, Our own Blessed Mother, who was witness to the passion of her only Son, this mother's cross is far heavier than her son's. I pray that God shall raise this gentle mother into the arms of His own Mother Mary, there to be pressed close to the Sacred Heart of Christ, her Son—there, at last, to find peace!

In closing my plea for your prayers and protests on behalf of Cardinal Mindszenty, let me tell you a story that will, I believe, touch your hearts just as it touched a spark within my own when first I heard it. It is a story that I heard told by an American of another faith, a Jewish gentleman whose parents emigrated from a country which was then, as now it is again, held in bondage.

"My parents came to these shores about 70 years ago," this gentleman said. "They left behind them an old world filled with bitter hatreds and ruled by despotism. Here they found a new world filled with wondrous things—freedom, justice, opportunity, kindliness. Not things you could touch or eat, but—when you've never had them before—things that are more real than a pair of shoes or even a loaf of bread. As long as they lived they never stopped wondering at the glory of America. They were two of the best Americans I've ever known.

"Seventy years ago, they came here with nothing but the clothes on their backs and great courage. Today their boy," this gentleman continued, "is speaking before a gathering of the leaders of America. In one generation our family moved from steerage to distinction. That's not one man's story," he added, "it is the American story. Multiply it a million times or more for every race, creed and color and you begin to sense the miracle of America!"

And this, my friends, is the America I beg Americans to save!

THE CARDINAL'S STORY

Let us have the faith that right makes might, and in that faith let us to the end dare to do our duty as we understand it.

—ABRAHAM LINCOLN

BOOK I

✠

IN THE FOOTSTEPS OF SAINTS

In the shadow of the ancient walls of the Mönchsberg, surrounded by the towering summits of the Austrian Alps, two women kneel in front of a tiny homemade altar, in a small shack that has served as their refuge. Forgotten is the outside world, forgotten the storms of the years past; they are clasping their rosaries, deeply immersed in prayers; only an occasional murmur breaks the devotional silence.

Mother and daughter are kneeling before the picture of Mary ever Virgin, saying the same prayers—if in different words.

A simple postcard adorns the place next to the Virgin Mother, the benevolent face of a man: Joseph, Cardinal Mindszenty, Archbishop of Esztergom, Prince Primate of the Hungarian lands.

Both women found refuge here for their tormented souls and bodies, refuge from the everlasting adversities of a world in flame, of a humanity gone berserk. Life has cut deep furrows in the face of Christine, the mother; a life that began with so much promise and sunshine in a little village nestled safely in the rolling hills of the county of Vas.

Erdöd was her birthplace. Yes, Erdöd, a little village with only one dusty road, the peasants living in the mud-built houses flanking both sides of it. The acacias planted along the roadside provided a narrow pathway for pedestrians.

The road itself, ancient like everything around Erdöd, had once had cobblestones which had disappeared from sight. When it rained, the road became a quagmire through which the horses' hoofs and the wheels of the peasant carts cut deep furrows that vanished as they passed. Many a Sunday, Christine sat by the small single win-

[1]

dow. Here she watched the world pass by, because when it rained there was nowhere to go by foot.

The road brought the good things of the world to the village, as well as the bad. When the weather was dry and nature was pleasing, Christine's father and brothers came home along this road from the fields.

At sundown, when the bells rang, a huge cloud of dust approaching along the road indicated that the cattle were returning home. Or perhaps it was the flock of pigs driven by the village swineherd. No one had to call the animals or guide them, for as they neared their home grounds they veered off in the right direction; all that had to be done was to close the gate after them.

Then the women went to fill the feeding troughs and milk the cows. By the time the menfolk returned from their arduous work in the fields, the savory odors of the day's hot meal filled the house and small yard, greeting the tired laborers.

This was the road where, every morning at seven and every evening at seven, two gendarmes marched, once up and once down the road, stepping in unison, in full service dress with bayonets drawn atop their carbines and their cock feathers flying from their leather helmets. This daily walk was a constant reminder of the authority of the state. Only on rare occasions did the gendarmes escort anyone; then it was a terrifying sight, for the prisoner's hands were tied or shackled as he marched between them, head hanging and eyes fixed in shame upon the ground.

There was one place in the village where the road widened. Some called it the village square. Here stood the Catholic church, with its tall spire. Seven wide stone steps led up to its door and its rows of benches, which had been hewn by the villagers from the adjacent great oak forest.

The church had three stained-glass windows which the lord of the near-by manor had given in memory of his mother. The beautiful, but simple, altar had stood there for time immemorial; it must have come to the village when the saints were still living.

Next to the church lived the priest, all by himself, a kindly old man who had served his flock well. They told stories about him, how strong he had been in his youth. Once when the high-piled hay-cart of Uncle Timothy was caught in a shower and slid through the mud into the ditch that served as a gutter, the young priest had crawled under the axle and lifted the cart high into the air with his shoulders. Now the children who were taught in the one-room schoolhouse, that stood next to his home, were his main interest and the principal recipients of his loving care.

The youth of the village were taught the three R's by a young schoolteacher. There were so many young schoolteachers within a generation that they were hard to count. All of them were young when they came and young when they left. They were very studious and were seldom seen anywhere but in school and at church, when they assisted the priest at Mass, or at one of the processions.

Hardly a stone's throw away, farther up the road and next to the house of the notary—the only "public official" in the village—stood the Presbyterian church. The preacher and his wife were kindly people, but very poor. It seemed as though they had more children than anybody else. At one time some cynic had called them the or-gan-pipe family because the oldest boy was taller than his father and the youngest child could hardly stand. They were a hard-working couple, and even though the preacher tilled his three acres of land with his own hands, it hardly fed the family. How could it? For at one time there were eleven mouths to feed.

The preacher's wife worked a small garden in the back yard. Here she grew many flowers and some of the vegetables for the table. She also tended a flock of chickens and geese which wandered all over the neighborhood. Nobody minded, and if any kindly neighbor noticed her "poultry" a few handfuls of corn were always spread before them. "If they have wandered away from home, they must be hungry," was the saying.

The preacher was a learned man. Frequently the villagers could see him and the old priest wandering off together, on a Saturday afternoon, to the meadows, discussing the affairs and the fate of the villagers or, possibly, of the world.

The old priest had the wisdom of the ages, the younger preacher the enthusiastic eagerness of youth. This is the way they impressed the village council, where they sat with the elders, the notary, and the storekeeper to decide questions essential to the life of all the villagers.

The storekeeper was a quiet man. He was almost as poor as the rest of the peasants, yet he was the village banker. He furnished the scanty supplies needed by the peasants: nails, salt, cloth, scythes, and rock candy, and the other few things the peasant is not self-sufficient in, all on credit. Everyone always paid him, but not until harvest time, when the produce put hard money in the pockets of the villagers. If some extraordinary emergency compelled a member of a family to travel by railroad to the city, or even to the Capital, and he lacked the train fare, the storekeeper loaned the money for the trip too. The railroad station was some six miles away; if the horses of the villagers were busy plowing the traveler had to walk all the way to meet the iron horse. If one did not have a team and someone was sick and had to be taken to the hospital located at the county seat, a neighbor's pair of horses was always there to make the journey, for there was no physician in any of the near-by villages.

The priest, the preacher, and the midwife together combined the attributes of the doctor in the village. The wisdom of the elders had cured many an ailing person. They knew which roots, leaves, and bark had curative effects; how to brew and mix them, how to administer them; their mothers had done it and their grandmothers before that. The natural art of caring for the sick had come down through the ages.

The priest and the preacher visited the sick and acted as the family physician for mind and soul. On rare occasions, such as the time when young Luke stepped onto a scythe, gashing his foot, the preacher performed minor surgery while the priest assisted by quieting the patient. For many years treatment consisted of fresh water, a little home-distilled spirits sprinkled over a wound, and a torn pillowcase or a part of a sheet serving as a bandage.

The midwife was called when the hour arrived for a child to be born. The neighbors, mostly the grandmothers, gathered at the home of the mother-to-be and held extended discussions with the midwife about the best way the newcomer could be helped into the world. If the mother had many hours of labor and pain overshadowed the joy, the priest or preacher was called. He would hold the mother's hand, wipe the sweat from her brow, and speak words soothing to both the ear and the mind.

It was difficult for some of the families to raise their children. A new child kept the mother away from the fields for days and even made it hard for her to do the work at home. Still, all of them gave birth joyfully. Even when Esther died in childbirth, her last rational words were: "The Lord hath said: Suffer children to come to me, for·of such is the kingdom of God."

There were two cemeteries. One was quite a distance up the road, on a hill. A narrow path, cut through the bushes and just wide enough for a cart, led to it. The setting was beautiful. One could see far across the plains, over the thatched roofs of the village, across the meadows and the winding brook. On an exceptionally clear day the chimneys of the next hamlet, nestled below another hill, could be seen. On that far-away mound stood a lord's manor in all its splendor.

Sitting under huge trees that enshrined the cemetery was the favorite pastime of the young people in spring. Here they could talk undisturbed, learn one another's thoughts, and dream of their future lives, forgetting that tradition determined the course of their lives. Here, on a Sunday afternoon in spring, after the day's chores had been done, boy and girl would walk among the tombstones, speaking of the beauty of nature. As they passed from grave to grave, they avoided the one thought which imbued both of them and which they were too bashful to express.

Here some of the youngsters, instead of going home after school, played hide-and-seek. One day the preacher, coming to tend some of the graves, found several of the culprits and after a stern lecture led the boys to his friend, the old parish priest, for additional ad-monitions.

The Catholic cemetery was directly behind the churchyard; it had a fence and a gate with a lock. No boy ever dared enter it, for the old priest could look out from his home and see the grounds. It was much larger than the Protestant cemetery because there had always been more Catholics, and many of the villagers who went away returned home to rest.

Some of the girls went to the cities, but only to serve in the households of gentlefolk for a time; then they returned to marry. The young men who left for military service or to earn their living as hired help on some aristocratic estate also came back to the home of their fathers to continue to till the soil sanctified by ancestral sweat.

Peace reigned not only in and between the two cemeteries but in the religious life of the villagers. The Catholics and the Presbyterians respected one another's creed as the priest and the preacher respected each other's garb. The merchant's family was the only one which did not belong to one of the churches. They were Jews, and everyone respected them, too, and their belief.

Once a year, during the high Jewish holidays, the family who currently owned the best cart in the village harnessed their best pair of horses and drove Samuel and the members of his family to the city so that they could worship in the synagogue. It was a reciprocal gesture, because Samuel and his father and his grandfather had always taken a lively interest in the affairs of both village churches. While Samuel and his family never attended any church services, they lived and acted as an integral part of the religious life of the community.

When winter came to the village, life froze and work became harder. Most of the men went to the forest to cut trees, to haul wood by sled, or repair plows and carts and the other tools of their livelihood. When the time was ripe and the river, which was a half-day's drive away, frozen fast, they drove down with their sleds, cut the ice, and brought home the big slabs to be buried in an ice pit in order to keep the meat fresh and the wine cold during the burning days of the summer. When the snow was hard and the time right, the pigs were slaughtered, an event that kept the whole family busy for days, helping with the many chores.

But winter had many hardships. The days were short and much kerosene had to be burned in the early evening hours. Occasionally, when it became very cold and the wind blew sharply, some of the people, craving warmth, went to the small stables to sleep, for the hay was soft and the animals radiated heat.

Erdöd was more or less like any other village, near or far. The people and their life were no different than the people and the life in thousands of villages in Hungary. The main difference might have been that in some villages the peasants were richer and had more land; in others, they might have been poorer, with little or no land to their names, working as hired help on the estates of the land-owners; but life, as if predestined, was the same everywhere.

Life in Hungary was sedate. A people much tried throughout its history was enjoying the fruits of an era of long peace. There had been no real war since 1849, when Louis Kossuth led the nation to fight for liberty; and some of the older people were hailing the reign of "our old lord" Francis Joseph I, Apostolic King of Hungary and Emperor of Austria, as a reign of peace.

The face and the life of the village changed abruptly, Christine recalled. It was a sunny afternoon in the summer of 1914 when the village drummer marched along the dusty road, drumming to his heart's content. That was not unusual, because matters of importance to the villagers had always been announced that way; but this time the drummer was followed by two soldiers in uniform, as well as by the notary himself. All who were at home followed to the no-tary's house. There the drummer stopped and read a long, very long proclamation that no one could really understand, except that it was a message from His Majesty the King. Then the soldiers posted two placards, and within a few minutes the great bells of the church be-gan to ring. They brought a message to the people far and wide, a message everyone knew by nightfall:

"War has broken out! The king commands you to join the colors!"

All men of military age left hurriedly. In the village only the women and the children, the aged and the infirm, remained. The weeks and months of aching hearts, the time of tears had started.

Christine's two brothers had left with the others, singing and marching in a group down the road. They carried a side of bacon, a loaf of bread, and a bottle of wine tied in a kerchief which swung at the end of a rough walking stick across their shoulders. The red, white, and green ribbons—the Hungarian colors—were fastened to their Sunday hats and were blowing in the wind.

Andrew, the younger brother, never came back, and his young body rests forever on one of the bleak mountainsides of Serbia; but Mark returned.

It was summer when they brought Mark home. As usual just before sundown, the womenfolk of the village were out of doors, near the roadside, attending to all kinds of unnecessary chores. None readily admitted it, but they were there to watch for someone coming up the road. They pruned the little trees, or washed the windows, or swept the ever dusty hard-mud sidewalk, just to be there if "he" should come, for whoever came to the village from the train always arrived late in the day.

The sun had just disappeared behind a cloud nestling on the horizon when a peasant cart approached along the road and the women stopped their various activities to watch.

The cart entered the village slowly, the horses' tired heads hanging low, the sweat dripping from their bodies. Christine ran out when it stopped in front of the yard. The horses and driver were unfamiliar. No one seemed to know them, and all she could see was a priest seated on top of some hay, with Mark's head resting on his left arm. Just the way you hold a babe, she thought.

Because Christine's father was still in the fields, the neighbors helped lift Mark from the cart. Her mother was sobbing, and the neighborly women remained motionless and stared.

Mark was well wrapped in a blanket. The priest carried him in his arms, and Christine's mother was holding his hand, when he opened his eyes and smiled at her and whispered, "Mother."

The priest carried Mark into the house and laid him upon his mother's bed, the best one in the house. As they unwrapped the blankets, they faced his tragic lot: Mark had lost both his legs.

Christine stared at her mother, who took a deep breath and smiled graciously at Mark as she said softly, "Never mind, son, you gave your legs to the king; but the Lord, the King of Kings, sent you back to me." She turned to the young priest and murmured, "Thank you, Father, for guiding him home."

The young priest bowed and said, "I am Father Joseph; Mark is my friend."

Through tragedy, Christine met Father Joseph, the young priest who was to become Primate of Hungary and a prince of the Holy Roman Catholic Church.

During the long months when Mark was wasting away, Christine took care of him, and he told her about his friendship with Father Joseph. It had begun in the second year of the war, after he returned to the military hospital at Szombathely, badly wounded. Christine remembered when they received the first letter; his wounds had seemed so minor. At that time Father Joseph had not yet attained priesthood and was detailed to help nurse the wounded. He stood by Mark and all the other soldiers in their hour of great need. It was he who helped Mark find courage when they amputated both his legs. It was he who sat by his bedside and tried to mitigate the pain by wiping the perspiration from his feverish forehead, by moistening his lips when they were dry, by holding his hand until he fell asleep.

Yes, Father Joseph understood him well. They had so much in common, for Joseph came from a peasant family too, from Mindszent, a village of his own home county. It was near Erdöd. His father, John Pehm, was as hard-working a peasant as any of the villagers they knew, and his mother was a saintly woman. Joseph loved her dearly, and Mark understood that so well.

Both their mothers had received the name of Barbara in baptism, and it became a common bond between them. Mark admired Joseph for the many things he knew.

It was Joseph's eagerness for knowledge that paved his escape from the predestined trek of the average peasant. When he was ten years old and had attended the small village school for about four years, a rural dean paid them a visit. The intelligence of the child and the astounding extent of his knowledge amazed the visitor, who spent some time with him and even went to see his parents; they were very grateful when the dean indicated that he might try to find a place for Joseph in the Latin school of the city.

Joseph's father and mother were very poor and the family large; and when he went to the city he continued his studies under great hardships. He was in the fourth class of the Latin high school when he was asked by the dean whether he had decided what he wanted to become. Joseph said he had made his decision—he wanted to become a priest.

Joseph finished the eight years of the Latin high school in Szombathely as one of the best in his class. True, they had been lean, hard years. Each summer he returned home to help in the fields—to harvest, to reap, and to plow; and his greatest reward was the sight of his mother's face as she attended Mass with him in the small village church.

The outbreak of war found Joseph preparing for the priesthood, a student of sacred theology at the seminary of Szombathely. The military ordered all students to serve in the hospitals, to assist in caring for the wounded and the sick; and Mark was one of these wounded whom Joseph served with the humility of the faithful.

On the 12th of June, 1915, Joseph became Father Joseph; he had been ordained a priest of the Holy Roman Catholic Church. His first call was as chaplain to the little church in Felsőpaty, where he remained from the first of August, 1915, to the end of January, 1917. The benevolent dean, who always kept a watchful eye over him, exercised his influence with the bishop, and young Father Joseph received an appointment to teach religion in the State Latin School at Zalaegerszeg. It was the county seat of Zala, a place of some importance.

For more than a year he devoted himself to teaching the youngsters the history of Christianity and the true appreciation of the supernatural character of faith. He was happy in his surroundings and recognized the challenge of his task.

Vacation time had come, and Father Joseph, in the company of other priests, traveled to Szombathely to pay his respects to the much revered Bishop Count John Mikes.

Ready to leave for home, to help the family with the harvest, Joseph visited the military hospital to see how some of his wounded friends were progressing. There he saw Mark in poor condition. He had only one wish: to be taken home to his mother. Joseph spoke to the doctors and the commanding officer, arranged for a peasant cart, and carried his friend home—home to his mother.

Mark never left that bed, and when he felt the end near, his last wish was that Father Joseph should be sent for. He wanted to see him once more; he wanted to receive his blessings. Father Joseph came, and from his hands Mark received the last unction.

Father Joseph stayed for the funeral, took part in the last rites, and walked at the side of the old priest, through the rain and the slush, as they led Mark to his eternal rest. Christine never forgot how earnestly he spoke the words: "And we beseech Thee, O Lord, upon the sacrifice which we offer Thee for the soul of Thy servant, that to him on whom Thou didst confer the gift of Christian Faith, Thou mayest also grant its reward."

The war was going into the fifth year. The old king, Francis Joseph, had died in 1916, and a young king had come in his stead; but he brought no ray of hope for an end. There were fewer able-bodied men in the land, for the king had commanded even the older men to join the colors. A good pair of horses could scarcely be found; cattle were slaughtered young, and even bread became scarce. The war devoured it all.

Then came the fateful November, 1918. People did not know whether they should laugh or cry. The armies of the king had been defeated; the war was at an end.

The emotional storm that shook the peoples of Europe to their very marrow swept over Hungary, too; the revolutionary ideology, the same that led to the collapse of far-away Russia in 1917, was lashing at the souls and minds of the simple people. Incendiary slogans appeared on the walls of the buildings in the cities. From nowhere strangers appeared, spreading tales of horror from the front and throughout the land.

In Zalaegerszeg, a place of fifteen thousand souls, the impact was much more strongly felt than in the villages. Here lived a great many learned people, merchants, lawyers, and civil servants, not to speak of the officers who were in charge of the small garrison.

Father Joseph taught his religious classes with more fervor than ever before; in his public utterances he spoke for calm.

Then came the turn which decided the course of the Hungarian nation for a generation to come. The Revolution took hold in the Capital. A national council headed by the Socialist Count Michael Károlyi took over the power, and King Charles IV, who had been crowned at Buda two years earlier, abdicated. Count Stephen Tisza, Prime Minister when war was declared, was murdered, as a mob thirsting for blood demanded his death in revenge for the "heart-aches" caused by a war that engulfed five continents.

Embittered bands of returning soldiers, void of discipline and good leadership, joined hands with the revolutionary elements. No rational government could control the violently swinging pendulum of public sentiment.

Responsible to no one, one cabinet followed another; left-wing liberals, uniting with the Socialists, tried to counter the forces of anarchy, which finally, in March, 1919, seized power.

A Communist regime established itself. The teachings of Spartacus, Marx, and Lenin were spread by long-haired, unshaven strangers heralding the dawn of a new world, with a new "holy red star" emblazoned by the hammer and sickle. Wild-looking youngsters, men, and women rushed through the land in cars taken from unguarded army depots, shouting and shooting, waving the red flag.

"Oppressed workers of the world, unite!" was the call of the marching groups in the morning; "Down with tradition! Down with the feudal lords! Hang your oppressors!" was the chant of the "demonstrators," gathered from among the unfit, the vagrants, and the hoodlums. By nightfall it developed into "There is no God; the proletariat shall rule the world, tear the churches down, chase the priests away!"

Father Joseph watched the development in horror. He had had little occasion in the past to exercise his political acumen in matters beyond his immediate community. He had written and compiled a book on motherly love and he recognized in the acts of terror more than revolutionary sentiment: to him this was not a simple quest for liberty; it was the violent revolt of the son against his mother, the citizen against his own country, Hungary.

In the newspaper he edited he warned against the "forces of evil," and in February, 1919, he was arrested and imprisoned. Two weeks later, free, he spoke out publicly on "The Threats Against the Nation." When the Communist regime assumed power on March 21, 1919, he was rearrested and kept in prison for two months, until some of his own young students set him free.

Undaunted by his cruel experiences, by the beatings and humiliations suffered during imprisonment, he returned to his seat and with more vigor and even stronger conviction chastised the sinners; but to his faithful, who gather around him, his message is: "No hatred, but love, that love for which our Lord Savior died, binds us together and makes us strong to overcome the trials and tribulations of a sick world."

With the coming of August, 1919, the terror regime, headed by Béla Kun, and supported from Moscow by the Communist International, ended. The leather-jacketed "Samuely boys," named after the bloodthirsty executioner of the Communist regime, either had been killed or had fled abroad into the loving arms of the mother of all anarchists and nihilists: Moscow.

In Lenin's paradise they lived in the obscurity of studentship at the college maintained by the Communist International to "train national leaders for the coming world revolution."

The common people of the land had valiantly, and at times cunningly, resisted the revolutionary inroads on their lives; but weakened by the long war, with no material resources and a wavering leadership, they could not immediately end the reign of terror. The neighboring nations, fearing that the red menace might spread across their own borders and seeking their own advantage, one after another advanced over the Hungarian borders to such an extent that more than two-thirds of the former Hungarian territory, in the end, came under foreign rule.

The red terror had been defeated by the lack of roots from within and by armed forces from without. This was the political situation preceding the Peace Treaty of Trianon, which practically reduced the physical body of the Hungarian nation by two-thirds.

Father Joseph traveled far and wide during these days. Up and down the country he visited friends, classmates from seminary days, parents of the students he taught in school. The well meaning gathered around him, at times in the clandestine setting of someone's back room, with a single candle lighting the anxious faces. "The forces of godlessness are spreading evil. This is the time for us to be steadfast, strong and upright, defend not the Faith of our fathers only, but their sacred heritage of which we are the stewards." His words are remembered to this very day.

On the first day of October, 1919, when he became the "vicar" of the parish, his travail grew more strenuous and his responsibility for the souls of his parishioners more weighty. On the visits to his flock, seeing the plight of the people who, as a result of the continued upheaval and pillaging, were in permanent insecurity, had lost a whole year's harvest, or had been robbed of the small remainder of stock the war had left them, he spoke words of encouragement, spreading the light of hope into their hearts: "Economic distress has never defeated a people, never ruined a nation united in purpose. A people strong in heart, pure in soul, unswerving in faith and respecting the moral law of God will rise again."

In many places reaction to the Communist terror set in. The enraged population was ready to shoot or lynch anyone who had the slightest taint of the short-lived revolutionary period. The reaction was a bloody experience, and the population dreaded the new terror as much as it despised the red one. Because some members of the governing set of Communists had been born in the Jewish faith, but as good Communists heathenly professed that there was no God, anti-Semitic slogans were spread by irresponsible elements.

Father Joseph heard one day that on the outskirts of his own parish a group of men had arrived who, bent on revenge, were inciting the population to perform a "purge" by their own hands. He faced the gathering: "Thou shalt not follow the multitude to do evil! He who takes his brother's life shall perish by the same sword! He who disregards the law of God shall die a thousand deaths in Purgatory! He who has trespassed on the law of man shall be punished through the law of man! Peace shall never come to you if your hands are soiled by the blood of revenge. Trust the law; before all, trust the law of God, observe the Ten Commandments, and go home! Go, while there still is peace in your souls."

But in many places the words of Father Joseph were not, or could not be, heard. Individuals and even organized groups took the law in their own hands and declared: "Until we have finished what we set out to do, we are the law." Tranquillity crept only slowly into the minds and lives of the Hungarian people.

The year 1920 brought a great many sorrows and joys into the life of Father Joseph. A new shadow fell over the national life of the Hungarian people as the peace terms became known and formal peace was signed in June, in the Grand Trianon, at Paris. "The Peace of Trianon shall never prevail" echoed through the land, and the nation went into mourning, for the treaty had dismembered the "thousand-year-old body of the Hungarian Crown." The people followed an unseen banner which, in the national consciousness, was inscribed with the words, "No, No, Never!"

Church bells rang throughout the land, signifying a funeral, as the spokesmen from the detached counties took a public oath in Budapest, the Capital: "Two-thirds of Hungary is being torn from our national body! A soil unquestionably ours! We shall repossess it and retain it!"

Father Joseph found his joys in the very life of the people of the parish as he recognized their will to return to serene normalcy, as he helped them to build anew, to improve the present, and prepare for a better morrow. And one of his great joys was when he married Christine to Francis, a son of his parish.

Francis was a young man who had returned from the wars and in passing through Erdöd had come to see Christine's mother. He had been close to Mark; they had suffered together in the trenches; and when Mark was wounded, it was Francis who carried him to safety.

He had wanted to visit the mother of whom Mark had been talking all the time. And there he met, for the first time, Christine. Shyly he admired the girl who had grown to be a beautiful woman; and he came back again and again, never missing an opportunity to ride on a wagon that he knew would pass through Christine's village. Once, in spring, he walked fifteen miles to keep an engagement with her. He told her then that he wanted her to be his wife. It was on that Sunday afternoon that Francis went, with hat in hand, to Christine's father, asking him for her hand in marriage.

Christine had already reached the age of twenty. Usually girls of her age had been married long before; but the war and the continuing upheavals had changed things. A great many of the boys who had left to go to war had not come back; some died a hero's death, others were still in hospitals; still others were prisoners of war. There were few men of marrying age in the villages, and there were many girls waiting for a husband.

Francis was the eldest son in a family of five boys and a girl. His father died at the end of the war and left him a few acres of land on the outskirts of Zalaegerszeg. His youngest brother, too young to have gone to war, helped him in the fields. The others had hired themselves out on a near-by estate.

As if Fate wanted it that way, Christine found a happy home in the vicar's parish. (Everyone called Father Joseph, "Vicar.") Her simple house was roomier than the one she had left behind, and the roof had real bricks. Besides, the community had all those characteristics of a city of which she had heard: stone sidewalks, several stores and schools, a hospital, and many roads leading to it.

One Sunday afternoon the vicar had a sick call in the neighborhood and dropped by to see how they were getting along. He and Francis understood each other well, despite the fact that Francis was tall, heavy, and strong, and always had a smile on his face, while Father Joseph—for to Christine he always remained Father Joseph—was not tall at all, but lean and very serious, with clear, strong, and benign eyes. It was Francis who could really make him smile, not with tales men usually tell when getting together to "smoke a pipe" at the back fence, but with stories of his parents, his happy youth, and little childish pranks.

Somehow Mark was the common bond between the three of them. It was that afternoon that Joseph invited them to accompany him to the railroad station, where he had to receive a visitor. Christine had on her Sunday best, for she had never seen a train before, and with Francis they flanked Father Joseph as they walked along.

Everyone knew Father Joseph; and wherever they passed, men lifted their hats, women and children made the sign of the cross, and it made her happy to hear, over and over again, the traditional greeting: "Praised be the Lord Jesus Christ," and the answer, "Forever and ever, Amen."

At the railroad station Christine saw the train arrive and stop, the noise frightening her somehow. She was lost in amazement as she watched the people getting off and on the train. She felt a slight tap on her shoulder; it was Father Joseph, whose visitor, a priest, had arrived. She heard him say: "You remember Mark. This is his sister Christine, and this is Francis, Mark's brother-in-law." For an instant it passed through her mind how unusual it was: Father Joseph spoke of Mark as of a living person. Yes, somehow Mark was the common bond between the three of them.

The young priest, as he told them later himself, came to get advice from Father Joseph, because, as he said, all their classmates sought his advice and bowed to his findings.

In fact, everyone who knew him seemed to look up to Father

Joseph as a man of wisdom and sound judgment. A year later people were commenting upon it in front of the church. They said that the poor and the rich regarded him with equal respect, that his counsel was sought not by the peasant only, but even by the learned and the influential.

Christine had gone to Mass twice that day, because she wanted to be there when the "Te Deum" was sung as Father Joseph celebrated his first Mass upon becoming the head of the parish. To the second she came to ask for a certificate of her first-born, whom three weeks earlier he had christened Stephen. When she told about her anxiety at not having the paper, Father Joseph laughed: "Yes, we in Hungary need a certificate to prove that we have a name; that we exist at all."

During the next nine years Christine had occasion to repeat this very same visit three times. Each time she received a new certificate; in 1924 it was for John, in 1927 it was for Michael, and in 1930 her beloved Elizabeth was born.

This very same Elizabeth, who now, kneeling next to her, is praying for the life and salvation of the same Father Joseph, who prayed over her when she had hardly entered the world.

These years meant a great deal in the life of Father Joseph. As spiritual leader his interests in the affairs of the community increased; his contact with the everyday life of the people became even closer than heretofore. Zalaegerszeg came to regard him as its own, and he reacted in kind.

His activities became manifold. As pastor of the largest parish, he began to take a lively interest in the civic affairs of the entire county. Soon after his elevation to parish priest, the Bishop appointed him dean and he spent a great deal of his time visiting the parishes of the county. The work he did during this period laid the foundation for the great tasks he was destined to face.

These were trying times in Hungary. The constitutional crisis had been bridged by means of a law passed by the National Assembly, declaring the throne vacant. Government functioned "in the name of the Holy Crown," and the commander-in-chief of the armed forces, Admiral Nicholas Horthy, became Regent. Twice in the course of 1921, King Charles tried to regain the throne. The second futile attempt led to an armed conflict on the outskirts of Budapest, during which "royalist" troops, who were supporting the monarch, were facing soldiers opposing them on behalf of the "Holy Crown of Hungary." Eventually the king was interned, and a British monitor later took him to exile on the island of Madeira. Regarded as a martyr when news came of his passing in April, 1922, the simple people said that "he died of a broken heart." For nearly a quarter of a century, Hungary was governed as a kingdom without a king.

All the curses of a lost war and its aftermath were visited upon Hungary. Inflation upset the economic equilibrium of the country. After the reestablishment of monetary values, a new economic blow came from without, the collapse of the price of wheat. The produce of the peasant and landlord alike, the golden wheat of Hungary, had no market. The government machinery, geared to a prewar Hungary, had to be readjusted to postwar conditions, and numberless officials retired. Their pensions, no matter how small, allowed them to remain aloof from competition for the scarce opportunities in gainful employment; instead they bewailed the past and added to the instability of the political trend.

The haughty and the humble found the door of Father Joseph; he admonished, he encouraged. Above all, he was the caretaker of souls, the shepherd, devoting his special attention to the improvement of the care of the sick. Wherever he could he pleaded for more doctors, more hospitals; and he rejoiced in caring for the youth. Every year he collected shoes for poor children. He was never able to face a barefoot youngster. A dozen cows were kept in his barn for the sole purpose of providing milk for those who could not afford it. "How can you say grace over your own meal, with a clear conscience, when you know that some of your neighbors' children are hungry?" were his words.

His religious fervor bore fruit for the people and the Church. Honors were bestowed upon him. In 1924, the same year in which he led a pilgrimage to Lourdes, Father Joseph became the titular Abbot of Pornó. In 1927 he was appointed Bishop's Commissioner, with the authority to found new parishes; he accepted joyfully the additional burden, for it meant "more opportunities in extending the arms of the mother Church, letting more people partake in grace, enriching the family of the Lord."

While doing this work, he published *Zala Cries Out for Help*, a document designed to call the attention of the government, if not of the entire nation, to the plight of the common man in his district.

"The common man was always nearer to his heart than the wealthy and the powerful," Francis said of the Abbot. "He commands respect for those in power, but he truly feels with the poor, the landless."

Christine knew that by the "landless" he meant those whose fate was symbolized by his three brothers, living as the count's hired help.

One, the good-looking Peter, was a footman in the castle; the other two toiled in the fields and in the stables from daybreak till sundown.

In one way or another they were all taken care of. They had their two-room shacks to live in, a patch of land where they could raise corn or vegetables of their own, and the right to keep a cow and raise some pigs, chickens, and geese. Their pay came in the old traditional way, so many sacks of produce, corn, potatoes, or, if they chose, the monetary equivalent thereof; and, yes, they also received the cords of wood necessary to keep the stove fire burning, kerosene for the lamp, and two pairs of shoes a year.

All were married; the count looked graciously upon married couples and gave them a small dowry. There was also another consideration. The estate had no separate dormitory for unmarried men. If one was single, one had to sleep in the stables; if one had a family, one was entitled to one's own "home." If any member of the family got sick, the overseer told the manager, who in turn told the count's secretary. The doctor came and one even got medicine; and one did not pay for it, either. As many could live in the house as the floor space would stand, as long as each one behaved well and respected the rights of others, but first of all, that of the count and his rule.

The wife could take care of the house, the patch of ground, the animals and the children; except for one day a week. This day she had to serve in the castle, either washing dishes, scrubbing, doing laundry, or any of the many chores that go with the maintenance of a large establishment.

It was a life of comparative security. One did not have to worry about the sun and the rain, whether the harvest would pay, or whether one could pay for the seed and the midwife. The term of employment ran from St. George's Day to St. George's Day, and it was a handshake with the manager that sealed it. If one had no reason for leaving, no quarrel with anyone, one could remain with the estate all one's life in one capacity or another.

The children and children's children would grow up under the paternal wings of the estate and its owner or lessee, and they would always find the same employment with the count which their fathers and fathers' fathers had performed for generations.

They all would become the same, more or less, as their fathers had been, and their fathers before that, servants of a prince, of a count, or of any lord of the manor. It did not really matter whether one was young or old, there was a chore of some kind for everyone on these vast estates. Such was the life of the landless between the two wars.

The old herdsman was the best example; his great-grandfather's headstone was in the last row of the cemetery: before he died he had been a herdsman too.

Uncle Matthew, the herdsman Francis knew, had already seen eighty-seven springs pass by and was still spending eight long months of every twelve, from March to October, in the lowland pastures, watching the cattle wander over the meadows in search of fresh grass. He, for instance, left the hamlet in March and spent the days and nights in God's own nature, whether the sun scorched the earth and hay or the rains came down and drenched the soil. Then he pulled his shelter to one of the hummocks, where the cattle

had already intuitively assembled, recognizing the spot most protected from the vagaries of nature.

The "shelter," his summer home, was actually a hut about nine
feet long and five feet wide, resting on an axle with two large wheels.
It could be pulled by a man wherever he wanted to set up his "home."
Straw or hay was spread upon its boards, and the huge traditional
sheepskin cloak of the Hungarian peasant served as a comforter.
He kept his food in the straw, too, brought to him twice a week by
one of the women of the family, and a jug of wine but no water,
for water spoiled if kept for days.

For assistance he had two sheep dogs who, at the sound of his
whistle, attended to rounding up the herd, or called his attention to
a stray calf or to a fight between two young bulls. The dogs understood his every motion, the tone of his voice, the commands of his
whistle. He relied on them for most of the errands because he was
too old to run after or wrestle with a beast. The only time he devoted
his personal attention to the individual welfare of an animal—he
knew them all by name and their ancestry—was when one of them
got sick, which was a rare occurrence, or when a calf was born. The
old man knew how to treat the sick and how to teach the newborn
calf to nurse.

For company he had one of his great-great-grandsons who was
not yet of school age. The youngsters vied for the opportunity to
live out in God's open with the "ancestor." He knew a collection
of never ending stories, tales from the heroic history of the Hungarian people. He taught them all about the soil, the earth, the birds
and the bees, the grass and the trees, and about the great miracle
of how things grew. He taught them prayers and songs before the
sanctity of nature's eternal altar, the star-laden evening sky. He convinced them of the magnificence of faith, of the supremacy of the
reign of the Lord, the Master of all. He answered their unending
queries the way his fathers did, and their forefathers before that.

There was also another consideration behind all this, for if anything happened to the old man, the child could run and notify those
at home. Then he would be laid to rest in the little cemetery at the
lower end of the hamlet, the end opposite to where the lordly manor

overlooked the scene. The crosses carried the names of only seven generations, because the plot for the cemetery was set aside seven generations ago.

In the midst of a huge park stood the castle of the count, with its forty rooms.

Peter, as a personal servant to the count, wore a uniform, a shirt with a collar and a black tie, socks, and soft black calf-leather shoes. He had his hair cut regularly and had to shave every day. When there were guests in the manor, or for special occasions, he had a frock coat; but generally he wore a white linen jacket with gilded buttons bearing the crest of the count's historic family.

At first he felt very uncomfortable, because, having gone barefoot most of his life, he was annoyed by the tight shoes. At the beginning he also revolted against the suspenders, because hitherto he had simply used a piece of string to hold up his pants. In his soft, or starched, white shirt he felt like a dressed-up doll; sometimes he was not quite sure whether he was not one. But he quickly made up his mind when he saw the clothing worn by the servants whom the visiting dignitaries brought along with them when they came to visit the count and his family. For there were many visitors. Some came alone, to keep the count company, and stayed for weeks; others brought their families and stayed for a few months, for they were "relatives."

All this went on, however, for only six months a year. During most of the winter, except for the hunting season, the count and his family were away, because it was too cold and dreary to stay in the castle; during the heat of the summer, the family were away at some cooler spot, in the mountains or abroad, because it was too hot. As one of the family once exclaimed: "The trouble with living here is that in the winter the nights are too long and too cold, and in the summer the days are too hot and too long."

Peter could not understand how anyone with the power of lordship over so much wealth and so many souls could feel uncomfortable at all.

At the end of the right wing of the castle, surrounded by beautiful hundred-year-old oaks, was the chapel. The count and his family worshiped here, as well as the people of the hamlet. Mass was read every Sunday by a priest from one of the near-by parishes who was brought in the count's carriage, if among the resident guests there was no priest.

It was on such an occasion that Peter learned to revere Father Joseph. It was right after Pentecost that the latter had come to visit the count. He had arrived on Saturday, stayed overnight, and on Sunday morning celebrated Holy Mass, for all, in the chapel.

There were many guests that Saturday at the dinner table, friends of the count's and some visiting "relatives," forty in all. Peter himself was serving at the table, assisted by six of the servant girls. Even the countess's French maid was helping out. It was a most interesting assemblage, for it included an uncle of the count's who had once been very rich by virtue of the income of the huge entailed estate which he had inherited from his father; however, he was known to have gambled away this patrimony for many years to come. This uncle became much excited during an exchange of views with the Abbot. Peter overheard the answer of Father Joseph, "the Abbot":

"It must be recognized that we are living in an age which may be called the age of liberation. Nearly a hundred years ago serfdom was abolished by the pressure of the popular trend that swept over the Continent.

"The choice now is whether amends are to be made by those who have the power to make them, or whether they will be forced by popular demand to give up what they have. A satisfied people does not bear, does not foment, and is not receptive to uprisings. Our Hungarian people have made very slow progress on the road leading to the recognition of the absolute freedom of the individual. True, we have had some cruel experiences: the revolution at the end of the war and the inroads the forces of antichrist have made on our national and individual life during the Communist terror following it. Today we still have agitators boring at the very foundations of our social structure; and who is it who gives them justification?

"Our people are land-hungry. True, some land has been distributed to our deserving soldiers who returned from the war, and some to their widows and orphans; but it was a very small drop in a very thirsty bucket. The land they received was mostly plots nobody wanted, acres where they could harvest nothing but rocks, meadows where the oxen would sink knee-deep in the swamp and the plow not take hold. Yes, some got plots to build homes for their families on—plots nobody clamored for, at the wrong end of the village, where the spring floods covered their garden and sapped the foundations of their homes.

"The descendants of the people whose blood, sweat, and toil made this earth sacred—made it the garden spot of all Europe, where wheat grows that has no equal in the world, where the corn is sweeter, the fruit tastier—these people want an opportunity to call some of this land their very own. They want an opportunity to buy a patch or two with the money they have earned by their swollen muscles and their aching backs.

"A way must be found to still the people's hunger for land; but the way must be shown by those who possess the land. We must be conscious of the faults that exist. The entailed estates are out of step with our time; in fact, some who inherited them are very desirous to sell land. They should be enabled to do so.

"Your argument that the bishoprics of the Roman Catholic Church represent, as a unit, one of the largest landholdings of the country, is valid. These lands were never acquired. They came to the Church throughout the centuries and stem mostly from grants and deeds. These lands were received by the Church for specific scriptural purposes. They enabled the Church to perform its functions, to establish, build, and maintain educational institutions, hospitals, homes for the feeble, the aged, the sick, the blind; to take care of the orphans, the wayward, the fallen, and the needy. Yes, it enabled the Church to educate countless millions throughout the ages; to seek knowledge and spread it throughout the world; to explore the past for the benefit of the present and the future; and to become the foundation on which culture, a world order was built; a civilization which it has established, nursed, supported and, above all, defended against the onslaught of the heathens, the pagans, the godless and the forces of destruction!

"The Church has endeavored to put the fruits of this land to work for the benefit of all. Despite all this, the Church will never refuse to give up some of its land if it is destined for ownership by the common man and is not to become an addition to some already existing large landholding, to enhance that economic power already wielded by them."

A stony silence followed the words of the Abbot, but the warmth of gladness filled Peter's breast. He had recognized in Father Joseph the shepherd whose heart was aching for his flock.

No one dared to touch the social structure; no one cared to introduce economic readjustments. Every wrong supposedly originated with the Treaty of Trianon, the dismemberment of the country. Schoolchildren were praying in an unusual manner:

> "I believe in a God!
> I believe in a Fatherland!
> I believe in the resurrection of Hungary!"

The people throughout the land were dreaming of a new dawn, the return of the lost territories.

While Father Joseph spent his days in the service of his people, most of his evenings, and some of the long nights, were occupied studying the history of Hungary, particularly the history of its Catholicism. Years of painstaking effort, research through archives, and the study of thousands of ancient parchments bore fruit. In 1934 his two-volume *The Life and Times of Martin Padányi Biró* was published. The subject was dear to his heart. It was a valiant Bishop of Veszprém, a great leader whose period was that of the religious renaissance in Hungary.

News of his accomplishments traveled far; it reached Rome. In recognition of his beneficial work, the Holy Father honored him, and in 1937 Father Joseph became a papal prelate.

Politicians, recognizing his influence with the great masses of his district, courted his favor, paid their respects to him, and sought his counsel; and not during election time only, for as they discussed affairs of state with him, his interest in the political trends of the world rose. Nevertheless, he continued to devote his best energies to his first interest, his own parish and his immediate community. Occupying a seat on the municipal board and in the county council, his voice was heard, his proposals weighed, and his wishes considered. At times his sincerity and devotion to purpose even seemed to govern these assemblies.

Despite all honors and offers of transfer to more important parishes, Father Joseph remained in his beloved Zalaegerszeg. He even refused a bid to become a member of Parliament when the government party assured him the election. "It is the wish of God that I shall remain among my people, where I can serve them the best I know; only He can call me away from them! I have no aspirations for political office, no desire for worldly power," was his answer.

The dark days following the Munich crisis cast their shadow over the world but brought a false rejoicing to the people of Hungary. The Germans and Italians had already chained the Hungarian economy to their own, by buying her produce, and were now drawing the Hungarian nation into political debt; between them they decided to slice a part off subjugated Czechoslovakia and return it to Hungarian rule. (The same thing was done later in the case of Rumania.)

The psychological effect was as could be expected. Some of the population saw in these acts the partial fulfillment of their prayers, rejoiced, and did not recognize the gift of Danaüs they had received. Everyone who had the slightest part in the "recapture" of the lost territories was hailed as a popular hero; Prime Minister Béla Imrédy was given, in gratitude, the "honorary citizenship" of Zalaegerszeg.

Soon, however, the Hungarians awoke to the fact that a price had to be paid, in blood and honor. First, Hitler's emissaries suggested that Hungary should pass more stringent anti-Jewish laws; then the request came to gear the entire Hungarian economy to the needs of Hitler's National Socialist aims.

The European war broke out. Hitler marched into Poland, setting the world aflame anew, and the Hungarian nation began to feel the impact of the dynamic forces of totalitarianism.

The second time Christine and Francis went with Father Joseph to the railroad station was when Francis was leaving. It was in May of 1940 that Francis had been called to serve the colors again. Her first-born, Stephen, was already in the army and was stationed somewhere in the northern mountains. He wrote long letters but never gave a hint what he was doing.

Father Joseph explained to her that soldiers could not tell all the things a mother wanted to know. But Christine felt a tearing ache: her own boy was keeping secrets from her. He could tell her—she thought—she would tell nobody else.

Anyway, things had progressed to a point where the neighbors were no longer given to chatter. New fashions had developed in private relations between people. Political differences had become more acute—over the deputy in Parliament, or the way the government collected the taxes. Novel arguments had been introduced into the life of the common people: arguments about race and creed.

People were inquisitive about the grandparents of other people. Some even dared to say that anyone who did not consider the Germans as the greatest nation in the world, was "in the pay of the Jews." Some people who had German-sounding names held their noses high in the air and considered themselves as a privileged class.

One day Christine spoke to Father Joseph about that. He smiled: "We are all Hungarians, no matter what our name or creed. Take me, born Joseph Pehm. It is a German-sounding name, but my father's ancestors were all good heart-and-soul Hungarians. When the time came that I wanted to have a Hungarian-sounding name, I chose the name of my birthplace, and changed from Joseph Pehm to Joseph Mindszenty!"

As time went by Christine saw her second son, John, in uniform. The Germans had passed through Hungary to invade Yugoslavia. All the land was excited, for the news had come earlier that Prime Minister Count Paul Teleki, having refused the Germans transit, had committed suicide, for he would not break the treaty of friendship with Yugoslavia. Hungarian honor gave a tragic answer to the demands of the Germans.

Despite the missing men, the home was not empty. Christine's house, like the others, was full of refugees. Father Joseph had asked her to take them in. There were refugees from Poland, from the Ukraine, from all over the map; and they brought tales of horror, both of the Nazis and the Communists. Some had walked hundreds of miles, pursued by men and machines on the ground and in the air, to find a haven.

Yes, Hungary during these days was a haven. At least some people considered it as such. Even after June, 1941, when war with Russia had started, no fighting took place on Hungarian soil. The bombings came later.

Hungarian National Socialism—the Arrow Cross—with help from Hitler was propagandizing the country: "Have no fear—you are allied with victorious Germany!" In the elections of 1939 the Arrow Cross gained some political strength at the expense of the Smallholders and the Social Democrats, increasing from a diminutive handful in Parliament to a noticeable—in fact, loud—minority. It was riding high on the wave of slogans; demanded anti-Jewish laws and, with the help of German diplomatic pressure, put them through, although execution of some of these was delayed by the government. Soon untold thousands of Jewish citizens were forced into labor battalions, administered by the army; sent to Russia, to help win the war for Hitler. Tens of thousands of them, ill fed and ill clothed, perished in the Russian wastes.

The majority of the population disliked and distrusted the Germans, by tradition. But they also fostered the fear of the Russians—the Slavic danger—that had been imbued in the Hungarians for countless generations.

In Zalaegerszeg and Erdöd as in all the cities, villages, and hamlets, men and women young and old distrusted the broadcasts of the Hungarian and German radio stations and listened to the news reports broadcast by the Allies. Curiously enough, any time the Germans were beaten the tidings spread like wildfire through unidentified channels. The more doubtful the German victory, the more numerous the clandestine meetings; the longer the war lasted, the larger the groups.

At one of these gatherings, Father Joseph himself heard the "voice" from America declare that the great powers had agreed on an Atlantic Charter, signed by the leaders, guaranteeing a new bill of rights for men; and he said:

"Human society—we all, you and I—cannot lose this war. Troops may be defeated on the battlefields; but, by the facts you have just heard, the creation of a new charter of human freedom, a new era will dawn for all the peoples of the world, and the rights of men, as proclaimed by our Lord Savior himself, will prevail."

The words of Father Joseph found echo everywhere in his district, for most of the citizens had lost faith in their political leaders and were looking more and more to the Church for an answer to their questions.

There were many questions and needs to be answered. Father Joseph tried to answer the theoretical ones by thoughts and meditation, the practical ones with deeds.

Many deeds were necessary, for, as 1944 dawned, the wants of the people knew no end. Some who could afford it showed their gratitude, and on the day before Christmas, 1943, the parish house of Zalaegerszeg was filled with gifts large and small, ranging from priceless black cloth for a suit to a pair of live geese. But none of them was to remain in the parish house.

Tears came to the eyes of Father Joseph as he entered his home that night. Deeply touched, he knew what he had to do. After the Holy Mass of Christmas Eve he had his carriage loaded with all the presents except the handkerchiefs his mother had embroidered for him with her own hands. He could not part with these.

The carriage was driven to the poorest of the poor in Father Joseph's acquaintance; and on Christmas morning these good people found at their doors or windows the presents passed on by this unknown benefactor. The geese he left in the kitchen of the children's hospital.

Whenever want arose he gave away everything—even things he needed, so that when March of 1944 came he had only one coat, one good pair of shoes. He had given all for the benefit of the poor.

But in return he could point to the results of his labors. In the twenty-five years in Zalaegerszeg and the district, he had created eighteen new parishes, built nine new churches, thirteen parish houses, and six new schools. He could look proudly back to his achievement in Zalaegerszeg: a new church and chapter house for the Franciscans; a great educational establishment for the Sisters of Notre Dame; a home for the aged, a printing house, and a bookstore. These monuments of stone were built by faith, conviction, perseverance, and humility, by a great shepherd, a shepherd of souls.

Then came the fateful night of March 18, 1944, when German armored columns, crossing the Hungarian border in the dark, invaded the land of the so-called "ally," occupied its government buildings, and actually if not openly took over the running of the country. When people awoke on March 19 to find that they had lost their independence, that foreigners had seized control, there was a silent upsurge of grief. Father Joseph was stunned by the betrayal.

A few days later important visitors arrived at the parish house of Zalaegerszeg. They were visitors from Rome, from the Holy Father. They carried a message from the Vicar of Jesus Christ—a message symbolized by the ring.

On March 29, 1944, Christine saw Father Joseph consecrated Bishop of Veszprém.

The Cathedral Church of Veszprém was thronged with the faithful, priests and dignitaries, as the coconsecrators, bishops of other dioceses, preceded Father Joseph to the main altar. The great Litany of the Saints was sung, calling on the Blessed Trinity, and the arches of the ancient cathedral echoed with the response "Ora pro nobis," the heartfelt seeking to be prayed for; then the invocation followed: to the great Lady of Hungary, the Blessed Mary ever Virgin; to the Archangels, to St. John and St. Joseph, to the apostles and evangelists, to the doctors and the martyrs and the bishops. True to the times sounded the petitions for deliverance from spiritual and temporal evils; those in the name of the mysteries of the life of Jesus, and on behalf of the Holy Roman Catholic Church and the faithful. There lay Father Joseph prostrate, his forehead touching the steps of the altar. Then they laid hands on him, and there sounded "Receive the Holy Ghost." All in the Cathedral went on their knees and sang "Veni, Creator Spiritus" as the head and hands of Father Joseph were anointed.

Then he received the pastoral staff, the ring, and the scriptures, and in turn he offered the wine, the bread, and the candles. After receiving the miter and the gloves he was led to the throne, and they all sang the Ambrosian hymn, the "Te Deum."

The new Bishop of Veszprém gave his blessing and received the kiss of peace.

A prayer for peace was on the lips of all as they filed out of the Church to the sound of the great organ, returning to their homes.

But peace did not come for a long time.

The German Nazis exercising the power over Hungary, through a puppet government, made no more requests, no more demands; they commanded.

Their actions drove the refugees into hiding. Systematically, they denuded the land of its supplies. The Gestapo arrived, and with it the persecution of all who did not bow to tyrant's rule. Any inclination to resist, past or present, meant prison or firing squad; political leaders, even immune members of Parliament, were incarcerated, kept behind bars, or deported to concentration camps beyond the national border.

Men, women, and children of Jewish faith or descent were rounded up and herded into stone quarries or brickworks, or loaded into cattle cars and taken to Auschwitz or some other extermination camp.

The nearer the Russians advanced their front, the more reckless became the behavior of the Nazis and of the Hungarian Arrow Cross. When news came that the Allies had landed in Normandy and were advancing on Germany, inhumanity knew no bounds, and murder and pillaging became the rule. Every prayer, every day, concluded with the thought, "Deliver us from the evil—at any sacrifice."

Conditions taxed the strength of the new Bishop of Veszprém heavily. Countless numbers of his flock, and all the people living in his diocese, were looking to him for relief and help, for protection and refuge. Whomever he could help, he did, whether Catholic or not; wherever his influence reached, he improved the lot of individuals, the conditions in the community; and wherever he could make his orders effective he voiced the word of God, to counter force.

The overseeing of the diocese itself was a great responsibility. The population was over four-fifths Roman Catholic, and the Bishop had jurisdiction over three hundred parishes, nearly six hundred priests, and more than a thousand schools maintained by the Church. The burden was not light.

Despite living in the impressive episcopal palace the Bishop's own ways grew even more simple, more frugal. Land reform had become a burning internal political issue, and he ordered that plans be worked out to distribute to the landless parts of the estate belonging to his office—a plan that never materialized, for history moved too fast.

In the late summer the Russian armies had advanced into Hungarian territory, the puppet government of Döme Sztojai was exchanged for a cabinet led by Géza Lakatos. Lakatos, an army general, tried to stem the German tide, and he and the Regent, Nicholas Horthy, decided to enter into armistice negotiations with the Allies. The armistice commission reached Moscow, and on October 11 the terms were signed.

On October 17 Admiral Horthy was scheduled to broadcast the news of the armistice and corresponding orders to the troops. Through some indiscretion the news seeped out on October 15, and by noon his son was wounded and abducted by the Germans; the regent became himself a prisoner and his government was supplanted by an executive headed by a fanatic named Francis Szálasi. While the radio station was under siege, its courageous director Andrew Hlatky broadcast the proclamation.

Some of the superior officers of the Hungarian army received the news of Horthy's intent and of his imprisonment, and acted accordingly. This enabled the Russians to advance more speedily into Hungary; but the war on Hungarian territory continued, the Germans decided to fight there.

The slow retreat of the Germans was devastating the eastern half of the country. The Bishop of Veszprém, after a conference with the Bishops of Transdanubia, decided to call on the men in power to end the bloodshed. He traveled to Budapest and presented to the Prime Minister the plea, which read in part:

"As the Shepherds of Transdanubia, cognizant of our responsibility as Hungarian Prelates, we ask the present administrators of the fate of Hungary not to deliver Transdanubia, intact as yet, a prey to the battles of retreat. With such a step, the last piece of the Hungarian Fatherland and with it the future and the last hope for recuperation will be lost.

"This region will become the stationary and active battle front of two powerful armies. There will perish three and one-half million natives and the countless refugees from other regions; the beautiful cities, villages, unestimable wealth, historical values, and the last food supply will be destroyed. This can be expected the more, as the evacuation between fighting and conquest becomes more desperate and the scorching and the thirst for blood increases. Starvation awaits the remainder of the population. Because of lack of housing, frost and contagious diseases lie in wait; for medical service in Transdanubia is practically non-existent.

"An individual may sacrifice himself for his nation, but a nation cannot be used as an object of suicidal principles. Sense of responsibility and conscience do not permit it.

"Should it be asked why we deem it our right to raise our voice, we answer with head erect: We are Hungarians, we live and want to continue to live in an indivisible unity with the nation. We are factors of legislature, of government, as decreed by God, King St. Stephen and the laws of a millennium. The question of life and death that has arisen today is not political but, transcending everything, is a moral one.

"This is why we should not only speak—more than that, it has become our sacred duty to make our voice heard on behalf of the population of Transdanubia, by conscience, before history and the judgment of God."

Bishop Mindszenty was stared at. Without daring to call him openly a traitor, the men in power treated him as such. Ignoring his plea, they answered his courageous act of presenting it. His steadfastness in conviction, his daring to call on the government to change its fatal course, and his resistance against the outrages in his own diocese had been a thorn in the side of the men who had usurped the local authority. On October 31, 1944, the prefect of the county ordered his arrest.

When the commander of the detachment read the order of arrest at his residence Bishop Mindszenty asked permission to retire for a few minutes. This was granted. He returned in the full episcopal insignia, surrounded by his immediate staff of priests. The prefect and the detachment commander wanted to arrest him alone; but his priests insisted on being taken with him, and he could not be loaded quietly into a van and made to disappear from public view. The arresting officers were forced to heed his will, and they had to march the Bishop of Veszprém in full insignia followed by twenty-seven of his priests, through the streets of the city to prison. The people, comprehending swiftly as they saw their Bishop escorted by police through the streets, went on their knees to receive his blessing as he passed.

This was the first time that a tyrant's power dared lay hands on the person of Joseph Mindszenty; and on November 21, 1944, the Bishop and his entire priestly staff were taken to Sopron-Kőhida and imprisoned in the penitentiary.

The See of Veszprém was without a shepherd.

While the retreating German regulars defended every inch of Hungarian territory against the onslaught of the Russian armies, Hungarian Arrow Crossists, encouraged and directed by German Nazi Party functionaries and supported by the German Gestapo, staged a blood bath that had had its equal in Warsaw only.

Persons of the Jewish faith had practically disappeared from the countryside; those few who had remained were being hidden. Others fled with forged identity documents to communities where they were unknown, to lead a clandestine existence.

Anyone hiding the persecuted risked his own life and that of his family. Nevertheless some truly Christian clergymen, both Catholic and Protestant, found ways of hiding women and children; convents, hospitals, monasteries, and other religious institutions were among the havens.

The Germans herded into a ghetto all the Jews of Budapest they could not transport to concentration and extermination camps. This multitude lived under conditions unfit for animals, surpassing Dante's imagination. Some few were in "protected buildings," nominally declared extraterritorial by neutral legations, which issued protective passports. But the German and Hungarian Nazis broke into these as time went by and chased the unfortunate residents along with "useless" groups of humans from the ghetto to the edge of the Danube, where they lined them up and shot them so that their bodies would fall into the river.

The Danube had become the river of death.

"Useful" men in the ghetto were marched off hundreds of miles to contribute to the defense of the retreating German armies. Protected against the sub-zero weather only by rags since their good clothes had been taken away in the ghetto, they were put to work digging tank traps and ditches for the last stand of the infantry.

But the terrorism extended beyond the Jews. Anyone resisting the man with the Tommy gun, even indicating resistance, found him prosecutor, judge, and executioner all in one; and bullets knew no argument.

This continued to the very end, as the battle lines slowly moved through Hungary, leaving devastation and misery behind.

By Christmas, 1944, the Russian armies had surrounded the Capital. The grapevine spread a proclamation of a new democratic government that had been formed by Béla Dálnoki Miklós, a high-ranking army general, with no political background. The government had its seat in Debrecen, in the eastern part of the country, all of which was already occupied by the Russians.

The siege of Budapest began on Christmas Eve and lasted seven long weeks. The Germans, having decided to sacrifice the city, defended tenaciously every street, every block, every house, and even every inch. Bombs and mines rained over the city continuously. The population of the Capital moved underground, into cellars, shelters. Soon the emergency food supplies ran out, and anyone was considered lucky who could hack a piece off the frozen carcass of one of the dead horses lying around. Melted snow served as drinking water.

The dead lay unburied, mercifully frozen, in the snow. Even hospitals and churches suffered in the holocaust. In their retreat the Germans dynamited the bridges over the Danube, set the royal castle aflame. At the end of the siege Budapest, one of the most beautiful cities of the world, became a smoldering waste of ruins.

It was not the Capital only that felt the destructive impact. The greater part of the Hungarian land lay devastated by total war.

These were the conditions as people were praying for delivery and "liberation."

Christine with her daughter Elizabeth had gone to her husband's people, when news reached Zalaegerszeg that the Russians had crossed the Danube and were heading west. The never ending stream of refugees brought frightening tales of the excesses of the Soviet troops.

Hundreds, perhaps thousands, of peasant carts loaded high with bedding, the daily necessities, and sometimes the most useless pieces of furniture had passed through Zalaegerszeg, drawn by tired horses and driven by frightened humans. Some of them who had experiences in the battle lines, and had been "liberated" by the Red Army, were terrified to the point of fleeing the land; they were ready to go anywhere, as long as it meant escape from the red terror.

Christine had not heard from her husband, Francis, for two

months. Her son Stephen had been reported a prisoner of war, and John was missing.

Her brother-in-law, Peter, who had served together with the count, had returned wounded and was convalescing when he decided to bring Christine and her two children out to the estate. At least there they were not by themselves. Christine's youngest son, Michael, insisted that he be permitted to go to Erdöd: "Grandmother needs protection too," he said.

The battle front soon moved near the estate. Suddenly, the Germans retreated, even leaving their artillery behind. The countess and her daughters gathered the womenfolk of the hamlet and led them to the icy forest, where they stayed three long days and two long nights. On the third evening, one of the boys came with the message that it was safe to return, "the red soldiers were treating everybody nicely, and gave candy to children." During the night they went back to their homes. There were very few troops in the hamlet itself. Most of them seemed to be on the hilltops, where one could see the flash of their artillery. Soldiers came and went. Most of them wanted food; all wanted wine. Receiving it, they left for the front.

The next day the Germans came back in force, and there was fighting in the street; then the Russians withdrew.

The Germans had brought mechanical monsters like railroad cars, in which one could not see any human being. They moved swiftly, and one spat flames right through the window of a house from which Russians had been firing. The battle lasted a few hours, but to Christine it seemed like days; then it moved on, with the Germans occupying the hamlet again. They did not stay long.

The day after, the sound of the triangle in the barnyard called for assembly; the sweet, thin-voiced bell of the chapel had gone, a long time ago, to war. A German officer was shouting orders through an interpreter. Every house, all the barns and stables were to be evacuated. The people had fed the Russian troops; and that must not happen again. He gave the people two hours to gather their belongings, load them on whatever conveyance they could find, and start westward. The livestock was to be driven ahead by the soldiers.

Terror took hold of the people; but the countess said they should do as they were told.

Peter, the loyal servant, was taking care of the countess and her daughters. He drove the large hunting carriage, into which they had managed to load all the traveling bags. His wife drove an ordinary wagon filled with their few things, and all the members of the family. On it, Christine and Elizabeth found a ledge for sitting. The travel was hard and slow. Most of the carts were drawn by oxen, but these at least made a good hard track in which the horses could follow. Behind this pitiable procession trailed those who had not been able to get a cart and were pulling small sleds through the snow or pushing wheelbarrows loaded with their meager belongings.

Two hours later the hamlet was afire, and the flaming roofs of the homes and the barns with their straw and hay lit the dark winter sky. The column stopped to look back once more, and tears were frozen on the faces of the homeless.

Christine spoke to Peter; he in turn spoke to the countess, who had decided to head for Erdöd, seeking refuge in Christine's old home. Great was the joy when they arrived there the next day. Christine's mother and her son Michael were well, and there were no soldiers in the village. As there was not enough room for all, Peter and his family drove on to his wife's people, two or three villages farther.

On the following day an entire German column entered and left the village within an hour. At their heels came the Russians. The first two detachments stopped hardly long enough to demand food and wine. Alas, they were followed by more Red Army troops, more demands for food, and more insistence on wine, and these remained; they were the "liberators" destined to occupy the village.

Then came the call: all males between the ages of fourteen and fifty were to report at noon at the Kommandatura established in the notary's house.

Not all of the men went; some hid. Young Michael was there when the commanding officer of the troops in the village examined them. Their names and ages were taken by a man who spoke Hungarian and interpreted every word to the officer. Then they were told to wait in the back yard, where Russian soldiers with machine guns kept guard. Some of the older and sick men were sent home and ordered to see that plenty of food was produced for the liberating army.

In the afternoon the priest and the minister called on the officer. Through the interpreter, they were told that this detachment had captured 284 prisoners who had escaped a week earlier when during the mobile battles the Germans advanced; but the number of prisoners had already been reported to the high command, and here the priest and the minister could see for themselves were the "escaped prisoners."

Thus Michael became a prisoner of war without ever having been a soldier. Christine never heard from him, but one neighbor got a letter from Siberia saying that they were all very well, just like the Takács family.

It nearly broke Christine's heart again to read it; for the Takács family was the poorest of the parish; it was never without sickness and was known to have meat on the table only when some good soul gave it.

Her heart had broken that very night, when strange voices were heard in the yard. Then the strangers tried the door; finding it bolted, they pushed it in. They were soldiers of the Red Army. Two of the fifteen had electric lamps; one spoke broken Hungarian. Some came with guns in hand. Christine hid Elizabeth behind the stove; the countess and her daughters were in the front room. Christine and her mother faced the intruders alone; all knew two words in Hungarian, "food" and "wine," and they demanded it.

Suddenly the countess appeared, admonishing them for their rudeness and threatening to report them to their commanding officer, if they did not leave instantly. When the threat was translated they broke out in laughter: "To him, ha! He is very busy at another house."

The soldiers wanted to know if there were any men in the house; then, how many women there were. A stony silence followed.

Then they began to search. Three of the men went into the next room, and grinned as they pushed the trembling daughters of the countess through the door. Another, with an electric lamp, discovered young Elizabeth behind the stove and tried to pull her out.

Christine defended her young like a lioness. She asked what they wanted, and they told her. Then she begged, going on her knees. Finally, she offered herself instead of her child. One of the soldiers laughingly accepted, on the spot. Christine resisted; everyone was staring. "If it will only save the child!" she prayed. But it was all just a cruel play. They violated her and violated the child, over and over again; violated the three women who had found refuge in the home; and they did not even spare the grandmother.

The more the women resisted, the more they cried, the more they yelled for help—the more soldiers came. More and ever more.

When Christine finally pushed her nails into the eyelids of one of her attackers, they bound her hands and feet and made her look on while the suffering of her daughter continued.

The nightmare of rape only ended when the dawn came. Elizabeth and one of the daughters of the countess were unconscious. Christine and the others were hysterical from pain, in body and heart.

Grandmother finally gathered her senses and went to call the priest. He did not have to be told, he already knew: it had happened all over the parish.

Later he arrived with a horse cart bearing others, and took the two unconscious girls to the hospital.

This was the night Christine's heart broke. It never mended.

What happened that night was repeated a thousand times in thousands of villages, towns, and cities; only the degree of cruelty varied. Untold numbers of Hungarian men died, trying to defend the honor and the bodies of their womenfolk.

Women and girls fled from their homes to caves and forests. Some sought refuge in convents, believing that even men who had turned into beasts would stop before the holy signs. They did not; they violated the nuns.

Baron William Apor, the Bishop of Györ, opened his episcopal residence to the women of the city and had the doors locked before the entering Red Army. They demanded entry, threatening to set the buildings afire. The Bishop, with his miter on his head, his staff in hand, and the other hand extended, appeared on the steps and said, "You can pass here only if you kill me first!" They did. Trampling the murdered body of the heroic prelate, they staged a never ending orgy on the sacred grounds.

But it was not only the bestial lust that had to be satisfied. The Red Army had to be fed, for they had brought no food with them. The country—already bare, through the pillaging of the Germans —had to deliver supplies to an occupation force which amounted at one time to more than a million soldiers.

One of the last cities to be evacuated by the Germans was Sopron, near the Austrian border. Their leaving meant freedom for Bishop Mindszenty.

The four long months in prison were not uneventful. On St. Ambrose Day, December 7, he performed a ceremony remindful of the days in the catacombs. Within the walls of the prison he had prepared the souls of ten young candidates who had accompanied him; and there, after they had had full opportunity to consider the step, he ordained them. Among them, the ten had one vestment and one candle; but each participant had a personal attendant at his side; a guard with a loaded gun. The Bishop's heart was overflowing as he kissed them one by one and spoke words of encouragement, reminding them of great trials ahead. It was a most unusual ordination.

The Russians came to Sopron on April 1. They were polite to the Bishop as they were polite, at first, to anyone who had been imprisoned by the Nazis; but they expressed regret that they could not arrange transportation anywhere.

At the first opportunity, the Bishop set out for his diocese, using every conceivable means of conveyance, even freight trains and oxcarts, and walking part way.

His cathedral and residence had been plundered and partly destroyed. The Germans had taken everything of value, and the Russians had used the furniture for firewood. What pained him most was to find the almonry emptied of all the clothing and underwear he had been keeping to distribute after the war, when the danger should have passed that they would be seized from the poor.

The Bishop considered it as his first duty to visit all parishes of the diocese, examine their needs. Traveling continued difficult, for train services were not reestablished for a long time; all motorcars in sight had been taken away by the Germans, and those in hiding were seized by the Red Army. He was able to secure a team of horses and a cart with which he went from village to village, from parish to parish.

Great was the astonishment and joy of the parishioners when they recognized in the dust-covered traveler their beloved Bishop.

Wherever he went conditions were appalling; and everywhere he sought to help, encourage, and strengthen the faith of a distraught people in a better tomorrow.

It pained him greatly to hear in April of the passing of the Archbishop of Esztergom, Justinian, Cardinal Serédi, Prince Primate of Hungary. Earlier, three other bishops had fallen prey to the war, and scores of priests had sacrificed their lives in the service of their flocks. Countless believers had died in the defense of the church.

Bishop Mindszenty distributed the little that was given to him, for the Church itself had become poor. On March 15, 1945, the provisional government decreed the long awaited and much wished-for "land reform." The aim was commendable, but the decree itself, a product of Soviet preparedness, had been hurriedly drawn and even more speedily executed.

The Communists dominated the scene wherever they could, from the time the law was written to the announcement to the new land-owners that their parcels came to them through the generosity of the glorious Red Army and the intercession of the Communist Party. The large estates, whether owned by persons or by institutions, were broken up without any careful planning in the interest of the recipients—the landless peasants. This failure to plan was a premeditated part of the master plan of Moscow, to drive the new owners, when the time became ripe, into a cooperative of the Russian type: the kolkhoz. In less than five years it was to come true.

Most of the land owned by local parishes had not been touched.

No parish owned more than a hundred acres. Later, Bishop Mind-szenty himself received a grant of 450 acres of diocesan lands for his "brave personal resistance" against the Nazis.

The provisional government had little authority. It was the crea-tion of the Red Army and the political entourage that had arrived with it. Among these were the three "refugees of 1919": Ernest Gerö, who had fled as Ernest Singer; Zoltán Vas, who twenty-five years earlier had escaped as Zoltán Weinberger; and Mathias Rákosi, who had not changed at all. With short or long interruptions, all three had spent years at the training school of the Comintern in Moscow, being prepared to help in the conquest of Hungary by Communism. Gerö had become the expert in organization; Vas had the last word in economic matters; and Rákosi decided the political issues. At least it seemed so. Actually, they were only subaltern ex-perts as far as Hungary was concerned; their decisions and authority depended on the orders from Moscow. It was not difficult for them to exercise this authority, for it was backed up by striking power of hundreds of thousands of Red Army bayonets, and the presence of Marshal Klementi Voroshilov, himself a member of the Politburo.

The cabinet consisted of a minority of Communists and crypto-Communists, who knew what they were planning, and a majority of more or less well meaning people who were tools of the minority. Its existence—for democratic eyewash—had been sanctioned by a National Council hurriedly selected and summoned by emissaries of the Communists, who, naturally, had the motorcars of the Red Army at their disposal.

In accordance with the solemn agreements signed by the Allies, an Allied Control Commission had been set up. It had as members an American and a British general, the chairmanship being reserved for the commander of the Russian occupation troops; he exercised the authority of the Control Commission. Soon, the American and British generals were made to understand, that they were there in no more than an advisory capacity.

The valiant determination of the Hungarian people to lead a na-

tional life again, bore fruit; but the first steps on the road of con-
valescence were hard.

The economy had been bled white. Whatever the Nazis had been
able to take from Hungary, had been removed. Not only the gold
treasure of the National Bank, the contents of private vaults, of store-
houses, of institutions, both public and private, but most of the equip-
ment of industrial plants had been dismantled and carried off. The
priceless collections of the museums had disappeared, including the
Holy Crown of Hungary, the Coronation vestments, and the great
relic of Hungarian Catholicism, the mummified hand of the first king
of the country, St. Stephen.

The relic was found by the American army in Austria, and to the
joy of the population it was returned in time for the traditional St.
Stephen's Day procession.

The return of the relic had a magic effect. It symbolized somehow that there was hope for return—from the West; for whatever
could still be extracted from the devastated land, was being moved
East. The country, not yet able to sustain itself, was groaning under
the load of "reparations." Livestock the peasants had been able to
hide from the Germans were being rounded up and driven to Russia.
The meager harvest, which could have solved at least the most urgent
food problem of the country, was loaded on trains and shipped to
the Soviet Union. About the same time the first shipments of relief
arrived from America.

The fall came, and with it, a dread of the winter.

In all dioceses, problems mounted upon problems. The very sur-
vival of the population was the question that returned every morning to the minds of those who had the fate and future of the people
at heart.

The country was saturated with the soldiers of the Red Army.
They were quartered in the cities, in the towns, the villages and
hamlets. Wherever one went, they bivouacked in the fields. And
they all lived off the ransacked land. In the cities starvation claimed
its toll; contagious diseases were rampant.

The nation went on its knees. It prayed more fervently than ever before; prayed for deliverance from the new evils.

Yes, two conquering armies had to come to unite the entire nation in prayer and unite it in purpose. For it was the prayer not of the weak but of the strong in heart, with an unbending spirit to resist and with a will to live for a better morrow.

With untiring efforts Bishop Mindszenty had been proceeding on the road of moral reconstruction; religious life in his diocese received a new impetus as the common people saw him make their cares his own, bring order into the communities, and, wherever needed, fearlessly let his voice be heard on behalf of the right of man.

In Rome, Pope Pius XII had been anxiously watching the developments in Hungary. For nearly half a year, since the passing of Justinian, Cardinal Serédi, the bishops and the more than six million Catholics of Hungary had been without a primate.

On the second day of October a messenger from the Holy Father arrived bearing the pall.

It had pleased the Holy Father to select Joseph, the Bishop of Veszprém, to become Archbishop of Strigonia, and, as such, Prince Primate of Hungary.

On October 7, 1945, he was enthroned in the Basilica of Esztergom. After the ceremonies, when he was alone, he returned and knelt at the gate of the altar:

"Father, Thou hast chosen me to lead Thy Hungarian people. Make me be their righteous shepherd . . ."

Humbly, the new Archbishop took up his residence in the great historical edifice. The seat of the Primate—known in the Catholic world as the See of Strigonia—housed one of the most impressive neoclassical cathedrals of Europe. Now it showed the scars of the war; part of it had been destroyed.

Esztergom had been the seat of the first Hungarian kings, who about the end of the twelfth century had caused the erection of a most magnificent Romanesque basilica that was partly destroyed by the Turks. In 1822, on the very same site, a new cathedral rose that was completed in 1886. It included within its walls the old Renaissance chapel built during the Archiepiscopacy of Thomas, Cardinal Bakócz, at the beginning of the sixteenth century.

In this magnificence he lived a life of the utmost simplicity. He slept on a hard bench; his study had no ornate furniture, but only necessary pieces.

On October 14 he presented himself to the faithful of the Capital. The words he spoke in the Basilica of St. Stephen were heard far beyond the walls; they called on the world:

"As your most graciously designated new shepherd, I come to you in haste. It is here that the wounds are most numerous, on the walls and in the hearts. This city is fighting valiantly, suffers and bears its burden and the hours—months—of hardship in exemplary fashion. I have come so that shepherd and flock may meet, face to face, that they may read in each other's heart, that we, together, may draw further strength from our God, the Almighty.

"The thunderous storm of the war passed over us more than half a year ago. We might rejoice at its passing; however, the Danube valley, though no longer a valley of blood, still is a valley of tears, a valley of suffering, a valley of sorrow. A gigantic vulture ready to embrace its prey, the coming winter—maybe the most terrible winter of our entire history—hovers over us.

"When I look at the prospect of this winter, I shudder as a human being, as a Christian, and as a citizen of this land. The newspapers print reports of starvation; reports of the political battles have almost become secondary as the papers cry over the lack of food supplies, over the approaching stoppage of the public utilities, over the ever climbing curve of inflation.

"We can see the windowless, heatless homes on snow-whipped nights, the innocent infants hanging withered and forlorn on the dried-out breasts of their mothers.

"I am fully aware of the self-respect and noble pride of the Hungarian people. It is not easy for a Hungarian to beg or to show his wounds. Instead of the people, the Primate of this land, at the occasion of his first visit to the capital city, standing under the war-wrought ruins of ancient Buda, comes to call on the world, on the civilized peoples and nations everywhere, holding the beggar-bag of this nation; he is sending the cry to the four corners of the globe: Save the perishing Hungarian lives!

"You promised us humanity after the war. I know your hearts are open, since you have already helped other defeated nations.

"We did not wish for this war; our geographical position, our historical misfortune, the logic of warfare have plowed over us.

"For a thousand years, our blood and our soil have defended the peace, the civilization, the culture, and the wealth of the Western world; this is why *you* could remain at the gates of life."

The Primate was imbued with the urgency of action. He felt that no time could be lost; that action was needed.

From the window of his study he could look across the Danube to the shore which after the Second World War had again become part of Czechoslovakia. This sight was a constant reminder of the fate of his brethren across this border.

As Bishop of Veszprém, he already had concerned himself with their reported persecution; now as their own Archbishop he deemed it his duty to speak on behalf of the suffering:

"And the hand of the Lord was heavy. Were our sufferings expressed in sound corresponding in intensity to our pain, they would leap to heaven even under the burden of our crosses, the crosses carried by individuals, families, communities, and cities—indeed, by the entire society over the whole Hungarian land.

"And yet, we must admit, it is not our cross which is the heaviest, it is not our wounds that burn most deeply. From the northern part of our Archdiocese—with which for nine hundred years we shared the communion of the sacred faith and sanctified traditions—news comes to us of untold sufferings following in the wake of the contaminated spirit of the world, fountainhead of hatred and vengeance. Their sufferings are brought about by means and methods which had been tried out and practiced on the ill-fated Jews, and which are practiced on them even after their return from concentration camps.

With the same methods, by practically the same men—but under different colors and under somewhat different sponsorship—Hungarian Christians have now been persecuted for weeks, in the spirit of National Socialism.

"Armed guards drive sisters and servants of the Lord through the streets of cities and villages to prisons and to the new frontiers established by the Armistice Convention.

"For many months, several hundred thousand people have been awaiting fearful events with strained nerves during every hour of the day; especially during the night. According to one of the reports, in the district of Ipolyság, over five hundred people were driven to an unknown fate between 5:00 P.M. and 5:30 A.M.; among them were infants, old people, families with four to five small children, all of whom were stripped of their possessions. When they could finally stop for a rest, their temporary lot was a house without doors or windows.

"As a result of the actions of church-denying individuals, politics has begun to interfere with the affairs of the Church; Hungarian and Catholic schools are being taken away from the families, and the children are forced to attend foreign schools. Consecrated statues in front of churches and on façades of buildings are being defaced and destroyed. Family fortunes are being confiscated, institutions are being dissolved, Hungarian signs are being ravaged and demolished.

"The ancient archives and files of the parishes are being pillaged and plundered. Family shrines sanctified by the joys and sorrows of a long line of ancestors throughout many centuries are being robbed, their inhabitants, like so many driven beasts, are chased out of these homes and deported.

"As for the few who might be left behind to arouse the conscience of the humane world, even if they happen to live in purely Hungarian communities, they are likely not to have Hungarian priests and Hungarian schools; thus they will lose today, in our twentieth century—which brought the world most welcome human rights, such as the Atlantic Charter—the precious right to worship in their own way.

"They will strike the shepherd, and the sheep of the flock shall be dispersed. The flock is the great Hungarian people.

"But we have to perpetuate the virtues of today's Hungarian priest whose history goes back in tradition a thousand years; like a good shepherd, he stayed with his flock to the very last; in all cases he left only under coercion and threats. There were even some who came back to this world of agony. The flock, too, merit praise for their loyalty to their persecuted, faithful shepherds.

"You ask me, my dear brethren, Why am I informing you of this lamentable situation? Certainly not to kindle hatred in your hearts. Of hatred there is enough as it is.

"I have shown you a horrible, outrageous, accusatory example of the mishandling of human rights, of the mistreatment of the weak, an example which bears within itself its own retribution.

"The world without fear and want has not yet come to us here. You should feel sympathy and compassion in your hearts and souls for the victims who are your fellow men and brothers-in-faith. As for those who perpetrate all this because they are contaminated by the spirit of an inhumane world, strive to save them with the words of the Savior: they know not what they do.

"I ask you to pray for your suffering brethren, for the repentance of the torturers of your fellow men redeemed at the cost of our Lord's dear blood; for truth, life, righteousness, brotherly love and for the land and a world of peace."

The letter was made public on the 15th of October, causing consternation in political circles, but it drew the attention of the world to an injustice.

Having done this in his own right, he called a conference of the episcopate, to evaluate the conditions in the homeland. Two days later, on the 17th, the Primate issued his first pastoral letter:

"As teachers and guardians of the revealed truth, of the spiritual laws of nature and the moral law laid down by men, the bishops of the Holy Mother Church, the descendants of the Apostles have raised their voices from time to time throughout history whenever society or the general trend of a given era was found to be in contradiction with these fundamental truths or laws. Thus, the Church spoke in protest against slavery, against the unjust treatment of labor and more recently against the persecution of the Jews.

"When last year on the Day of the Apostles our pastoral letter concerning the Jews was published, despite the government and the general spirit of that time, few people understood the real meaning, and those concerned most even took offense.

"In fact, all we did was to condemn those measures which, because of race, deprived one group of Hungarian citizens of their inherent rights and rightful possessions, stigmatizing and humiliating them, throwing them into ghettos and deporting them without establishing, by legal procedure, their guilt as individuals.

"Today, public opinion in this country is well aware of the fact that by defending the Sacrament and the individual we only acquitted ourselves of our duty. The country as a whole was only harmed by what happened, and had it listened to the Church instead of following the ignis fatuus it could have been spared the harshness of this lesson.

"But if we raised our voices in favor of the baptized and the non-baptized, cross-bearing Jews, we cannot keep silent about the accumulated suffering of our own people either; we now refer especially to those hardships which were not brought about by the unavoidable consequences of the war, but which are germinated by anger, hatred, vengeance, and evil passions.

"If they punished only the guilty we would not protest; but they brand those upon whom no crime can be fastened as friends of the wicked and deport them. They even blame them for things that constitute their natural rights, such as their mother tongue. Let us not commit any deed which we survey with indignation when it is committed on the other side of the frontiers, set by the Armistice, and which, when it was perpetrated against us, we found unbearable.

"Unless competent tribunals have pronounced a final verdict based on valid proofs against individuals, these cannot, by sheer force of authority, be despoiled of their rightful property, cannot be ejected from the homes of their ancestors, and cannot be torn from the land rendered fertile by their forefathers' sweat and their own.

"We also raise our voices on behalf of the innocent children, the old people, and the sick, against the national ghettos, the ceaseless resettlements, which eventually will lead to complete legal insecurity, and which are driving the country into poverty and destitution.

"We consider as capable of settling these matters only impartial, experienced men who are imbued with the historic responsibility of their task, and who, guided by their own conscience, rise high above the heated passions of our times.

"The state cannot, arbitrarily, because of fashion and the spirit of the era, take the place of the natural laws, more specifically of the individual liberties, of freedom from fear and freedom from anxiety. In the matter of minorities the wisdom of our King St. Stephen has traced the road we must tread; today, as ever, we should be conscious of the sublime knowledge that in a country inhabited by several nationalities there is room only for brotherly love, mutual understanding, and respect. We are harming ourselves if, instead of acquiring friends, we make enemies of our fellow citizens. Who knows whether what is done on one shore of the river will not be turned against us on the other bank?

"Let us reestablish the supremacy of the law, the spirit of love, peace, and understanding: grace to you and peace from God our Father and from the Lord Jesus Christ. There should indeed be at least peace for all men of good will, whence will come glory to the Lord of all things existing."

Fearlessly he expressed his convictions on every issue. His utterances, both public and private, became signs pointing the way in the wilderness of the political life of the country.

He knew that the people were turning to the wise road, for about the time he was enthroned in Esztergom the municipal elections had been held in Budapest, and the population had voted overwhelmingly against radicalism. Nationwide elections were held on November 4. The first secret ballot in eastern Europe; an experiment of the Soviet masters. Indeed, they had certain conditions.

Marshal Voroshilov desired of the political parties a single electoral list, guaranteeing the majority to the leftist combine of Communist-dominated Socialists, crypto-Communists, and Communists. The Smallholders Party, conscious of its strength, refused all offers, but had to agree, whatever the outcome might be, to continue in a coalition with the henchmen of Moscow.

The people went to the polls. The result of the first unfettered elections surprised the world. Despite threats and terror, the people voted overwhelmingly for democracy and against the Communists, the latter receiving less than 17 per cent of the votes. Conforming to the preelection agreement, a coalition was formed; the cabinet consisting of nine Smallholders, four Communists, four Socialists, and one representative of the crypto-Communist, radical Peasant Party. Zoltán Tildy, a Protestant clergyman, became Premier; Mathias Rákosi, the Communist, and Árpád Szakasits, a renegade Socialist, secured indirect control by vice premierships. The greatest fault of this and of all succeeding coalition cabinets was the fact that their basic character was not representative of the will of the people, as the key ministries, including the all-powerful Ministry of the Interior, were by force—exerted by the Soviet occupation authorities —in the hands of the Communists and their henchmen.

The average man did not recognize the faults and was ready to support the new government. The provisional regime had bowed out gracefully, one of its last acts being the declaration of martial law throughout the country in an effort to counteract the spread of looting, rape, and murder; committed mostly by "criminals in stolen Russian uniforms."

On New Year's Eve the Primate at the microphone weighed the past and pointed to the future: "Men of Hungary—fight and hope with trust!"

Among the many issues confronting the nation and, by historic implication the Church was the question of changes in the form of government. The kingdom was to be abolished, a republic established. Popular support, the will of the people, could not be gauged; no plebiscite was proposed. The majority—even some who would have liked to see a republic—were of the opinion that no such constitutional change should take place while the country was occupied by a foreign force. But the Soviet wanted the monarchy to be abolished.

Hungary had been a kingdom for a thousand years, with the short interruption during the revolution following the First World War. Since 1920 it had been a kingdom without a king, ruled in the name of the "Holy Crown" by a regent.

The crown and the coronation vestments were abroad, having been taken by the Germans. The popular, mystic concept among the people was that without possession of the Holy Crown there could be no claim to recognition as a constitutional executive.

To understand this, one must know its history.

The Holy Crown of Hungary actually consists of two crowns. The upper part, a caplike dome with a cross atop it, was sent by Pope Sylvester II to the first king of Hungary, St. Stephen, who later was canonized. Historians believe it to be one of the magnificent masterpieces of jewelcraft as exercised by the goldsmiths of the Benedictine monastery of Monte Cassino. The enamel ornaments show a painting of the Lord Savior and of eight of the Apostles; its unique character is supposed to symbolize sovereign royal powers, independence of all secular heads, and apostolic and absolute prerogatives. The lower part, an open crown, was sent by the Greek Emperor Michael Ducas to King Géza in 1072, in acknowledgment of his generosity toward his enemies. It is one of the finest examples of the Byzantine goldsmith's craft, and its highly ornamental design contains enamel portraits of Emperor Michael, the giver, King Géza, the recipient, Crown Prince Constantine of Greece, St. Demetrios, St. Michael, and St. Gabriel. The blank spaces are decorated with pearls and precious stones; heavy gold chains hang from the sides.

The two parts were joined before the end of the eleventh century and together compose the Holy Crown which has been used ever since to crown the kings of Hungary.

It was traditionally an important factor in the historic development of the Hungarian constitution, as early as the thirteenth century. The Holy Crown has been the uniting symbol of constitutional kingship and statehood, denoting king and nation as a unified organism. No dynasty or famliy has any proprietary rights to the crown, its ownership being vested in the Hungarian nation. It does not denote the king without the nation nor the nation without the king.

In the year 1401 the assembled leaders of the Hungarian people declared that "the power of the state is singly vested in the Holy Crown." Embossed in the seal of this charter is "Sigillum † sacre † corone † regni † Hungarie."

The more modern constitutional concept has been that the king wearing the Holy Crown, and the nation as a unit, are two parts which together constitute the "body of the Holy Crown": the state. The state itself and every one of its organisms are in direct relation to the crown. In this manner the territory of the state is the territory of the crown. The sovereign rights are not inherent in the person of the king but are vested in the crown, and their exercise is temporarily transferred to the person of the king, through the act of coronation. Legislation, as the highest expression of sovereignty, is reserved to the unified complements, the Holy Crown and the nation, together constituting the state: its authority—as every function of the executive—is exercised jointly by the king and the members of the nation, the citizens, represented by Parliament. The right to give royal assent to legislation is transferred to the person of the king only through the act of coronation—a ceremony through which the living personality of the king becomes a part in the unity of crown and nation.

For this reason no king is recognized without an act of coronation; and without a king there is only a transitory stage in the life of the nation. It was because of the first that, when the Austrian Emperor Joseph II succeeded his mother the Empress Maria Theresa on the throne and refused to be crowned King of Hungary, he became known among the common people as the "ruler with the hat." And it was because of the latter concept that, the throne having been declared vacant through laws passed by the constitutional assembly, Hungary was governed from 1920 to 1946 "in the name of the Holy Crown," its sovereignty maintained, sentences passed in its name, and bills sanctified on its behalf.

As there had never been any question in the past, the relationship of the office of the Prince Primate and the physical body of the crown had never been clarified; his office had political significance, for it was the Prince Primate that performed the coronation ceremony and, together with the Prime Minister, placed the crown on the head of the monarch. By tradition and by law, he was an integral part of the legislative body, having a seat in the upper house; in the structure of public functionaries, he was considered as the "first dignitary of the land" and had precedence before all, except the representative of the crown.

In January of 1946, as preparations were being made to bow to the inevitable wish of the Soviet, which through the Communist propaganda machine had manufactured a "popular demand," the Prince Primate did little to retard the establishment of a republic. Eventually he considered it as an untimely act, executed under duress, regarded it as an existing condition and never raised the question of its constitutional legality. He did not deem such a step to be in public interest.

At the turn of January, Parliament passed the law creating the republic, and a few days later Zoltán Tildy became its first President; Ferenc Nagy, the leader of the Smallholders Party, a God-fearing, devout Presbyterian, became Prime Minister and Monsignore Béla Varga, a canon of the Roman Catholic Church, followed him in the chair as President of the Parliament.

The same day, the Prince Primate turned to one of the burning issues of the day and sent from Esztergom his pastoral letter asking to help heal the Hungarian wounds:

"In the course of the last few decades, when we, the bishops of this land, standing on the unshakable foundation of the laws of God and nature, spoke to you collectively, we did this at almost each occasion to point out the errors being made in the national life of our country and thus to help bring about a much desired improvement and solution. This time we point to burning, open sores and ask your help in the healing of the 'Hungarian wounds.'

"The final outcome of the war brought untold misery and suffering. There is hardly a family in our country—be it in city, town, or hamlet—which has come through the ravaging war without freshly dug graves, close by or far away, without a new widow, without new orphans, without loss of members as prisoners of war or just prisoners, without deportees to the West, without humiliated ones, without mentally sick, without cripples or without some measure of destitution.

"There are families on whose shoulders we observe almost all the crosses mentioned; but aside from these families there are, in our national life, hordes of people who not only suffer such agonies but also feel unceasingly the torments, unknown in our land up until now, of indigence and privation. It is to those that we wish to call your attention, my dear brethren, not only to make you share at least in spirit the terrible ordeal of these agonized masses, but also to kindle your brotherly love into active help.

"This winter brought to hundreds of thousands in our nation serious lack of clothing, heatless homes, and frightening shortages of food. Strong, grown people can at times withstand the pangs of hunger for days; not so the aged, the infants, and the children. As for the strong, where is their strength today?

"In the destiny of the individual as well as in that of the family infinite destruction in our already diminished national life will be the deadly aftermath of misery. The cities of the living are disappearing rapidly while graveyards are spreading with frightening swiftness. We know very well that the quantity of food supplies in our land has shrunk to a disastrously low level since the rapacious war devoured the food destined for our people; and especially along the main highways the gleaning assumed gigantic proportions.

"And now, after having made all possible efforts at the right time to secure outside help which, mostly because of general insecurity, arrives with great delay and only in promising dribbles, we have to reduce the radius of our SOS signals; we ourselves must also partake in bitter but essential rescue work; especially must those help who are in regions where general destruction left some little more than an agonizing void. In such cases the true Catholic who aspires to this sacred title must not shrink from sharing his last mouthful of bread.

"The slogan of each heart should be, 'At least one parcel to our starving brothers in Budapest.' You can well imagine what it means when after weeks of gloom and privation the mother of the homestead can offer to the children and to the aged something to eat more than the dreary emptiness of tasteless soup. The help given until now has been a great comfort: God bless the senders. We beg you to continue.

"We are asking for winter homes for city boys and girls from four to fourteen years old. This winter, the warmhearted Catholics of the counties of Somogy and Baranya have already been host to fifteen hundred children. We might mention that each child, as a token of gratitude, will bring ten pounds of salt granted by the authorities to each foster home.

"We know the generous hearts of our people from the past, from better times. It was not in vain that at the country houses in Zala there was a so-called lean-to, a beggar shed. When the family took their seats around the table, any strange wanderer was given a hot meal and kind words; he never left a Hungarian home with empty hands.

"Foreign countries also know Hungarian generosity. If, in the course of the past few years, it was Hungary that gave 70 per cent of the alms collected all over the world for the rescue of the Western countries suffering under the German occupation, this time we have to speed to the assistance of our own whose misery lies before our very eyes, those who are blood of our blood, bone of our bone, whose good and ill fortune we have shared throughout our thousand years of history and of whom not one should perish because of your failure to help."

February of 1946 brought one of the greatest events in the life of the son of the humble peasants of Mindszent. For some time Joseph, the Archbishop of Esztergom, had been selected, *in petto*, cardinal of the Holy Roman Catholic Church. He had received the scarlet cap. Now that the sacred college was meeting in consistory, he was to travel to Rome to receive the red hat from the Holy Father in person.

The brave stand the Primate had taken in matters of public concern had not only earned him the hate of the leaders of the Communist party in Hungary, but the displeasure of the Soviet occupation authorities. The Hungarian government itself had a little to say as to who was permitted to leave Hungary; the passport it issued was good for travel abroad, but permission to leave the country depended on a clearance issued by the occupation authorities at their convenience and pleasure. The chancellery of Esztergom had requested such clearance for the Primate and his secretary, but it had not been forthcoming. The Russians claimed to have "mislaid" the first request and to have "lost" the second. The consistory had already opened in the Vatican when finally, through the energetic intervention of Prime Minister Nagy himself, and of General William S. Key, the American member of the Allied Control Commission, the clearance was received. The Cardinal was flown to Rome in a United States Army Air Force plane held at the personal disposal of General Key.

Among the newly created cardinals was Francis, Cardinal Spellman, the Archbishop of New York; and a lasting personal friendship ensued between the two princes of the Church.

While he was abroad, hundreds of people paid their respects to him; and he pleaded with all the case of his people, asked for patience, for understanding of the problems facing the Catholic Church in Hungary and the nation in general.

Within a few weeks he was back in his Archdiocese, hard at work. Conditions in general had become very difficult for everyone, as inflation was playing havoc with the country's slowly recuperating economy.

For his own person he made no demands. The bins in his kitchen were notoriously empty. He insisted that his table should be as frugal as that of the poorest of the land. As it became known that there were days when the cook did not know what to serve, people came from near and far with their offerings for the Primate's table. As soon as he received such gifts, he had them sent to the orphanages. The priests serving with him actually had to hide some packages so that their contents would reach the Cardinal's table. To adapt the household to the difficult times, he ruled that on Mondays a single dish of food only was to be served. During Lent he ate no breakfast; for the noon meal he had soup and a piece of bread; at night, one piece of bread only, spiced with paprika.

To compensate him for the income of the fields the Archdiocese had lost through the land reform, the government voted him a grant equal to the Prime Minister's salary. He never made use of it, never accepted it. Once when he was asked how he expected to manage without any income, he answered: "One of my sisters sent me a calf; another, a pig; my mother brought some chickens: thus the Primate is provided for."

The family of the Cardinal retained the simplicity of their village life in Mindszent. Just as for three hundred years they had been part of the community in their simple way, they did not change because Joseph had become the first shepherd of the land and a prince of the beloved Church of Rome.

Soon after he received the scarlet biretta, one of life's hardest chores faced him: his father died, and he laid him to rest in the simple cemetery of Mindszent.

Even in these difficult days the family of the Cardinal had kept close together. Mother Barbara, having already passed the biblical age, still oversaw the busy household, filled with life and the laughter of her children and fourteen grandchildren. The fact that a brother was a Cardinal brought no change to the life of the men of the family, who continued to dig the fields and force the produce from the reluctant soil by the sweat of their brows.

When vacation time came, they would find brother Joseph among the busy workers. Just as he had done for all the years since he had become priest, even as a Cardinal, whenever he visited his old home, he continued to take part in the common work. After celebrating Mass at daybreak, he left with them for the fields; and one could see him in a simple long black cassock pushing the plow into the soil to dig a deep furrow, driving the oxen, or swinging the scythe to cut the golden wheat, the Hungarian's staff of life. No toil was too hard, no chore too lowly for his dignity.

Once he was asked by one of his young priests why, as the

Primate of the land, he still continued to work like the lowliest peasant; and he answered:

"I have come from people who have toiled on the soil for hundreds of years; my ancestors' sweat sanctified this Hungarian earth; I shall not change because of an office granted to me by grace.

"Among my predecessors as primates of the land were many plain people; they never denied their fathers. Archbishop John Simor's father was a bootmaker; Kolos Vaszary's was a furrier; Justin Serédi's was a pottery maker—men as simple as my elders who tilled the soil."

At sunset he used to sit out in the courtyard with his mother. Neighbors came to seek advice; for his counsel was sought at times on many earthly matters, some even asking him what to sow. They brought their children to him, and it made the mothers happy to see their young receive his blessings. He was always benign to the good and stern to the wayward.

Above all, they regarded him as their own. Joseph, the Cardinal, was one of their sons, of their blood and of their mind. They recognized in him the qualities they had striven to attain; and whenever they sang a "Te Deum" their hearts overflowed in gratitude to the Lord for the grace He had shown in exalting one of their own.

He spoke to the men of the cities in the same manner as he spoke to the peasants:

"When Pope St. Pius three hundred seventy-five years ago sent the Christian armada to the sea battle of Lepanto, he first prayed and then prepared for his activities. He banned from the inns of Rome the addicts to alcohol, gambling, and other harmful pursuits. He freed the city of women of dubious character, equipped his lodgings with simple furniture, slept on a hard straw bed, and ordered general fast and penance. With such measures came a new world order which he proclaimed and initiated.

"We, too, want nothing more: merely decency, justice, love, peace, and harmony. Particularly at the present moment, when peace is in the offing, all saber rattling seems superfluous and may even prove to be harmful. There are already too many ruins on Hungarian soil. To cause more destruction would show a lack of responsibility on our part. *Concordia parvae res crescunt, discordia et maximae dilabuntur.* (In harmony even the smallest values grow, in discord even the greatest decrease.) According to the Revelation, every house divided against itself will ultimately fall.

"Herewith we offer the hands and the strength of our Catholics, who constitute two-thirds of our country's population. Their moral capital, built up in a thousand years, is now offered for the rebuilding of our nation. We do expect all people, in all walks of life, to give the best of their strength and skill for this purpose. However, since no undertaking of man can succeed without the grace of God, we stand ready to pray for His aid! We, representing Catholicism, the most religious of all religions, shall fight with prayers. Could we imagine any communion, in these fateful years, at which the suffering image of this country was not evoked?

"Trusting in God, we work for this country, giving all our physical and moral strength. So help us God!"

When speaking to the students of the University of Budapest, he reminded them of history, that some of the spirit of the past had become timely:

"You are all acquainted with the illustrious fame of the Congreganists. When the hour for liquidating the Turkish dominion was about to strike, the Congreganists assembled on Hungarian soil. The great army sent from abroad by Pope Innocent XI joined Hungarian troops 24,000 strong. Heading the former army was the Congreganist Charles of Lorraine. The Hungarian soldiers were led by the Palatine, Prince Paul Eszterházy, who wrote the beautiful prayer to Virgin Mary beginning with the words, 'Be mindful, blessed Mother of God, Our Lady of Hungary.' The majority of the officers of both armies, as well as a considerable number of the rank and file, were Congreganists. At dawn, on September 2, 1686, trumpets sounded beneath the disconsolate walls of Buda. Battle cries pierced the air. The Congreganist soldiers invoked the aid of Virgin Mary. Those who first scaled the battlements of the fortress, led by gallant Captain John Fiáth of Györ, were Hungarian soldiers bearing the banner of Our Lady. While another Hungarian army stood idle in the country, following a so-called 'realistic' policy, Congreganist soldiers took Buda and fought for thirty years to regain the rest of Hungarian territory. And the territory of the country was reconquered, its freedom established.

"Some may hold that these are not timely words. After all, the war is over; we wish to devote ourselves to reconstruction. But even in times of peace and reconstruction, the spirit of the Congreganists is timely; our young men and young women should be imbued with it.

"As long as the dignity of man remains part of the Magna Charta of youth, as long as the worth and accomplishment of the individual are to be respected and safeguarded, as long as this nation wants life and resurrection, the Congreganist ideal of life will continue to be as important to us as the light of our eyes, as the last bit of crust that nourishes us.

"Live in accordance with your faith. 'Estote factores verbi, et non auditores tantum.' And may your life and example and apostolic zeal cause the love of our Church and country to permeate to the farthest reaches of the nation. People all over the world dare to love their country. We Hungarians dare to love our country, and this love of Church and country shall become the salvation of our souls and the resurrection of this nation."

Dark clouds began to gather over the schools of the churches as early as 1946. The Communists had believed that, because the Church through the land reform had lost the financial basis for the maintenance of her institutions, these would fall like ripe fruit into their lap. The willingness of the population to sacrifice without stint for their maintenance resulted in a disappointment for the Communists; they were forced to rearrange Moscow's timetable. Then different methods were tried.

Catholic youths were accused of having killed Russian soldiers; Catholic teachers and leaders of youth organizations were accused of complicity. In the Communist press banner headlines announced the crimes. The Communist Minister of the Interior, backed by the threat of economic sanctions by the Soviet against the whole of the

country, finally succeeded in dissolving all Catholic youth organizations by simply revoking their licenses. Despite the country-wide
protests, their properties were given to the Marxist youth.

The Communist press "discovered" conspiracies in the Catholic
schools, hidden depots of ammunition. The accusations were proven
false, but the battles went on.

The fight for the soul of the child had begun, and the Cardinal
spoke:

"To whom does the child belong? In Hungary both children and
parents agree in saying that the child belongs to his parents. The
deed is entered in God's registry. Parents have a primary, inalienable
right with regard to the education of their children. No one can
justly deprive them of that elemental right—not even the state. For
the family comes before the state. The relationship of the family to
the child takes precedence over that of the state.

"The Church, too, has a right to the child, a divine and historic
right.

"The two-thousand-year-old historic right of the Church Universal and the thousand-year-old historic right of the Catholic
Church in Hungary stem from divine right. Through the ceremony
of baptism, the Church becomes the child's spiritual father. And the
Church, Sancta Mater Ecclesia, by virtue of being the Mother
Church, is also the child's spiritual mother. The Church stands beside
the earthly parents as the child's God-given parents. This is the basis
of the rights of the Church in the field of education. Now someone
may ask: Do we allow no rights to the state? Let no one imply such
an attitude on the part of the Church. The Church recognizes the
rights of the state and desires that it live up to its obligations by giving support to the schools, the teachers, and their pupils, so that
nothing may obstruct the work of the schools. Furthermore, in places
where, to this day, no schools exist, and where competent organizations are not in a position to establish schools, we ask and desire the
state to set up schools, so that even in such regions no Hungarian
child should grow up in ignorance. Allow me to remind you of the
action taken ten years ago by a British minister of education, who
had a bridge built from one island to another, in order that the life

of a solitary English schoolchild should not be exposed to the daily risk of an open-water crossing.

"Our poor Hungarian children are not in this situation. We are happy if—as the official statute prescribes—schooling can be provided wherever there are thirty or forty children in one place. We not only approve, but urgently demand such facilities for Hungarian children. However, we Catholics do not recognize the right of the state to a monopoly in the field of education, not because we itch to contradict, but simply because it would conflict with the teaching of our Lord Jesus Christ.

"A state monopoly means the secularization of religious schools. From the moment of its inception, only state schools could exist or be established.

"Against this endeavor we Catholics protest, citing the precepts of our Lord Jesus. The Church is very old, far older than trends that crop up from time to time.

"It goes without saying that the parents who have entrusted to us their dearest treasure and holiest legacy, the immortal souls of their children, will be behind us one and all."

The parents and the people, mindful of the fact that their own future and that of their children was dependent on the rearing of the young, rose in defense of their beliefs.

Speaking in the capital city of the country, the Cardinal called attention to the character and accomplishments of the Church's schools:

"The Church carries on a tremendous work in education. Down through the centuries the Church of Christ has displayed many wondrous qualities, but as the educator of nations she shines with the endearing charm and glory of motherhood. Throughout human history she has been fruitfully active in this task. Ever since the words of our Founder, 'Going therefore, teach ye all nations,' this mission has inspired the Church. Ex scholis omnis nostra salus.

"Our present concern is with Hungarian church schooling. This was carried on, at first, in the churches themselves. Here our ancestors were taught the rudiments of agriculture and the industrial arts. By 1526 we had a thousand schools, all Catholic. The monastic schools were in a class apart. On consulting canonical visiting books of the eighteenth century, we find that the school was twin sister to the Church, the village schoolmaster the partner of the parish priest. The state, engaged in recruiting soldiers and gathering taxes, showed scant interest in schools. The Latin high schools were in the hands of the Piarist, Jesuit, and Paulist orders. Nuns supervised the education of girls.

"What characterizes our schools?

"Their pedagogical worth and their foundation of religious morality. Their basic principles—not formulated yesterday, but existing from the very beginning—are: absolute truthfulness, respect for authority, community spirit, devotion to duty, justice, and neighborly love.

"These are the ideals by the light of which the traditional pedagogy of the Church guided youth past the hidden reefs of puberty to the firm shores of manly and womanly character.

"In the realm of church schooling, the letter to the Romans still applies when it says, 'Be not overcome by evil, but overcome evil by good.' Yet another feature is the harmonizing of precept and example. Count Albert Apponyi notes in his memoirs that his Catholic training revealed the fact that his teachers were not motivated by material reward, but by dedication to a cause. For centuries the Church has invested in her schools not only tremendous resources, but also an infinite amount of devotion, skill, and self-sacrifice. No other form of education is able to invest so much, for there is no way of giving what one does not have.

"Now, during the second period of occupation, the work of the state schools is disrupted; but the church schools are intact; and until this very day we have been struggling with our utmost strength to preserve them."

The direct attack veered off; popular resistance forced the Communists to choose a more arduous road.

The official Soviet representative, Minister Pushkin, began to exert pressure on the government—during conversations with Prime

Minister Nagy—to agree to optional religious education, with re-
vised religious schoolbooks. Ferenc Nagy recognized the magnitude
of the issue, for he could foresee that if the publishing of schoolbooks
should be made a state monopoly, as it was suggested, the teaching
about God and the supernatural would soon be according to the
tenets of Moscow. Economic and political sanctions were in the
offing again, and he seemingly agreed to entertain the issue, knowing
that, as soon as it became public, resistance in Parliament and by the
masses, could be counted upon.

It turned out that his plan worked. The Russians and the Communists were furious; but time was won.

In general 1946 had been a year of continuous trials for the people
of Hungary. Since the elections the population had been increasingly
anxious to return to normalcy; everyone was feverishly working to
restore the ruins and re-create the destroyed.

Money had been depreciating rapidly, and on July 5 the government had to print bank notes with the astronomical figure of five
sextillion pengös, which corresponded on the day of issue to about
ten cents in United States currency. Reparations were an ever increasing burden, Soviet Russia having taken 24 per cent of the entire
national income in 1945 as its supposed legal booty.

In April Prime Minister Nagy flew to Moscow and pleaded with
Stalin for a breathing spell. The concessions he received were disregarded by the local Soviet occupation authorities, willfully or by
instruction. In June he visited Washington. The American government generously returned the $32,000,000 of gold of the Hungarian
National Bank captured from the Germans, which enabled the Hungarian government to stabilize the currency, and in August, the
Hungarian florin (forint) was issued.

A peace treaty had been written in Paris, with terms even harder
than the treaty of Trianon.

The Cardinal felt it to be his duty to voice his plea for a just
peace:

"Hungarian eyes turn toward the West, as we await the decisions
of the peace conferences, watching anxiously to determine the extent

to which the oft proclaimed principles of a just and lasting peace will apply to the land of St. Stephen.

"Here in Central Europe, Hungary is the last branch of the tree of the Church, which embraces so many lands. For two thousand years this great tree has been producing the blessed fruits of civilization, gladdening the hearts of peoples and nations. It would hardly be a matter of indifference if the Central European branch were split in five or six ways and allowed to wither away, instead of continuing its thousand-year-old mission with full vigor.

"I send this thought by way of the World Church which today, too, beyond symbolizing the unity of faith and love, is the mighty pillar of justice.

"In the past, Hungarians distinguished themselves in defense of civilization, though, in the main, their eminent service has gone unrecognized. Continually, since their arrival in the Danube basin, but especially from the thirteenth to the seventeenth century, they defended with their blood the peace and integrity of the West. Thus, Michelet in his history of France refers to Hungary as the 'blessed deliverer' of the West.

"Hungarian blood has flowed in a never ending stream. While Michelangelo worked undisturbed on the dome of St. Peter's, while London applauded Shakespeare's dramas, our warriors of the border castles fought valiantly to defend the very gates of Rome, Paris, and London.

"In the Middle Ages, England, France, and Hungary were about equal in population. England today has forty-four million people, France forty-one million, and Hungary but ten or twelve million, because Hungarians, over a period of five hundred years, have ceaselessly bled for the world, and for Western civilization. In consequence of this blood bath, Hungary was reduced from a great power to an impoverished and dismembered little nation. By way of gratitude, they have carved three and a half million people from her living body, apportioning them to the Italians, Czechs, and Slovaks, whose defense we had been for centuries; and to Rumanians and Serbs, to whom we had granted asylum.

"For five hundred years we have been awaiting some sign of

appreciation. So far, our only reward has been the dictate of Trianon, which took from us 63.5 per cent of our population and 71.3 per cent of our territory, leaving us the legacy of poverty and a new war.

"Innumerable statesmen have since acknowledged that it was a prejudiced decision based on concocted statistics.

"Do they intend to repeat an admitted injustice, and cap it all by rendering millions of our compatriots homeless? Is the twentieth century to mark the death of civilization? Are we to suffer thus for our guilt in not subduing the mighty German war machine that it took the united nations of the world seven years to conquer?

"During the recently ended global war, we heard the promises of many charters and declarations. The war, they announced, was being fought to defend truth, freedom and human rights from the forces of organized oppression. So, now, let us seek these human rights, along with the principle of self-determination, and freedom from oppression.

"There is hope, if these words are truth, not propaganda; if the victors are superior to the vanquished; if the spirit of brotherly love refuses to allow human millions to revert to animal existence; if tortured humanity meets with charity, instead of partnership in crime and base revenge."

The words were strong and sprang from noble thought, but to no avail: as a result of Yalta and Potsdam, Soviet Russia dominated the conditions of peace for Hungary.

More than a hundred thousand of the faithful assembled to hear the Cardinal turn back to Hungarian history and refer to the stations of suffering:

"Defending the faith of St. Stephen and St. Gellért is equivalent to loving one's country. Speaking out in defense of this faith and maintaining it is equal to carrying the Cross for one's country. Spilling one's blood on behalf of this faith is the same as dying for this sacred country of ours.

"But we have no desire to be blind in the national fashion of to-day; nor do we wish to identify ourselves in any way with the nation's present record in world affairs. Our hearts bleed for and go out to those both near and far who are rotting away; and our hearts ache for every Transylvanian, for everyone persecuted in Slovakia, and for those suffering all over the world, even though they do not happen to speak Hungarian. We condemn all illegal greed and moronic cedings. As among the Galatians we have enmity here, quarrels, anger, secession, envy, murder, immorality and the like. And because we are continually tearing at one another's throats so do we destroy one another.

"We love freedom but not the freedom of inequality and strife.

"We learn easily, but we wish only to be part of enduring truth such as God, the immortality of the soul, and brotherhood; we do not feel that fashion can be accepted as a truth to be followed.

"Our flag has the picture of the Virgin Mary on one side and the Hungarian coat of arms on the other, with the inscription: 'Cum Deo pro patria et libertate.'

"Our ideals, as expressed by the bishops at the millennium, are: mutual understanding, brotherly love, moral health, and piety that is expressed in action. To this I add, as very timely ideals, the Church, the sacrament of marriage, and the family. In the spirit of St. Gellért, we wish to be faithful to these ideals in life as in death. Amen."

But suffering was not to end with that year, or any coming after.

On Christmas Day, the Communist Minister of the Interior announced that the secret political police had discovered a "conspiracy" and arrested a number of "conspirators."

Soon, everyone who displeased the Communists became a "conspirator"; trials were held at which most of the unfortunates "confessed"—their confessions implicating others; and these again "confessed" against the next. The public was stunned; respectable, upright, honest men were failing to stand up in court, were "confessing" to crimes they never could have committed, and accusing others.

The few who stood up in court, and whose behavior refuted their extorted "confessions," found their trials interrupted. For shorter

or longer periods they were returned to the care of the secret political police, or to the special detachment of the Russian N.K.V.D.
stationed in Hungary. When their trials were resumed they "confessed" and accepted their sentences without arguments. Among
those accused of crimes were Catholic priests and nuns. The persecution of the individual, under the cloak of legality, increased from
day to day.

Wherever the Cardinal could help, he attempted to improve the
lot of the persecuted. When he was once asked whether such unusual steps would not cause unpleasantness, he answered: "My son,
unusual steps are necessary in unusual times. I do what I believe is
right. The Lord Savior did not ask what His reward would be when
He set out to do unusual things."

The Cardinal did not turn away from any door. Once, without
advance notice, he appeared at a district prison where the warden,
guards, and prisoners were equally surprised by his presence. "My
children," he said to the prisoners, "happening to be in the city, I
wanted you too to partake in the blessings of Our Lord." And he
prayed with them.

He gave much time to visiting the dioceses, the parishes. Occasionally he would appear without announcement at some parish
church and, unnoticed, observe the life of the community. The
parish priest and the vicar would learn of his presence only after
he already thoroughly evaluated everything. He enjoyed the opportunity to express approval; would chastise when it was unavoidable. He never failed to express his feelings. For this he enjoyed the
respect of all.

The Cardinal insisted that whenever a bombed church or parish
house could be rebuilt the priest should see to it. Any priest
who failed to improve conditions soon found himself without a
parish.

Many a day the Cardinal would travel great distances, perhaps
celebrating early Mass in a city in the western part of Hungary,
speaking in the Capital at noon, and reaching some community in
the north or southeast in the afternoon or evening. Once his chauf-
feur, noticing that he looked tired, asked whether the next stop

should not be canceled. The Cardinal answered: "By no means, my son. There is so much to do—and I have so little time."

In his own archdiocese he expected his clergy to set the best examples in the way they lived. Above all, he demanded fervor and devotion. To create a closer tie between the priest and his parishioners, he divided up large parishes into smaller ones. No doubt ever entered his mind that the divided parishes would flourish.

He sent young priests out to unchurched communities with no other earthly asset than their own religious fervor. Imbued with the spirit of the apostles, they set out to places where there was no church or chapel, no parish house, not even a social hall—only the latent religious hunger of the communicants.

He was overjoyed when a young priest presented to him a new church; and proud, even though that church were only a transformed shop or garage. And other young priests, seeing such examples, set out gladly to do his bidding.

Words he spoke in his own basilica at Esztergom when he ordained some young candidates have remained in their hearts:

"The last ordination I was privileged to officiate at took place in a dark, catacomblike part of the Veszprém prison. A strange ceremony! He who officiated was a prisoner; those about to be ordained were also prisoners.

"The ten candidates had one candle, one cassock, and one surplice between them, but each had a separate armed guard watching over him.

"Present at the ceremony were the brave, faithful president of the Criminal Court, sixteen jailed priests, and over twenty lay prisoners.

"I began the high ceremony, knowing that it might have to be cut short. In that industrial region an aerial attack might be expected at any moment, or the near-by forces of occupation might appear on the scene, or else a promised police van to transport me and the candidates and certain of the communicants to the Csillag fortress at Komárom, or the penitentiary of Köhida.

"It was God's will that none of these events should take place then.

"On the occasion of the ordination at Veszprém, I repeated the words of our Savior: 'Behold I send you as sheep in the midst of wolves.'

"To you, my sons, I can only say the same.

"In any case, even today, you go out into the world clothed with illustrious power.

"Let the words ring in your ears without ceasing: *Sacerdotem oportet offere*, sacrifice yourselves, and even your lives. *Benedicere*, and bless those that mistreat and persecute you. *Praeesse*—you may say with the Savior, 'I am a worm, not a man,' but if there be five, or ten, who desire to be saved, they will kneel before you. *Praedicare*— to preach Christ and Our Lady, the Mother of Sorrows. *Baptizare*— the world is stiff-necked, but you open before it the gates of life everlasting by way of the cross and through the sacrament of repentance and remission of sin.

"You have steeped yourselves in holy knowledge, and enriched your souls with virtues, like all candidates before you. Continue in this spirit. Many muddy boots may be wiped on the robes of the Church—it matters not. The cassock of a priest is still man's most imperishable raiment."

As neither the decent members of the Hungarian government, nor the people as a whole were willing to become Soviet tools, Moscow decided to apply the thesis of Lenin and Stalin: "Disintegrate your opposition; then you conquer them one by one."

The Communists, gaining control of both the secret police and the political police of the army, used them to spread terror throughout the land, within the government, and eventually even in the cabinet itself. They arrested at will, questioning and threatening individuals. Protests were without avail, for they always claimed to be acting "in the best interest of the state" and, if necessary, would produce a "confession" by someone implicating in a crime the person arrested.

Such moves usually were preceded by headlines in the Communist press attacking the individual, giving the signal to the police to take action.

The most flagrant case, which developed into a matter of international importance, was the arrest of Béla Kovács. Next to Ferenc Nagy, Kovács was the most respected personality in the Smallholders Party. An ardent Catholic, a son of the soil, natural in his reactions, he had been an outspoken critic of both Communists and the Soviet system. He believed that he could afford it, for the other two members of the triumvirate of the Smallholders Party, Ferenc Nagy and Béla Varga, were Prime Minister and President of Parliament. For long months Kovács had been a thorn in the side of the Communists. At the end of February, 1947, they suddenly claimed that he was implicated in a "conspiracy." Brave and undaunted, he voluntarily went to the police to be examined; during his second appearance, he was abducted by the Russian N.K.V.D.—never to be seen again. His arrest became a *cause célèbre* of the world, for he was a deputy of a freely elected parliament, and as such protected by immunity; except, if that body had decided to suspend it, which it never did.

In December, 1946, the Cardinal had approached the American Minister in Budapest, asking him to use the good offices of the United States to prevent the flagrant violations of human rights in Hungary.

Now in March, after the arrest of Béla Kovács, Washington dispatched several strong notes, directed actually against the government of the Union of Soviet Socialist Republics, suggesting that the sovereignty and prerogatives of the freely elected Hungarian government were not being respected. It led to emphatic Soviet denials, and Kovács and numberless unnamed persons continued to suffer in prisons.

Some of the "conspirators" were brought to trial, and even though they delivered in court their manufactured "confessions" and were sentenced, no crime was ever proven, except by the corroborating "confessions" of other defendants. To the public it becomes clear that any who dared to meet in a group to discuss peacefully any ideas or plans for the time when Hungary would be free again—for the time after the Russians should have left Hungary—was a "dangerous conspirator."

The future concerned the Communists more than immediate problems; for the present, the might of the occupation force and the political backing of the Soviet Union were enough. The future was dependent on how thoroughly they could inject the Communist ideology into the youth.

The Communists considered the Church and religious teaching as the main bulwark against their ideological onsurge. As they could not afford to attack the Church in the open, directly contradicting their own proclamation of respect for the Church as an institution, the question of religious instruction was raised again. The Communist press began to publish "popular demands" for a law making religious instruction in the schools optional. Everyone knew this meant that in most of the smaller communities religious instruction would be prevented by force or terror.

During the discussion in Parliament, claims were made that the Church had already agreed to accept the optional religious instruction.

The Cardinal wrote a letter to Béla Varga, the President of Parliament, informing him that such statements were contrary to truth, and that the bishops of the land were opposed to it. To the public he authorized a statement in the *Catholic Commentary* which read, in part:

"The first principle must be the protection of the freedom of conscience of the individual. This principle can be formulated as follows: No one can be forced to do anything against his conviction unless the rightful interest of others so requires. In our case, this conviction is our deeply rooted religious faith. Three kinds of individuals must take a stand: the faithful, the religious, and the irreligious. One is faithful if one believes in a revealed religion; religious if, although not accepting this revelation, one believes in natural morality and God; irreligious if one accepts neither of these.

"But can a godless, irreligious point of view be the ultimate result of honest search for truth?

"The existence of God can be proved rationally. Therefore anyone who fails to find his way to Him is of inferior mentality. The objection arises, however, that among godless people there can be found many with superior mentality. It can be conceded that these people possess a good mind; but there must be something wrong with their will power. They refuse to believe in God because they do not want to assume the obligation imposed by this belief. Seldom do these practical atheists lead a moral life.

"There is no form of government, nor can there ever be one, which is not concerned with the morals of its subjects. It is also clear that there can be no moral concept without religion. Irreligious morals cannot lay the foundation of a moral order. Although it exists *per se*, the moral order ultimately returns to God, for all secondary consequences eventually return to a primary cause. There can be no law without legislators. Take away the primary cause, and the effect will be suspended in air without the foundation. Thus, irreligious education renders the moral order itself irrational. Society cannot remain indifferent to the moral make-up of its component members, lest anarchy result. Therefore it is the right and duty of society that its members be valuable, ethically thinking individuals.

"This will be no easy task for politicians who talk forever about freedom of conscience and at the same time violate this principle by prescribing the books to be used in Catholic schools. Such people are unable to see other points of view, and are therefore unfit to deal with the problem.

"The first step then is to eliminate the politicians. Priests, educators, sociologists, psychologists, and lawyers will have to debate the problem. Those who proposed optional religious instruction did so in order to accomplish their special political aims. This becomes clear from the fact that educators who would be most competent to take a stand in the matter were forbidden to do so under the threat of being instantly dismissed. This is tantamount to letting a patient be examined by everyone except a physician.

"No doubt the task of finding a solution satisfactory to all concerned is not an easy one. It is especially difficult to determine who is entitled to freedom of conscience."

The storm around the question of religious education subsided, and it seemed that political life would become somewhat tranquil. Through the "conspiracies" and the resulting fear of terror that had spread again, the Communists seemed for a while to have been satisfied.

The Cardinal had received an invitation to attend the Marian Congress in Canada, and had decided to make the journey overseas. As his passport had expired, he had to apply to the Communist Minister of Interior for a renewal. This was first promised by May 10, but excuses were made for delay in issue; and he did not receive it until the grievance was made public in the newspapers.

In all simplicity, he traveled with his secretary Andrew Zakar to Ottawa. On the return trip he made a short visit to his brother prelate the Archbishop of New York, Francis, Cardinal Spellman.

By the time he returned in July, conditions in Hungary had undergone a drastic change.

On May 14 Prime Minister Ferenc Nagy and Mrs. Nagy had left the country to visit their daughter in Switzerland and take a vacation. It seemed that he could afford to be absent from the political scene for a short while. In fact, the Communist members of the cabinet had urged him to take a rest abroad.

About the time he was ready to return, he was suddenly informed that his best friend, Béla Kovács—in the hands of the Russians—had confessed that Nagy had been a "conspirator." He decided to return but was advised that his immediate resignation was imperative, with the hint that he would never reach Budapest as a free man. When he refused to resign he was told that his six-year-old son was being held as a hostage. The father's love outweighed all political considerations, and Nagy agreed to resign if his son would be delivered to him in Switzerland. The Communists finally delivered the child. They needed the signed document of resignation in order to maintain a semblance of legality for a puppet who had already assumed his office of prime minister.

Then the political disintegration began. With only two exceptions all Hungarian envoys abroad followed Ferenc Nagy and refused to recognize or represent the new regime; they chose exile. Canon Béla Varga, President of Parliament, was forced to flee in dark of night. In the days, weeks, and months following, everybody who could took to the road of escape. The iron curtain was closing on Hungary.

Ferenc Nagy had become a symbol to the peasants, two-thirds

of the entire population. He had risen from their ranks to become a deputy in Parliament, voicing their wants, their fears, their grievances, and their hopes. After the war, first as Minister of Reconstruction, then as President of Parliament and finally as Prime Minister, he represented their tenacity and determination to see the country rebuild, a democratic, constitutional government assured; and they trusted his wisdom at the helm of the ship of state. He had hoped to outride the storm and guide the nation safely to the ultimate goal, the regaining of complete national independence, for after the peace treaty should become effective the Soviet was supposed to remove its occupation forces.

But the Soviets had planned differently. The political conquest of Hungary had been badly delayed already, through the resistance of the population and the democratic leaders. The ideological assault had failed completely.

With the elimination of Ferenc Nagy, and the complete disintegration of the political leadership trusted by the common man, the next bastion of strength to be attacked was the Church and the spiritual leadership it exercised. The final goal was to be the complete subjugation of the citizen and the peasant, which was to come true eventually.

By July, 1947, the Kremlin's timetable had become very obvious.

The Cardinal was in New York, preparing to return home when someone suggested to him that his very life might be in jeopardy. Astonished by the underlying suggestion, he answered: "The Shepherd's place is with his flock. . . . If to protect them demands my life, I have but one life to offer for my Church and my country."

He returned to his beloved Hungary and faced all issues squarely. He chastised politicians who failed to execute the will of the people, and he was always prepared to defend fearlessly the rights of the individual and the Church. The words still ring, even in the ears of his adversaries, that he spoke of the pillars of justice and strength:

"The American magazine, *Newsweek*, published once a very strange picture: On the globe, burned out by the atomic bomb, a scorched man talks on the telephone: 'Hello, hello, is there anyone left alive?' Actually, even before the atomic bomb had been released, at the time that the mighty ones of the world only fooled one another with the idea of the bomb, we could have asked ourselves, Is there any brotherhood left on earth, because man has become an animal of prey?

"That the shattered hopes of today have not been able to extinguish tomorrow's hopes, neither in this poor, persecuted Hungary nor in Poland, nor in nineteen other European countries that have been desecrated and drenched in blood and sin, is due entirely to the fact that the Mother Church, the eternal Church, which is the pillar of justice and strength and is the anointed one of Christ's love, is in our midst. If we are ever able once more to celebrate real freedom, if we are again ever able to live without want or fear, and if the rights of man within these Carpathians cease to be on a parity with worthless money but are considered as good as gold, then the celebration will acknowledge the triumph and freedom of the Church throughout the world.

"It is through the Church that the words inscribed on the obelisk in the Vatican will become a reality: Christus vincit, Christus regnat, Christus imperat."

After the war Hungary had already experienced a religious renaissance. The churches were overflowing. As the Cardinal, at the head of the assembled bishops of Hungary, on August 15, 1947, opened the Marian Year, throngs such as had never before been seen at religious affairs publicly demonstrated their faithfulness to their creed.

Undoubtedly the Catholics' courageous show of strength angered the Communists, who were still claiming for purposes of propaganda that religious worship was an individual, permissible affair.

The Cardinal had dedicated the Marian Year to the patroness "Our Great Lady of Hungary"—Holy Mary ever Virgin. This was not unusual, for throughout the world Actio Catholica designates a new religious thought each year, to deepen the Catholic conscience. But the Communists took a different view. They had decided to consider anything the Cardinal did as an affront, and prepared to prevent the exercise of religious functions, by whatever means they could employ.

The Cardinal, recognizing the difficult position of the parish clergy, traveled throughout the Marian Year to all communities, wherever his presence was requested. Tirelessly he celebrated at the Marian Festivals every Sunday, except when inclement weather made it impossible for him to reach his destination.

On August 20 the traditional St. Stephen's Day celebration took place in Budapest. Six hundred thousand faithful took part in the procession, despite the fact that the Communists prevented uncounted throngs throughout the country from reaching the Capital.

This was part of the political campaign that had already begun, for Parliament had been dissolved, a new electoral law decreed, designed to disfranchise countless voters. The Communist press tried to drag the Catholic Church into the campaign, and several declarations by the Cardinal and the bishops became necessary to emphasize that the Church was not backing any political party. The bishops only reminded the voters of "their moral obligation to go to the polls and exercise their rights as citizens, for a truly representative legislature can only be created if each citizen fulfills his obligations as a voter."

The Communists reacted swiftly and took precautions. Employing diverse subterfuges, they had hundreds of thousands of voters disfranchised before election; and wherever unsuccessful they simply falsified the results of the ballots. And still the country voted against the Communist combine. Despite the falsifications the democratic parties polled 54 per cent of the popular vote.

Later, Mathias Rákosi, by now the absolute viceroy of the Kremlin in Budapest, "purged" the Parliament of all opponents by employing personal terror against the individual deputies. Some were thrown into prison, others—among them one of the most fearless fighters of this era, Zoltán Pfeiffer—had to find refuge in exile.

As the peace treaty was about to become effective, the Cardinal issued the following letter to the parishes:

"After long years of suffering, this fifteenth day of September,

1947, is a great day for us despite the fact that the Paris Treaty has brought us no joy and much sadness.

"Nevertheless, this is a great day, for Hungary has won back her national sovereignty and has become one of the free nations. We Hungarian Catholics, constituting nearly 70 per cent of the population, prayerfully turn to Our Lady of Hungary to bless and to guide her people. May we find the right road which will lead Hungary, our beloved country, truly to freedom and peace. All church bells will toll as soon as we receive official word that the treaty documents have been deposited."

While public officials tried to hail the peace treaty as having regained for the country and the people "the complete freedoms," including religious freedom, the government issued one decree after another curbing the freedom of the press; two months after, no printed or mimeographed matter could be distributed without specific government permit.

The Cardinal was pained to see the further inroads on the freedoms of the individual. He found specifically that the forcible expulsion of Hungarians from Slovakia and of Germans from Hungary, and the methods by which these expulsions were executed, were in flagrant violation of all human rights.

On October 2 he issued a pastoral letter:

"The basic rights of human beings were formulated in the following words by Justin, Cardinal Serédi, of revered memory, who distinguished himself by even daring to flaunt his views regarding the persecution of the Jews in the face of Hitler's regime.

"Every person is born with inalienable rights: the right to live, the right to human dignity, the right to personal freedom, the right to freedom of religion; freedom to seek employment, freedom for a craftsman to follow his trade, and the right to own private property. Neither the dictates of a party, nor laws passed by any state which violate these rights, can go unpunished.

"The Hungarian bishops raise their voices in warning against all unlawful and violent acts, and remind all violators that these rights have not been given to man by an individual, nor by a party, nor by a state, but by God Himself. No earthly power possesses the right to curtail or abrogate these rights except by just and lawful means. Only those people to whom God has delegated legislative, jurisdictional, and governing power can touch these rights.

"All power originates with God. All delegated power must be applied with justice—which means that it must conform with the moral laws. God has given no one the right to be unjust, or to sanction acts of terror by the individual.

"Throughout history the Church has always raised its voice against anyone who has infringed upon the rights of God, and has always protected those in danger of persecution. And it is not permissible to punish anyone for his race or religion, if he is innocent of any unlawful act.

"What happened to the Jews during Hitler's regime is taking place today in our country on a far greater scale. People are being dispossessed of their country, their homes, and their property, and are being made homeless and miserable."

Characteristic of the existing conditions was the letter the Cardinal addressed on October 24 to the Prime Minister of the Communist-dominated cabinet calling his attention to two facts: first, that individuals were forced to join the Communist party under the threat of losing their livelihood, and persons subject to punishment were seeking refuge in the Communist party because its membership card gave protection; second, that the spy and informer system was spreading. The secret police summoned individuals, even priests, without any cause and through unfounded charges, trying to induce them to spy on the Catholic community, in the residences of the bishops, in Catholic educational institutions and ordering them to report to the secret police periodically whatever they might hear.

"Such spying," wrote the Cardinal, "is incompatible with the Hungarian soul. It is an absolutely superfluous activity in ecclesiastical circles, for in our ranks it is needless to smell for a 'conspiracy'; we would not be party to one, as we air our opinions openly. Witness to that are our public meetings and our rarely appearing publications."

As an answer, the New Man, a weekly of the Catholic Church which published the Cardinal's letter, was confiscated. This paper had constant difficulties in reaching the public. It either was confiscated for publishing the Cardinal's letters and addresses, or did not even go to press, for the printers—at Communist command—simply refused to set the type. If it did appear, its circulation was entirely controlled by the government, through withholding of newsprint.

The Cardinal voiced his reaction from the pulpit in Szombathely: "Everything around us can tumble—but truth will survive forever."

Still, to the uninformed it seemed that the tension between Catholic Church and the Communist-dominated government had lessened; but it was only a breathing spell, and a slight detour in tactics. Communist brigades went to villages to help rebuild some of the churches still needing restoration work. Mathias Rákosi and other powerful leaders of the Communist party were photographed shaking the hands of priests; attending some of the functions of the Marian Festivals. Individual Communists were trying to join in the community life of the Catholics. The Communists needed a little time to consolidate their own position after the political and economic upheavals of 1947.

At the same time, wherever they could, the Communists were attempting to spread distrust of the Cardinal. They insinuated that no difficulties would exist for the Church, aside from the person and the attitude of the Cardinal.

Christmas of 1947 found the Cardinal in Esztergom. The residence of the Primate of Hungary did not echo with the joy so common in the lands of the free. He had only one guest at his table, his mother —the person he respected and revered most. Dressed in somber black, with the traditional black kerchief of the Hungarian peasant tied around her head, she had remained the same simple peasant woman, even though her son had reached exalted office. Someone asked her once, how she felt, as the mother of the Primate of the land: "Much happiness came to me through my son; I was happiest when he became a priest. Later I cried much about him; I cried when he went to Veszprém, and I cried when they called him to Esztergom."

With her natural instinct for the right and the just, she instilled strength into him.

Talks with his mother were the Cardinal's only real relaxations, for when he was in residence at Esztergom he wasted little time on himself.

Whenever the pressure of affairs permitted he prayed and meditated. Hardly ever did he take a walk, and on the rare occasions when he strolled in the archiepiscopal gardens on the shore of the Danube, he carried his breviary to recite it in the solemnity of God's own nature.

His gait was light, and even when dressed in the heavy insignia of ancient times he seemed to walk as if suspended in the air.

When contemplating he used to stand at the window of his study, overlooking the Danube, facing Slovakia. He could see the Czechoslovakian border patrol pass along the river, and the fate of his flock beyond the frontier was thus kept constantly in his mind.

Since he had occupied the historic palace of the Primates of Hungary, he never had it heated. In the winter of 1948 a visitor called to his attention that his own hands and lips were blue from the cold. He shook his head and said: "As long as countless brethren are suffering the cold—some on foreign soil, without even a home or a shelter—I could not bear the comfort of heat."

Valiantly he bore their suffering and defended their rights.

By the beginning of 1948 the direct attact on the Church had been resumed. The terror increased, and threats became more open. Rákosi already had indicated what was in the offing in a speech to the Communist party functionaries:

"The endeavor of the Hungarian democracy to include Catholicism also in the work of reconstruction of the nation did not succeed. The leaders of the Catholic Church do not recognize the Republic and are preventing the reconstruction. . . . The Hungarian democracy up to now has solved all its problems. When the hour comes it will tackle the reaction, too, which hides behind the Catholic Church."

On February 15 the Cardinal spoke out in judgment:

"Lies remain lies, even though millions may spread them . . . We defend the rights and the freedom of the Church . . . and we are taking part in the reconstruction of our nation. . . . There is no reason for human existence if we go on hating one another, wounding one another—individuals and peoples. Catastrophe is already ripening. We Hungarian Catholics desire peace, and we cannot resign the desire so entwined in our spiritual concept; should we not find peace, we shall turn to our inner self prayerfully: 'And in the shadow of thy wings will I hope, until iniquity pass away.' "

These words spoken at the annual commencement of St. Stephen's Academy were used by the Communist press to unleash a new series of violent attacks on the Cardinal. They accepted the last sentence as relating to them. Again the Catholic weekly carrying the text of the address was confiscated.

To the Communist claim that Catholicism stood in the way of progress, the Church answered:

"The Catholic Church does not devise the return of old times. But it does expect to function freely and openly for the benefit of the Hungarian people. It expects to seek for all its members human rights, particularly the right to work. The Church wishes that economic and political life be imbued with and guided by those eternal divine rights which it has been teaching, and without which no society can live in peace."

As the pressure on the individuals began to increase again and the terror spread, the Cardinal wrote on March 5 to the Prime Minister:

"The Prime Minister declared in Parliament on October 7: 'The government is doing everything in its power to reestablish good relations with the Church and to settle all problems that have arisen.'

"At the present moment, too, everywhere the willingness to establish pleasant relations with the Church is preached. At the same time, without reason attacks are launched against the remnants of Church institutions. From the hospitals they remove nursing sisters; priests caring for the unfortunate blind are kept from work. Teachers of religion are prevented from teaching as guaranteed by law. The students' right to receive religious instruction is violated, even though the cost of such instruction has been provided by Catholic population through taxes paid as 70 per cent of the citizenry. I do not wish to enumerate further at this time.

"All this is in direct contradiction to religious freedom and the oath of government officials."

The Communist press continued the campaign. Its clear aim was to prevent the Catholic Church from exercising its charitable functions; to abolish all parochial schools; to secularize Catholic institutions and nationalize all properties that had been used for these purposes.

The Cardinal recognized that the attack now was directed at the very heart of the Church.

In the small communities, agents who had been installed when the Soviet armies first conquered the country began to organize "popular demands" for the secularization of the schools. With threat and terror they tried to induce the population to sign petitions. Priests were terrorized, attempts made to prevent them from reading to their congregations the pastoral letters of the Cardinal.

The newspapers printed the "popular demands," some originating from non-existent societies and from faraway hamlets, places difficult to verify.

Obviously the popular reaction took an entirely different trend. Masses appeared wherever the Cardinal spoke. Tens of thousands turned out to demonstrate, with their very presence, fealty to the Church.

At Easter time the throngs became so large that priests were forced to serve day and night. The celebration of the sacrament of Holy Communion took place in one of the churches of Budapest three continuous days, as the faithful spent the nights waiting in line.

By the end of spring the attack against the schools had crystallized. On May 11 the Cardinal released a pastoral letter in the name of the bishops of Hungary. In it he gave a clear picture of the position of the Church and warned that the loving Church might punish too. On May 23 a second pastoral letter followed:

"With our heads held high, publicly and before God we declare that we are witnessing a spiritual tyranny that has not been initiated by us, although we are blamed for it!"

On May 29 the pastoral letter quoted the lies that were being spread to mislead the public and to misinform the communicants of the true state of affairs:

"The State's monopoly of the schools is to be imposed upon us. But we are going to do our utmost to prevent the immortal souls of our children from thus being violated. We sound our warning once again: Do not dare to interfere with the rights of parents to human freedom! Do not interfere with our freedom of religion! Do not take our time-honored schools from us! Do not lose yourselves on the road to totalitarian methods!

"Lies, misrepresentation and violence—it must be said to the disgrace of our country—have never, in the course of history, reached as high a point as now!"

The protests against the government's policy regarding the schools were rising throughout the country. Thousands of congregations sent petitions to the government, telegrams to the Prime Minister and the Minister of Education. But no one paid heed. No one dared. The Communists had set the goal, and Communism never gives up.

On May 30 the voice of the Holy Father came over the air waves in a greeting on the occasion of the tenth anniversary of the Eucharistic Congress:

"The Christian religion which you have received in precious heritage from St. Stephen and from your glorious forefathers, and which you guard with jealous care, inspiring source as it is of all the virtues, places you on a singular level of nobility and excellency which reaches the fullness of its splendor in an hour, when those who would deny the name and majesty of God attempt to delude you through cunning, falsehood, and deception.

"The secret of the Eucharist, which is the bond of love you confess and cherish, shall always be your strength and joy, that in union with the Catholic Church, obedient to your consecrated pastors, steadfast in your faith and rich in good works, you may cause flowers of true beauty to blossom in the midst of adversity and thus prepare for yourselves and for your children an age rich in the gifts of peace and prosperity."

On the 15th of June the Cardinal protested to the Minister of Education:

"We feel it our duty to enumerate our latest grievances:

"These are sad times indeed, when the faithful praying to God are attacked by arms.

"To disperse people standing outside the church is a flagrant violation of religious freedom.

"Verbal and written statements inspired by the government in the press, at political meetings, and over the radio start an avalanche of lies, calumnies, and vituperations of the prelates, priests, and faithful of the Church. This is no way to pacify anyone; on the contrary, it is the best way to alienate people.

"Against all . . . abuses, we protest most energetically, and we wish that for the sake of the reputation of our country these malpractices be forthwith stopped."

The Communists having recognized that the popular trend might endanger their chances, suddenly decided to act. On June 16 the puppet Parliament, in a single eight-hour session, passed a law practically confiscating the educational institutions of the Church. The schools of the Church and their properties were nationalized. The vote in Parliament was 232 yeas and 63 nays. The courageous members who voted against the law soon lost their seats; some went into hiding, others succeeded in escaping abroad.

On June 19 the bells in all the Catholic churches rang for a full hour. Their sound echoed the pain of the Church. The Catholic Church of Hungary was deeply wounded.

The only measure the Cardinal could take was to excommunicate all who had taken part in the action against the schools.

On June 20 a pastoral letter signed by the Cardinal and by the fifteen archbishops and bishops of Hungary was read in all the churches. It said: "We shall never cease endeavoring, with all lawful means at our disposal, to have our rights restored."

During the summer the festivals of the Marian Year continued; but the celebrations and processions encountered increasing difficulties. The Communists increasingly objected to anything that was said at the Marian meetings.

At first in 1947 it had seemed that politicians whose audiences were less enthusiastic and less numerous objected not so much to what was said there as to the movement itself. Now, systematic country-wide efforts were made to hinder the celebrations. Simultaneously, political parties held meetings within a radius of fifteen to twenty miles. For these they gave free transportation, particularly to the people of the town where a celebration was to be held, using special trains and requisitioned trucks. People were coerced to attend political meetings held in the same county as the Marian celebrations and at the same time. Those who were in charge of arrangements for such a celebration were terrorized on the eve of the event. In many instances the use of loud-speakers, indispensable in view of the large open-air crowds, was prohibited.

Tickets were refused to people planning to travel by rail; trucks for carrying pilgrims were taken away by the authorities. On official order, stores were not to sell bicycle parts before Marian Days. Mandatory horse inspection was held in order to prevent peasants from attending. The inspection was not held or, in lack of veterinarians, local members of the Young Communists performed it.

In several cases the people were notified that two hundred to five hundred soldiers would be quartered in the villages and were "urged" to remain in their homes. On the way, pilgrims had to pass road blocks and identify themselves individually. The secret police made a list of all who attended.

When, despite all attempts against it, crowds appeared in several places, they were told that because of an epidemic of meningitis no traffic was allowed and a quarantine was ordered. People were threatened with concentration camps. At the same time, in the same localities, permits were granted for dances, and public officials were ordered to attend party meetings in the Capital. In the "quarantined" territory public meetings were held at which cabinet members spoke.

Even those who had recently received land grants from the government failed to attend, saying, "We are sick in the brain." The people laughed off the official regulations.

When the bicentennial of the Abbey of Celldömölk was celebrated, twelve hundred soldiers prevented the people from attending church. As the assembled bishops proceeded from the church to the abbey, the crowds demonstrated around them. In answer military trucks drove into the people.

Before the Marian Day in Földszentkereszt, the town clerk called the people in and informed them that they would lose their jobs or would be interned or sent to Russia if they attended the celebration. For a whole week, machine-gun units blocked the roads leading to the church.

When none of these measures succeeded, a campaign of "country-wide protest" against the Primate was launched. The campaign enlisted the help of cities, towns, and counties. No communal or county elections had been held; the Capital was the only exception. A few Communist party members made declarations in the name of institutions silenced by terror. Everyone knew what was behind these resolutions. In one community of twenty-two hundred, the town clerk caused a verbal message to be spread among the people urging them to abstain from a meeting, and three Communist miners declared, in the name of the community, that the Primate was an enemy of democracy. After the meeting the clerk ran to the parish and said that he was unable to resist terror; he had been threatened with the loss of his position if he did not do what he was told to do.

Thus, fear governed all actions of the non-Communist officials.

In August the Cardinal would have traveled to Cologne to attend the seven hundredth anniversary of the ancient cathedral, but a passport was refused.

The government did not dare to cancel the traditional St. Stephen's procession, which always had taken place on August 20. To prevent this from being peaceful, it decreed the "Holiday of New Bread" for observance on that date and granted to the demonstrators "the traditional route of the procession of the holy relic." When word of it reached the Cardinal with the suggestion that "the Catholics should walk along some other route," he resented the indignity and canceled the St. Stephen's procession altogether.

The Communist propaganda machine was beginning at this time to prepare the ground abroad for events to come. A leftist publication in France printed an interview with the Hungarian Minister for Church and Education, which the Cardinal answered on August 24:

"The Primate of Hungary, himself a son of the people, has never opposed the ambitions or the progress of the Hungarian people. His life to date has been a series of unceasing efforts for the rights of the individual, for justice; for spiritual and material progress for his people—efforts made in his office as well as in prison amidst ceaseless unjust attacks.

"He demands that the crimes and usurpations cease, and that the respect for the basic laws in the best interest of the Hungarian nation be restored.

"The government actually does not practice bilateral negotiations. The distribution of land, the dissolution of Catholic organizations, the closing of Catholic institutions and schools, and all other steps are evidences that the government uses brute force unilaterally.

"The Minister for Church and Education repeatedly refers to the grants the state has made to the Church during two years. He fails to point out, however, that the state's contribution in 1945 and particularly in the first half of 1946, during our world-famous period of inflation, was sufficient to pay only for what the parochial schools of Hungary needed for stamps and matches. Likewise, he fails to mention what the government of the new order has taken away from the Church since 1945; nor does he speak of what the Church on her part has contributed in one thousand years. Like a grown-up son who for the first time in his life gives a thin slice of bread to his mother, the Minister for Church and Education refers to the state's grant as a magnanimous action which outshines all the earlier sacrifices of the mother.

"It is pointed out that the salary of the Primate and that of the Prime Minister are equal; but no mention is made that the Primate has never accepted payment—nor does he accept his salary.

"Secularization of Catholic schools in Hungary has not been accomplished in the same manner as in the West. While there is today not a single Catholic school in Hungary, there are many in the United States, Holland, France, Belgium, Sweden, etc. Except on paper, Hungarian Catholics have no right to found and maintain schools, Catholics of the abovementioned countries do.

"In our case, it is not the state that has nationalized the schools. Because, instead of a state, we have political parties. Not mere secularization has been effected; instead, our schools have been delivered to the whims of the Marxist party.

"Religious processions are preceded, accompanied, and followed by 'disturbing incidents.'

"The Primate has never complained that the government has not been represented at official religious functions. Their personal appearances, and the zealous photographing of their participation, for the purpose of misleading propaganda abroad, cannot be denied.

"Before each public worship service the more critical question is: Will the service be permitted, and will it be possible for the Primate to officiate and the faithful to appear? And, if the service has been permitted, will the permit remain valid, or will the service be dissolved?

"According to reports reaching me from various dioceses many Catholic priests have been arrested. Many have been prevented from exercising their functions. To speak only of the Capital members of 'the party' warned the priests of the different parishes not to read pastoral letters or toll the bells as ordered by their superior Church authorities."

At the beginning of the school year, in September, he addressed his now historic letter to the parents of Hungary.

On September 25 he wrote to the Prime Minister quoting some of the statements made by the political leaders:

"Let me state . . . that we consider Hungary as our country given to us by God, a country to which we have been loyal for a thousand years, whatever her lot has been. To elevate the country, we pray and work. Our churches, schools, and organizations, wherever you may still find them, teach nearly six million people who, regardless of sex, occupation, and political views, look upon us to guide their lives, to love their country and be loyal to her.

"When the rule of Hitler and his concomitant political system based on *Gleichschaltung* collapsed in our country and the nation began to look forward to an entirely new regime, the Church was sympathetic toward certain new aims of the new leadership, not only because she was stanchly opposed to antireligious Hitlerism, but also because the new leadership proclaimed principles which were in harmony with the teachings of the Church. For example:

"(1) Independence. 'We want a free, independent Hungary' (Rákosi in Parliament, September 6, 1945).

"(2) 'We want national unity' (proclamation of December 21, 1944). 'There is no difference between Hungarians and Hungarians' (Gerö, *loc. cit.*). 'Unity, unity, and a thousand times unity, of all decent Hungarians' (J. Révai, December 22, 1944).

"(3) Liberty. 'Instead of a Hungary of prisons, we want a free, happy Hungary' (Szakasits, September 6, 1945). 'We want an independent, free, and democratic Hungary' (proclamation of the National Council, December 21, 1944). 'We want freedom, happiness, prosperity' (Gerö, *loc. cit.*). 'We want freedom for every citizen, free press, the freedom to organize' (Szabó, December 22, 1944).

"(4) Self-government. 'We want local autonomy for the communities, towns, and counties' (proclamation, December 22, 1944).

"(5) The right of criticism. 'There can be no life without differences of opinion. We shall settle all differences of opinion through mutual understanding, as behooves comrades' (Révai, *loc. cit.*).

"(6) Love and brotherhood. 'Let our souls be free of recriminations: let us work for a better future. We consider every Hungarian our brother, we protect every Hungarian whenever and wherever need be' (Veres, September 6, 1945).

"(7) Honest government. "We shall fight to wipe out corruption from our midst' (Szakasits, *loc. cit.*).

"(8) Religious freedom. 'We want complete religious freedom' (proclamation).

"(9) Opposition to dictatorship. 'We shall not for one moment abide by a government or system which displays even the slightest tendency to rule dictatorially' (Zoltán Tildy, September 6, 1945)."

To the daily attacks on the Church and religion were added personal attacks on the Cardinal himself. The Communists accused the Church and the Cardinal of being antidemocratic. He answered with unmistakable definitions through the *Catholic Commentary:*

"The word 'democracy' has indeed several connotations. There is said to be democracy in the United States, in the United Kingdom, in Hungary, and in Soviet Russia. We have time and again stated what we mean by democracy.

"By democracy we mean what Pope Pius XII in his Christmas Encyclical of 1944 so clearly stated. His definition is exactly the opposite of that low state of affairs where the legislature gives absolute power to the state to mold 'democratic' government. This, despite all appearances to the contrary, is clearly and simply state absolutism.

"State absolutism rests on the false doctrine that the power of the state is limitless."

The attack against the person of the Cardinal began to reach full fury when the Communist newspaper *Free People* called him "the spokesman of death." From this point on, the terror increased. The Cardinal undaunted followed the road he had set for himself.

Characteristic of his determination were the words spoken months earlier, when he had been warned that his resistance might cost him his life: "A dead Primate is a greater power than a living one." That his mother thought the same way is proved by her words: "Son, I would rather see you a martyr than a traitor to the cause."

The Communist press published articles indicating that relations between the Cardinal and the bishops of Hungary had become strained. It was just a wish, disproved by the declaration of the bishops on November 3:

"That words of truth and of life have been given to the people is due to the historic service rendered by the Cardinal Primate, who, with strong faith and flaming love and unflagging spirit, has remained forever faithful, and who has proclaimed the creed of life and of truth.

"When the Hungarian bishops, in the name of religious freedom and human rights, raised their voices against those who attacked them, they showed their confidence in His Eminence, their compassion, and their desire to identify themselves with him in his work for the Church, the country, and the people.

"We ask the faithful to pray with us for the Church and its leader, so that we may be as one in our faith, in our love, and in the grace of our steadfastness."

To further counteract the continuous Communist propaganda abroad, some of which had even reached the pages of respectable British publications, the Cardinal released a statement on November 17 through the *Catholic Commentary*:

"The Hungarian clergy has not once raised its voice against the land reform recently carried out. In May, 1945, it bestowed blessings upon those who had acquired land. In a few instances only, it criticized the manner in which the laws were executed. However, its criticism was far from being as sharp as that voiced by several politicians of the coalition party.

"The Hungarian clergy never demanded that those who had obtained land give it back. It merely insisted that its impoverished institutions receive the compensation they were entitled to according to law.

"All accusations not based on the aforementioned facts are false and are aimed at separating from the Church those who benefited from the land reform.

"Those accusations claiming that there is a close connection between the clergy and certain 'feudal' tendencies, are equally baseless. The clergy is fighting to protect human rights, among them freedom of worship, and moral truth. This has been accomplished by the Church everywhere in this world in the degree made necessary by local and external circumstances."

Turning to his flock on November 18, the Cardinal sent his last pastoral letter to the Catholics of Hungary:

"For the past few weeks, in what remains of Hungary, certain factions have tried to enact resolutions against me. One hears that no attempt has been made to bring about peace between the Church and the state. Demands have been made to stop activities harmful to the people.

"The millions who have been asked to judge me, and who represent the public opinion of this country, have been subjected to methods which are unworthy, and which are in direct opposition to the democratic principle of religious freedom.

"The resulting 'resolutions' have no legal foundation. These resolutions have been extorted from the people by threatening them with the loss of their jobs and of their freedom. The country has been sentenced to silence. Freedom of speech has no meaning here except the right to give utterance to one dictated opinion, excluding all others.

"Look—I am calmly gazing at the angry seas that break all around me. Such turmoil, from where I stand, is not unusual. And I stand here, not by the good grace of any party, but by appointment of the Holy See. History lives by change.

"My own fate is unimportant when compared to the suffering of my people.

"I pray for a world of truth and love. I pray for those who, according to the words of our Lord, 'know not what they do.' I forgive with all my heart."

And he rose to true greatness in his letter for Advent:

"I come to you with the warnings of difficult times, in the name of our Lord Jesus Christ and as His emissary.

"What the world threatens me with, to put fear into my heart, I am disdainful of; and what they try to lure me with, makes me laugh. I beg you too most earnestly to resist with unshakable courage.

"The life of our Christian ancestors, including Hungarians, was not an easy one. The Apostle Paul, the man of sorrow, the chosen vessel of the Lord, sends us this message: 'For what things soever were written, were written for our learning: that through patience and the comfort of the scriptures, we might have hope.'

"Let us be beacons of light and let us be as active as possible, especially by the example of our lives and our behavior, so that the Kingdom of Christ, which is the Kingdom of Justice and Grace, may spread. On the road that leads there let us remember, in the words of Tertullian: 'The accusations of certain malicious people are regarded by us as praise.' Everything that happens conspires— toward the freedom of the Church, toward the safeguarding of our suffering people and of our youth, toward a fruitful peace, toward an interest in spiritual and holy matters, and not toward those things of which we are accused.

" 'Watch ye, therefore, praying at all times, that you may be accounted worthy to escape all these things that are to come, and to stand before the Son of man.' But prayer was made without ceasing by the Church unto God for him.

"Unto the hope of life everlasting, which God, who lieth not, hath promised before the times of the world: But have confidence, I have overcome the world."

The Communists turned to the last means to swing public opinion —within the Catholic ranks—against the Cardinal. Three well known laymen, two of whom had recently acquired definite Marxist leanings, were induced to present a petition to the Cardinal. It was indicated to them that there was still a possibility to restore peace between Church and state, if the Cardinal chose to retreat.

The petition was full of accusations, and he answered:

"The Vatican, the Papal Nuncio, and my predecessor have contributed to the alleviation of the plight of the Jews, in the Capital at least, as acknowledged by the well documented book by the Jewish writer Eugene Lévai. In my archives is preserved a letter addressed to my predecessor thanking him for his activities in behalf of the Jews. Also preserved in my archives are those cruel attacks in the press by the same people after his death. His Holiness has been twenty-two times attacked in the Hungarian press in one single month. The attitude of Parliament toward me is too well known to be discussed, as is the fate of members of religious orders and nuns, despite their charitable activities. I myself, as Bishop of Veszprém, repeatedly intervened in the affairs of Jews at the offices of the Prime Minister and the Minister of the Interior, sometimes successfully; but I can also safely say that up to that time I had never been exposed to greater humiliations. I shall not go on.

"At any rate, whether the Church has done little or much in this respect, it is more than has been done in behalf of the Church by the same people.

"It is held against me that I had no word of praise for the present; on the other hand, that I have not fought against certain groups (such as the big landowners). The truth is that I praised those who built bridges or, after the flood of the Tisza River, houses, etc. It is not my fault if my statements found no responsive audience.

"The fact is that I have stated my views on vested interests, but my opinions either could not be published or else have received no notice—as if certain groups did not allow it. If even cabinet members unscrupulously distort isolated passages and words of my writings, what can be expected from the secretary of the Communist party or from newspapermen? Distortions are born out of their rich imagination. They arise in such rapid succession that it is difficult to follow them. Moreover, their tone makes it impossible for Esztergom not to react to them.

"Nor should it be forgotten that the Marxist coalition created the Mindszentism which, if my interpretation is correct, constitutes a very distinct philosophical, theological, political, economic, and social system. Such a system widely discussed and dissected cannot be halted by authoritarian declarations. The widespread agitation against it seems to indicate that today therefore nothing is more logical in Hungary than Mindszentism. Propaganda is also being diffused abroad. Spreading untruth abroad may be patriotic and in the interest of the people; to tell the truth about it must be treachery and disloyalty.

"In my declaration I never dealt with purely political matters.

What I spoke of touched the Ten Commandments, morals, justice, love, and human rights.

"On the other side of the scale are such machinations as: the beginning of a wave of 'conspiracy' charges against the schools in 1946; the causing of a murder at Teréz-körut; the destruction of Catholic associations and the confiscation of their property; the expropriation of Catholic schools and boarding schools in 1948 despite popular opposition; introduction of materialistic doctrines in the schools; press campaign against the Primate; persecution of priests and members of religious organizations; arrests and court sentences disregarding legal measures; terror which can safely be called general, under which Jesuit orders and Catholic homes at the University are looted without any legal restraint.

"The letter urges me to change my stand. The reason given is that my attitude, the stand I have taken, is responsible for all the harm the Church has already suffered and will suffer in the future.

"In this connection I wish to point out two things which ought to provoke thought:

"(a) A whole month before I became Primate of Hungary—as a matter of fact, my promotion had not yet been promulgated— Prime Minister Miklós vigorously protested the agitations against the Catholic clergy. The new marriage laws, passed without consultation with the Church, already strongly attacked the sanctity of marriage. The publication of Catholic periodicals were prohibited. The buildings owned by religious associations were confiscated for the party youth. Legal protests were disregarded. Police were interfering with Catholic associations. A number of priests were arrested on the basis of accusations never subsequently proved. The terror mentioned in the memorandum was already manifest in crowded prisons and camps. I took office long after that.

"(b) Today in the countries of Central Europe the position of the Church is often discussed. The Hungarian press, and politicians returning recently from five Central European countries, have repeatedly stated that there the Church is patriotic; some of the higher clergy (Beran, Sapieha) behave patriotically; others celebrated Mass when 'democracy' came to power; others took the oath of allegiance, and their example was followed by their bishops.

"From all this one ought to conclude that the Church is flourishing there. Yet, at the present writing, both Archbishop Beran and Sapieha are called 'bad.' In Rumania four bishops were arrested at the same time. The Concordat is unilaterally disregarded. Catholic schools are confiscated, old bishoprics destroyed; and the bishops forbidden to communicate with the head of the Church.

"For these two reasons I do not agree with the writers of the letter that I should have remorse.

"In 1947 no one said that the Primate caused disunity. Mr. Rákosi blamed the party of Small Landholders and its two priest members for the introduction of optional religious instruction.

"The Marxist newspapers tried to deal with me during the election campaign for their own purposes. They mentioned repeatedly that the great majority of our people are deeply religious. In fact, prominent politicians declared: 'As far as I am concerned, I intend to settle any problem touching on the Church after consultation with the respective Churches' (Ortutay, April 24, 1947). 'We want peace with the Church, as can be proved by facts' (Farkas, general secretary of the Communist party, August 12, 1947). And Prime Minister Dinnyés declared in Parliament: 'The government is doing its best to reestablish peaceful relations with the churches and to solve all problems that have emerged' (October 7, 1947). Everybody felt that reestablishment of good relations meant, and could mean only, the remedying of old grievances and the inflicting of no new wounds. The Prime Minister even promised the Archbishop of Eger that the Catholic daily would be allowed to appear, within a week.

"In 1947 no objection was voiced against the Marian Days. On February 17, 1948, Mr. Ortutay promised to send us invitations to committee hearings. He broke his promise. When the budget for the expenses of the churches was discussed, the atmosphere was most inimical. From April on, there were strong objections to Marian Days, obstacles were created, even firearms were used. On the 9th of May, secularization of schools, a matter never even mentioned before, was announced. After the government endorsed the secularization of schools, we were invited to committee hearings. The government broke its promise about two bilateral agreements. Facts do not check with promises. For all this the Church was blamed.

"Then something happened last winter: either upon higher order or for some other reason, the government stopped mentioning this problem. Rákosi declared: 'Hungarians are still bleeding from a thousand wounds. We must avoid bringing up problems which may sow the seeds of anxiety or discord.' He advocated 'negotiations and agreements' with the leaders of the churches. He blamed the majority of the party of coalition and did not even mention the Primate.

"Christian authors and artists voiced, rightly, vigorous opposition against the first Jewish laws as early as March, 1938. It is a pity that the same people had nothing to say in Moscow or in Budapest, before June 16, 1948, when Christian institutions where they had received their education were taken away. This could have been expected, particularly because these gentlemen privately were very much opposed to secularization of the schools. Since then new grievances have been inflicted upon the monks and nuns, these most self-sacrificing servants of the Church. They are not allowed to teach religion —a function for which no one is better fitted. They were told of this measure after having taught religion for two months without any compensation. They are continually attacked, as Jews used to be by the Nazi press.

"The whole press and all political parties declared during the last election campaign that Church and Primate are not identical. To this we answer that we share the point of view of St. Cyprian: 'The prelate is part of the Church, the Church part of the prelate; whoever is not with the prelate, is not with the Church either.'

"We raise this question: How can three thousand monks and nuns collectively be treated in such a manner 'because of the Primate or rather bishops with whom they are not identical.'

"The Church has repeatedly declared its willingness to make peace. But the invitation to appear at negotiations reached us after a delay of three months. By that time it had already been decided not to negotiate. So far, each time the Church has declared its willingness to have peace, a new campaign against the Church has been launched.

"Toward the end of 1945, I induced the Vatican, upon request of the government, to send a Nuncio to Hungary. Still, nothing happened here. Now, in October, the Vatican was inquiring about the admission of a special envoy. A reply merely acknowledged receipt of the inquiry. Besides, the reply was sent too late. In two months no definite answer has been given. That is how the government deals with the Vatican and the bishops, who alone have a right to negotiate. At the same time, students and apprentices whose task is something entirely different, 'of their own initiative' urge the Church to make peace with the State."

But the Cardinal's answer never reached the public.

On November 19 the Communist secret police took a step closer to his very person. The Cardinal's private secretary, Andrew Zakár, had gone to the Viziváros convent church in Esztergom to celebrate morning Mass. Shortly after seven o'clock he was leaving to return to the Cardinal's residence when four men of the secret police grabbed him, pushed him into a car, and drove off. Very few people were on the streets at this hour; but suddenly, as if from nowhere, hundreds of strangers appeared in the city and remained posted at important points within Esztergom.

Those few who witnessed the arrest trembled. When the news reached the Cardinal, he retired to the chapel for prayers. In the afternoon he sent a priest of the chancellery to Budapest, to ascertain if the act was not the irresponsible step of some overzealous minor official. The next day the priest reported to him that there was no uncertainty. Zakár had been arrested on instruction of the highest authorities of the State. The Cardinal knew what this meant.

On September 9 the presiding bishop of the Lutheran Church in Hungary, Louis Ordass, had been arrested; and on September 30 he had been sentenced to two years of penal servitude, for "common crimes." All he had been guilty of was his refusal to sign on behalf of his church a dictate of the government legalizing the confiscatory acts. Broken in health, the aged presiding bishop of the Presbyterian Church of Hungary, Leslie Ravasz, resigned in face of terror. By now hundreds of priests and ministers had been imprisoned and "confessions" of the tortured were spread by the propagandists of the Antichrist.

The Cardinal could not be frightened by anyone. He feared his Master and no one else.

As the Communist press was now openly accusing him of "conspiracy against the state and demanding that he be "done away with," he recognized the increasing danger signals.

Mindful of the fate awaiting him, he took the precaution of writing a note in his own hand. Knowing of the cruel methods employed by the police in making individuals amenable to their will and in extracting "confessions," he stated explicitly that all the accusations published about him were falsehoods; that he "had not participated in any conspiracy"; that he "would never resign"; that he "would not confess"; that were the readers of the note "to hear about a confession [by him] by word of mouth or in writing" they should "consider this but a sign of human frailty and regard it as null and void."

The Cardinal placed this note in a sealed envelope and had it deposited for safe keeping with the head of the chapter of Esztergom. His instructions were that it be opened in case of his arrest and its contents be conveyed to the Hungarian episcopate.

Silence reigned in the See of Esztergom. Now the doors to the Cardinal's residence were kept closed, and very few visitors—only his closest associates—were received. He cautioned each of them that coming to Esztergom might cause the government to visit its wrath upon them. He spoke quietly about his own fate—courteous and modest when someone referred to his own affairs, but hard as steel when matters of principle were discussed.

The air of a cemetery had descended on the city; people hardly spoke to one another, and walked through the streets only when necessary. In most homes the shutters were drawn, as the population awaited the coming of Christmas.

Weeks before Christmas, armed police in uniform and secret police surrounded the residence of the Cardinal, asserting that the measure was precautionary, to protect his life against "popular dissatisfaction." Alas, the police boots on the pavement echoed the words spoken a few weeks earlier by the Communist minister Ernest Gerö: "We have put the liquidation of the Mindszenty problem on our agenda. We are going to accomplish it as we have accomplished all our tasks."

The Cardinal's mother arrived to spend the Christmas holidays with him. Together they listened on Christmas Eve to the words of Pope Pius XII broadcast from the Vatican:

"In all those countries where to profess the Catholic faith really means to suffer persecution, there have been and there still are thousands of valiant men and women who, undismayed by sacrifices, proscriptions, and torture, and fearless in the face of prison and death, do not bow the knee before the Baal of might and power."

Christmas passed. The Cardinal stayed up every night until the wee hours, praying and meditating. Peace came to his mind, but no rest to his weary body.

The sun set across the Danube on the afternoon of December 26. The residence of the Primate of Hungary was deserted as the clock struck the quarter before seven. The Cardinal and his priests and all other members of the household had assembled—as usual—in the chapel.

After the service he remained kneeling in silent prayer on the steps of the altar.

The attending priests and the members of the household had retired to their quarters. Only the Cardinal's mother had remained sitting in the chapel; she sensed the heaviness in his heart. She, the eternal mother, knew the thoughts that filled his mind. In the silent emptiness of the chapel's nave, the hearts of mother and son beat in unison.

The iron-gray twilight of the short day descended over Esztergom. Few lights had been lit, for economy had become a necessity at the seat of the Primate.

The Cardinal held lovingly the arm of his mother as they descended the great staircase.

Loud voices broke the quiet; the bell was rung. Impatient knocks followed on the great door bearing the arms of the Archbishop of Esztergom.

The Cardinal ordered the door opened, and faced the intruders— a multitude of armed police. An officer stepped up and read a paper: "Joseph Mindszenty, in the name of the Hungarian Republic . . . you are under arrest."

He ordered his coat and hat brought to him. The mother embraced her son, and the Cardinal bent one knee and kissed both her hands.

Clutching the very same rosary that she had given him when he first left the humble home at Mindszent, Joseph, the Prince of the Holy Roman Catholic Church, the Primate of the Hungarian lands, stepped as a prisoner through the door into the dark of night.

✠

BOOK II

✠

THE MARTYRDOM OF A SOUL

The Kremlin in Moscow had ordered its Hungarian viceroy, Mathias Rákosi, to "liquidate the Mindszenty problem" by the last day of the year. Rákosi, in turn, appointed a strategy planning group to consider the best possible means. It consisted originally of Minister Ernest Gerö, Minister of War Michael Farkas, Minister of Education Julius Ortutay, Joseph Révai, the chief ideologist of the Communists in Hungary, and the head of the Press Department in the Ministry of Foreign Affairs, Iván Boldizsár. The "Mindszenty elimination group" considered all aspects, and first it laid plans for the all-out propaganda campaign against the Cardinal, to create a situation in which the pressure on him from all directions would force him into retreat.

This having failed because of the Cardinal's steadfastness in face of threat and terror, the "planners" turned to more "practical" solutions. First, through *agents provocateurs*, they tried to induce the Cardinal to leave the country, arranging to have him arrested at the border as a "fugitive." This failed because he reacted in a negative manner to any suggestion, whether open or whispered, that he leave Hungary.

The next idea was to arrange an "accident" to the Cardinal while he was traveling through some deserted part of the country. This failed, for two reasons: first, because the Cardinal at this time traveled very rarely, and always with a large group intent on protecting him; second, because the planners were unable to agree on the methods to be employed, and the personnel to execute it. The minority opinion was that a mob of "angry citizens of the popular democracy infuriated by the misdeeds of the Primate" should simply lynch him.

[107]

No doubt Rákosi and his cohorts could have produced such a mob; but Minister Gerö vetoed the idea, declaring that it would lead to bloodshed throughout the country and possibly to civil war. Boldizsár opposed it too, arguing that it would harm the interests of the People's Democracy and the consequent publicity abroad would throw a bad light on the regime. The idea of murder was shelved.

At one meeting of the group, during November, a new man took part whom Gerö had brought along: Colonel Pavel Kotlev, Hungarian-speaking specialist from headquarters of the dreaded Soviet Russian secret police, the MVD. At this meeting it was proposed to manufacture criminal charges and stage a trial. Fourteen crimes were selected. Révai was charged with gathering a group of legal experts of the Communist party to prepare charges that would prove airtight to trained legal minds. Révai and Boldizsár were to evaluate, from the propaganda point of view, their credibility to the Hungarian people at large, to the Catholics in Hungary, and, last but not least, public opinion abroad. One of the men whom Révai selected as advisers in this matter was William Olti, a Nazi who had turned ardent Communist and had become one of the presiding justices of the "People's Courts."

The plans were ready when Colonel Kotlev returned from Moscow shortly before Christmas, introducing a mysterious Professor Gerson. He had arrived in Budapest with three of his personal assistants, and four hundred twelve trained members of the MVD.

The stage was set for the "liquidation."

*   *   *

On Sunday morning December 26 the chief of the secret political police, "General" Gabriel Péter, a former tailor, was called from his sumptuous home, to his headquarters to meet three visitors from the Ministry of the Interior. They were delivering the sealed orders for the arrest of the Cardinal; specific instructions as to the way in which it was to take place and the precautions to be exercised in case of any difficulties.

The arrest was to be made after dark, with pedestrian and vehicular traffic diverted from the surrounding area; guards were to be posted at all exits of the Primate's residence and everyone kept inside until after official announcement of the arrest.

Special detachments were to be kept in readiness in "critical" key places throughout the country; these were to maintain close touch with the newly arrived forces of the MVD, through the liaison officer of the Russian army stationed in General Péter's headquarters. Any demonstration, sign of protest, or uprising was to be immediately suppressed if necessary by the instant use of arms, and if by its size it should become generally known it was to be labeled as an act of "criminals," "enemies of the state" or as an "insurrection of individuals wanted for common crimes." Under no circumstance was such a protest to become known as a popular reaction to the Cardinal's arrest.

Péter also received a long list of persons who were to be arrested for complicity with the Cardinal. He was further instructed to issue a strict command to the political police to arrest any individual whose "behavior is indicative of a disturbance of the pacific conditions in the people's democracy." As a result of this command, during the days after the arrest to the end of January 3,314 persons found themselves in the dungeons of the political police, simply because "their behavior was indicative of a disturbance of the pacific conditions in the people's democracy."

*　　*　　*

The three police cars bearing the Cardinal and the seventeen arresting officers arrived from a near-by city to which he had been taken first, as a precaution, at three o'clock in the morning at "Andrássy ut 60," the headquarters of the infamous political police. Machine-gun crews were stationed in the courtyards of the two buildings comprising the headquarters unit.

The Cardinal was immediately taken to one of the detention rooms on the third floor, especially reserved for "prominent" prisoners. The staff had known that something special was in the offing, for on the preceding afternoon, the few prisoners there had been removed and special "watch guards" had been selected. Six units of four guards and an officer were chosen to keep uninterrupted watch. The guards took turns of one hour each, keeping their eyes glued on the Cardinal through the foot-square window. These detention rooms are quite large, sparsely lit from the ceiling, with a wooden slab for the prisoner to sleep on, a table, and a chair.

*　　*　　*

On Monday, the first day, a doctor and an assistant hitherto unknown in the prison arrived and were brought by a staff colonel to the Cardinal's room. They undertook a thorough physical examination and took samples of his blood. The Cardinal seemed undisturbed, ate some of his prison fare, slept little, and prayed a great deal.

The next morning two staff officers arrived with a stenographer. They first asked personal questions, then turned to the Cardinal's activities: whether he knew Prince Paul Eszterházy, whether Eszterházy had ever given large sums of money to the Church; whether he had received sums of money during his stay in Rome; whether he knew Cardinal Van Roey; whether he knew Cardinal Spellman and had stayed with him in New York; whether he knew the American envoys Schoenfeld and Chapin and had communicated with them; whether he knew where the Holy Crown of Hungary was; whether he knew a long list of persons, including Justin Baranyai, Béla Ispánky, Nicholas Nagy, Sigmund Mihalovics, Baron George Ullman, Emery Bóka, and who they were. As the last question, the Cardinal was asked whether Father Andrew Zakár had been his confidential secretary and, as such, had known of all his activities. Upon receiving an affirmative answer to all questions, they had pen and ink and paper brought into the room, and requested the Cardinal to write a *curriculum vitae* with special emphasis on the time since he had become Primate of Hungary. After indicating very politely that this was urgent, they left.

The very next hour the government spokesman announced to the world: "Mindszenty, under the weight of evidence produced against him, has made a confession. His arrested accomplices also have admitted the charges against him."

The supposed accomplices were Hungarians whose names had been on the list submitted to the Cardinal. According to Iván Boldizsár, who as both member of the planning group and head of the press department had the complete authority to be "government spokesman," "Mindszenty is accused of treacherous activities against the people's democracy, conspiracy against the republic, espionage, and foreign currency abuses."

While the world echoed with the propaganda slogan of the Hungarian government, "The Cardinal has confessed!" the victim was finishing the requested *curriculum vitae*, comprising more than forty pages, in his own handwriting. It was taken to the "chief" when the guard was changed, and that night he went to sleep early.

At four o'clock on Wednesday morning, shortly before the guard was to be changed again, a detachment from "downstairs" arrived. The Cardinal was awakened and taken to the largest of the "examination rooms" on the second floor. And here the ordeal began.

Three "examiners" in turn let loose on the Cardinal. They worked according to a pattern, in three-hour shifts under the direction of one of the colonels of the secret police. Occasionally General Gabriel Péter himself came in for a while. The mysterious Professor Gerson, Colonel Kotlev, and his assistants were present at times. Four guards were stationed constantly at the two doors.

The examiners read to the Cardinal his own notes and accused him of lying. Hundreds of times he had to hear the words: "Lies, lies. Understand, Mindszenty, these are all lies!" At other times he was reprimanded: "A priest does not lie; a priest tells the truth; a priest confesses; a priest cannot receive absolution for his sin of lying."

Occasionally the tune changed. It was impressed on him that he, as the head of the Church in Hungary, was responsible for the future of millions of souls. And again he was admonished to admit that all his statements, public and private, were false. Lies! Lies!

For hours and hours, the same questions were repeated again and again. The same demand was made.

A new set of examiners changed again the tune: What had he

done in Rome? What had he discussed with Pope Pius XII? What had he said to Cardinal Van Roey? How long had he spoken with Otto? How many times had he dined with Cardinal Spellman? Who had been his guide in Ottawa? What had he done in Rome? What had he said to Cardinal Van Roey? How long had he spoken with Otto? What had he discussed with Pope Pius XII? What had he— what had he—what had he—what had he . . . echoed from the walls. The Cardinal had stood looking at the examiners squarely.

Then they let him stand facing the brilliantly lit whitewashed wall, his arms raised high in the air for ten hours at a time, while new questions were repeated, and repeated, over and over again.

In some instances the same questions were repeated as many as two hundred times in succession; and no answer ever satisfied the examiners. Some of the questions were crude and referred to the life of priests and nuns. Some were even cruder and referred to the violence by the Soviet army of occupation against which the Cardinal had publicly protested. Others dealt with the life and families of his friends and associates. Others still concerned his own family. Questions after questions, that could not be answered. When did your sister . . . When did your sister . . . When did your sister . . . ? All that anyone could hear was the word "sister."

None of the questioners themselves could stand the strain for more than a half-hour at a time. None remained in the room for more than three hours. As one of the guards tattled, who had to attend inactively such a three-hour session: "My head whirled, my eyes were blinded, and for days I heard the same questions ringing in my ear."

On Thursday afternoon, after more than thirty-five hours of questioning, the doctor who had first visited the Cardinal arrived, and the questioning was interrupted while he made a cursory examination and consulted for a few seconds with Professor Gerson and Colonel Kotlev, who were present. Then the machine-gun questioning resumed again, with the Cardinal standing erect, with arms over his head facing the whitewashed wall.

All his answers were unsatisfactory to his inquisitors. With a firm voice he shouted denials. With a voice of pity he responded when they became crude. His voice never wavered until the evening of Thursday. Around eight o'clock, after forty hours of standing, he swayed slightly.

The Cardinal was told to turn. He did not move. One of the examiners walked over and pulled him around, seeing that his eyes were closed. He was left standing while a short consultation on the telephone was held. The doctor came with his assistant and two large glasses of coffee. A chair was brought, and the Cardinal was made to sit. The doctor, holding his head, put the glass to his lips. He gulped the contents and opened his eyes, their benign depth expressing gratitude. He was asked whether he wished the second glass, but did not answer. After a short while the doctor put the second glass to his lips, and he gulped it like the first. This time he spoke his thanks.

When one of the questioners asked whether he wanted some food he nodded. He was told that after he had answered all the questions satisfactorily he should have all the food he wanted.

He then had to stand again, and the questions were resumed. Seemingly refreshed, his voice became clearer, and at times he would shout his "No!" in a commanding manner.

*   *   *

It was during these hours that the news was broadcast throughout the world: Pope Pius XII had excommunicated, *latae sententia*, all who knew themselves, by their own conscience, to be guilty of the crime of "violently laying hands" upon the Cardinal.

*   *   *

The questions continued throughout the night. Shift after shift resumed the psychological torture. By Friday they were all read from sheets of paper brought in by each shift as it took over the relay. The Cardinal had twice asked to be permitted to take leave because of physical necessity. He was told that there existed no physical necessity; that he could attend to all that after he had answered the questions.

Whenever his eyes seemed to close, new coffee was brought for him, and the questioning continued. About ten o'clock Friday evening, when he had been standing sixty-six hours, he closed his eyes and remained silent.

The colonel in charge of the shift tapped the Cardinal's shoulder and asked why he did not respond. It has been recalled that he answered: "End it all. It is useless! Kill me! I am ready to die." He was told cynically that no harm would come to him; that he was not going to die; that all he had to do was to answer certain questions.

Afterward it was rumored at headquarters that the Cardinal had answered: "Your questions are no questions. They are suggestions of the devil!"

After more than three days and two nights of torturous treatment he still resisted like a rock.

As the time advanced he asked for more and more drinks, and they were given to him. On Friday night he drank twenty-seven glasses of "coffee."

From Friday night on the inquisitors hammered his eardrums with statements. Facts converted from his own *curriculum vitae* and added to it. They read the paragraphs to him again and again, asked him to acknowledge their truth.

By Saturday forenoon the Cardinal could be hardly recognized. He asked for a drink and it was refused. He was excited; his calm had left him completely; finally his legs gave way, and he fell down several times. During the forenoon his shoes had to be removed because his feet and legs had swollen and caused him intense pain.

After his shoes had been removed he was made to stand again. Then he first asked the question, "What do you want of me?" Colonel Kotlev, who had not spoken at any time, answered that he should sign the confession that had been prepared in accordance with his own statement. It was about the same as the one he had written, "with slight changes" because they had discovered his "conspiracy"—attempts to upset the tranquillity of the country, and plans to overthrow the government. Endless explanations ensued. The Cardinal did not respond.

Here "General" Gabriel Péter, with Moscovite training, took over. He began by asking the Cardinal cynically how it was possible—if the Church was so powerful—that he, the Primate, was in that room; how it was possible that the power of the Church did not protect him, had not freed him.

With a smirk he told the Cardinal that the people's democracy was mightier than the Church. Here was the best proof; here he could see for himself that no power, secular, ecclesiastic, or spiritual, could match the power of the people's democracy. Not even the American imperialists could save him or any of his "conspiring flock."

The Cardinal remained motionless: Gabriel Péter's words had no effect. He asked for a drink and was refused.

The examiners, taking turns, continued to read the statements to the Cardinal, who now could hardly keep his balance. His voice had become weaker and weaker; but to each question put, he still answered with his resolute No!

In the afternoon Colonel Kotlev returned again and told the Cardinal that it would be proved that all that had been read to him was true.

One of his assistants left, and Professor Justin Baranyai was brought in. The aged theologian collapsed upon seeing the Cardinal, approached on his knees, and cried like a child. Completely broken in spirit, he mumbled words no one could understand. He was led away.

Kotlev quietly spoke to the Cardinal at length; asked, not expecting to receive an answer, whether he wanted to see what was happening to others of the Church who had plotted against the "people's democracy." The Cardinal stared and did not answer.

At Kotlev's command the door opened, and the guards brought in two nuns. Their tortured faces and broken bodies beaten to pulp were a horrible sight. The Cardinal tried to bring his hands together in prayer, but the right hand could not find the left. A tear appeared in his eye. The nuns were carried away, and the Cardinal's secretary, Father Andrew Zakár, was brought in. His face was swollen beyond recognition; his hair was full of dried blood; his arms and neck were blue and brown from bruises. His feet were bleeding, and his right leg had a bandage that showed through the torn garment. Two guards supported him as he appeared. For moments there was a dead silence. It seemed as if the Cardinal did not recognize the mass of disfigured humanity, and Zakár, through swollen eyes blinded by the lights, did not recognize his revered Cardinal.

Colonel Kotlev spoke, saying that this was the secretary, who had confessed to every one of the statements they had been reading to the Cardinal. Zakár broke down, dragging himself on the floor toward the Cardinal, and implored forgiveness. When the two guards stepped to help him up, it was said at headquarters, he suddenly cried out: "No, no, do not hurt me. I beg you, I confess to anything you want. I cannot stand it. I beg you do not hurt me any more." And the Cardinal said, "My son . . ."

After Zakár had been carried away, the Cardinal asked for a drink of coffee. It was refused to him, as it had been all day. For two long hours he spoke no word. His eyes were like glass; his body, like stone.

Then, about four o'clock on Saturday, he was helped to the table on which typewritten statements had been awaiting his signature for days, and a pen was put into his hand.

He did not see the statements; he could not read them; he did not know what was in them; all they wanted of him was his signature.

After eighty-four torturous hours, at the dictate of his inquisitors, he signed the papers prepared for him.

He did not know that this statement began:

"I am a Hungarian nobleman. My original surname was Pehm. The Pehm family was declared noble in 1732. On my mother's side I am descended from the Hungarian noble family of Kovács which was raised to the rank of nobility in 1663.

"In February, 1917, I was sent to Zalaegerszeg as a teacher of religion. In 1919 I was appointed parson of that same place and I worked there in that capacity until March 29, 1944, when I became bishop of Veszprém. I was appointed Prince Primate in October, 1945. Recalling my public activities, I declare that I have always considered myself as a royalist. That is why I have always supported

to the greatest possible extent those political tendencies that helped
to realize that aim. After my appointment as Prince Primate I could
serve my aims all the more efficiently. My aim is the aim of the
monarchist movement in Hungary: a Federative Central European
Monarchy, with a personal union between Hungary and Austria, and
with other Catholic states, in the first place Bavaria, that might perhaps join it, and with Otto Hapsburg on the throne. I only thought
this possible after the overthrow of the Hungarian Republic with
foreign and, in the first place, American aid . . ."

The Cardinal was unable to stand up. Colonel Kotlev himself tried
to help him, without avail. Two guards lifted his limp body from
the chair and carried him back to the "detention room for prom-
inents," his cell.

Professor Gerson, the doctor, and his assistant came. The doctor
ordered the Cardinal stripped, and two guards washed his body.
Throughout, the prince of the Church remained motionless.

Warm soup was brought and some mashed potatoes. Professor
Gerson fed it to the Cardinal himself.

Then the doctor gave him the first of many hypodermic injections.
After watching for a while, they all departed, leaving the seemingly
lifeless prisoner to the guard detail, whose eyes remained ever
pointed at the Cardinal through the window.

For seventeen long hours, until noon of Sunday, the Cardinal lay
as if frozen, with his stary eyes wide open. Once during the night
the officer of a new shift of guards called the doctor, because the
prisoner was not asleep—his eyes were wide open and pointed at
the ceiling, his body rigid. The doctor examined the prisoner and
assured the officer that his ward was fast asleep despite the wide-open
eyes; there was nothing wrong, the body would recuperate.

The body did recuperate; but the soul of the Cardinal had received a mortal wound.

*   *   *

The planning group met on Sunday morning. General Péter made
the report on the Cardinal's confession, impressively unlocking his
brief case and putting the document on the table.

Iván Boldizsár had a cold shower ready for him: The document was typewritten and therefore carried little weight. The Cardinal must write it in his own hand. People would not accept it otherwise.

He explained his plans for the publication of the "confession." To prove that he had confessed, photostatic copies of a handwritten "confession" must be released to the world press; he believed that the best form would be a documentary pamphlet. All material prepared to convict the Cardinal in the eyes of the world would be included; documents that would infer his guilt, conclusive commentary that would suggest his guilt, and his own handwriting, which, even to the most skeptical, would prove his guilt. In this manner the Cardinal could be tried and convicted before world public opinion, in advance of any trial that might take place later.

The group was also informed that copies of the "documents found buried in the Primate's cellar" had already been published to prepare the public successively for the all-conclusive evidence: the Cardinal's confession in his own handwriting.

Bits of the "evidence" of the Cardinal's "guilt" had been broadcast day by day, and photostatic copies of the documents sent to newspapers abroad to support the broadcasts.

One of the ministers emphasized that, parallel to the moves to influence public opinion, all this would bear fruit for purpose of internal policies only if it led the Hungarian Catholics and the bishops to break away from the Primate. If at least a serious split in the ranks of the Catholics were brought about, it might hold the promise of a reversal of the Vatican policy. Anyway, such a split would make it possible to overcome the resistance of both clergy and the masses, eliminate the spiritual autonomy of the Church, and integrate its functional structure into the body of the people's democracy. As he put it, this would be the ideal solution.

Some expressed the opinion that sooner or later force would have to be used. The Hungarian episcopate and clergy had closed ranks behind the Primate. Of the episcopate one archbishop and four bishops had been summoned to the Ministry of the Interior; after an interrogation they were given to understood that the fate of the Cardinal might befall them too. Despite threats they remained adamant. The clergy refused to yield, and while not inciting popular resistance they preached sermons in which they asked for calm but inferred that the Primate was a martyr. Obviously the Catholic masses of Hungary who did not know the Primate personally would have to be convinced that he was a common criminal, unworthy of their respect and loyalty; and furthermore that his person and his false nimbus formed the only obstacle to an agreement between the state and the Catholic Church. Success in convincing the mass of Hungarian Catholics would have the ultimate effect of causing the Catholic Church in Hungary to secede from the Church of Rome and become the church of the common man, a purposeful functionary of the people's democracy.

Boldizsár answered that he had prepared a campaign for planting news items in the anticlerical press abroad which, when reprinted in the Hungarian newspapers, would carry the authority of the foreign source and as such would impress the population strongly. A group of forty-seven writers and "reliable" journalists had been assembled under the direction of an undersecretary to the Prime Minister to create and develop such news items. This staff might be enlarged as requests from the foreign press increased.

Directives had been issued that no permits to enter the country be granted to foreign journalists without the approval of Colonel Kotlev.

In the end, all agreed that special efforts must be made to discredit the Cardinal before public opinion, at home and abroad. "Convincing evidence" must be unearthed.

The Primate's character must be blackened to such a degree that persons who were not convinced of his guilt would at least be doubtful of his innocence.

"We know the secret," one of the members of the planning group stated then as he had done many times previously. "We know the secret, for we are experts in the mentality of the masses!"

*   *   *

They may be truly experts in the mentality of the masses bound by terror; of the beclouded mentality of subjugated, enslaved peoples; trembling with fear whenever the State's voice of command resounds. But they knew not the secret of the clear thinking, the sober judgement, the healthy mentality of the free peoples, living in free lands.

*   *   *

In the early afternoon Colonel Kotlev, General Péter, and Professor Gerson returned together to the headquarters of the secret police.

The Cardinal had awakened about noon and eaten a soup, some potatoes, and bread. After finishing his meal he complained to one of the guards of a headache and of pains in his legs, and the doctor was called, who examined the legs and prepared to administer a hypodermic injection. The Cardinal seemed to refuse. The doctor spoke awhile to him and then tried to insert the needle; but the Cardinal moved away, and resisted energetically. Two guards were instructed to hold him for the injection; but the third guard and the officer in charge had to be called on before the doctor succeeded. As the needle entered the Cardinal's body he gave a deep groan.

Then General Péter arrived with Professor Gerson and asked the Cardinal whether he had any wishes: he shook his head. When asked whether he could walk he tried to rise from the wooden slab, but failed.

After General Péter left, Professor Gerson sat down beside the Cardinal. He introduced himself formally and began to speak in a quiet, friendly tone as to a child, telling the Cardinal that no further harm would come to him if he were cooperative; that he himself had no control of what was done, and the ordeals of the past days might just be a taste of what awaited anyone who refused to cooperate. He described at length the tortures administered to the other prisoners, who had been arrested for "complicity." No one had to suffer such treatment, but a cooperative spirit was necessary. He expressed confidence that by now the Cardinal must have come to the conclusion that opposition or resistance was useless. As one who wished him well, he indicated the desire to hear any suggestions or wishes.

The Cardinal answered. Gerson was the first person to whom he spoke at length. He told of the injection he had received, against his will, for which there had been no necessity; and he became quite excited.

Gerson quieted him. The injections were necessary because he had been weakened by the experience of the past days. Everyone there was interested in his good health. No one wished to harm his health. No one really wished to harm him at all. The injections would keep him strong. He advised the Cardinal that it was best for him to ask for the injections whenever he felt weak. And he departed.

In the late afternoon a sumptuous meal was served, of which the Cardinal ate very little. Shortly after, the doctor and his assistant came. Another injection was administered. The Cardinal suffered it without a sound.

At eight o'clock that night he was taken "downstairs" to the interrogation room where he had previously been. He was seated at the table, with pen, ink, and paper in reach. Then General Péter told him that he was to make a handwritten copy of the statement he had made previously. He did not respond.

Then the colonel in charge of the team of "examiners" took over, and showed the Cardinal the statement he had recently signed. The Cardinal answered that he was unable to read it; it was all blurred. The colonel then began to read the statement to him.

The Cardinal excitedly interposed that he had made no such statement. The colonel continued. The Cardinal became more excited, and tried to get up from the chair; but his aching legs prevented him.

Then the examiners made him look at his own signature. The Cardinal answered that he could not recognize it; he was unable to see it clearly.

At ten o'clock at night, they placed him on his feet against the wall and made him raise his arms above his head. Then the recitation of each and every sentence of the statement began again. Every sentence was repeated over and over. By the time the shift changed, even the guards knew it by heart.

Thirteen hours later, the handwritten "confession" was delivered to the desk of General Péter.

Not until Wednesday were the interrogations resumed. For two days the Cardinal was allowed to rest, while his feet and legs were treated. Only the doctor and Professor Gerson visited him.

When the interrogations were resumed they took on an entirely different character. The Cardinal went "downstairs" twice a day for periods that varied at first but later became routine: two periods of three hours each, with a pause of three hours between.

The life of the Cardinal too became routine. He came under the constant care of the doctor, who even visited him during the night. The injections became accepted and regular, and once the Cardinal even commented that he felt much better after them.

Professor Gerson became a frequent visitor. The two had long quiet discussions on many subjects, most of them not connected with the Cardinal; many times they spoke of philosophy and of the human being as an individual. Occasionally the Cardinal would make incoherent statements, or give incoherent answers to questions; then Gerson would correct him and make him repeat the corrected sentence.

A distinct change in the Cardinal's personality could be observed from day to day. He practically ceased to act as an individual, and seemed to be in a daze. As time progressed, he became more and more dependent on other persons; most of his acts became responses to outside influence or a command.

Some of the guards had seen these signs before.

One day Professor Gerson brought a visitor. Most of the guards knew William Olti. He had no difficulty in passing through the complicated guard system of "Andrássy ut 60."

By this time the relationship between the Cardinal and Gerson had become settled. Gerson called him "Mr. Prince-Primate"—a uniquely Hungarian form of address—and he responded with a familiar "Gerson."

The guards overheard Gerson's introduction: "Permit me, Mr. Prince-Primate, to introduce to you my friend William. He has great interest in your case. I would like it very much if you two would understand each other."

William began to come and see the Cardinal every day. Sometimes in the company of Professor Gerson, at times without him. Usually, when he was alone with the Cardinal, he had the cell door closed. Only on rare occasions could the guard overhear their talk; then it seemed that William dominated the conversations; his voice was cold and his manner formal. Soon he began to attend the evening interrogations of the Cardinal.

The questions during these interrogations now dealt with details of the Cardinal's "confession." First his own statements were read to him; then the statements of the other prisoners accused of complicity with him; then again elaborations were read.

At times the Cardinal was morose; at others, greatly disturbed and excited. But he answered all questions willingly, repeated all sentences —once, twice, or even three times when he was told to do so.

The following Thursday, the 13th of January, the evening interrogation had to be interrupted. The Cardinal, after fainting and then recovering, had collapsed completely.

Excitement ensued, throughout all the floors. An hour later, the still limp body was carried back to the cell. The doctor and his assistant remained with the Cardinal until the next day.

Late that night, Professor Gerson arrived, and was followed by Colonel Kotlev and then General Péter. Gerson himself examined the Cardinal, performing the functions of a physician for the first time, and Colonel Kotlev conferred at length with the doctor.

Gerson, Kotlev, and Péter held a conference outside the cell door, in which the General was heard to say that "they gave him too much." Kotlev protested, and both he and Gerson began to speak in mathematical terms. Then the General turned on Kotlev and asked, "What are we going to do if he dies?" Kotlev answered, "Usually they do not die." The General proposed hospitalization. Kotlev demurred. They both asked Gerson, who replied that it was not necessary—"the man will come out of the coma."

The next morning it was whispered on the streets of Budapest that the imprisoned Cardinal was deathly ill.

In the evening he was well enough, and the interrogations were resumed. But the doctor remained with him all the following night.

With the morning of the 15th of January the account of the Cardinal's life in prison has to end.

All detachments charged with guarding him were suddenly exchanged. One officer and two guards had been put under arrest and removed to the Zsombolyai post of the secret police. Here the two guards were "accidentally shot while trying to escape"; the officer was sent to Russia, for "reeducation."

They had been suspected of tattling.

One officer who himself saw some of the happenings during the nineteen days and heard the reports of other guard shifts on the rest was sent to command an outlying post of the political police near the Yugoslav border. By the middle of March he had escaped from Hungarian territory.

*   *   *

In the case of the Cardinal more experts and more staff personnel had been concentrated at "Andrássy ut 60" than ever before. The officers of the guard were told that should he die in their charge they would pay with their own lives.

Of those who witnessed his first nineteen days in prison none believed it possible that any human being could stand the physical and psychological tortures he had to suffer. Later it was rumored in government circles that both Colonel Kotlev and Professor Gerson had stated that the Cardinal had been their most difficult and, as Gerson put it, psychologically most complicated case. Kotlev described it as the outstanding example of the obstinate resistance of the human spirit; but he added, "No obstinacy exists that we cannot overcome—no spirit that we cannot break."

Since "Andrássy ut 60" had become the headquarters of modern inquisition, no man had stood up for eighty-four hours under the treatment of the "examiners." Some had held out for seventy, even seventy-five hours, but then were "useless" for weeks, or even for life. Some others had collapsed; their nervous system had given up; some had died in that very room from exhaustion, or their hearts refused to continue to labor under the effects of the stimulating "coffee" that had kept them awake for days.

Some "confessed" and signed statements of crimes they had never known existed; involved others whom they had never known; denied their creed, their breeding, their friends, their loyalties. They "confessed" to anything, to gain the one favorable nod from the torturers: permission to leave, to go back to their cells, to the smelly dungeons below day, to rot—to rot alone or in the company of other victims, but without the blinding lights, without the physical lashings, without the depraved acts of men who had turned animals, without the endless beatings of body and mind, without the ceaseless hammering of voices on their eardrums, also without self-respect, or the wish for freedom, or the desire for the warmth of a human heart. Without all this—their only sigh being to be left unmolested, to rot.

Then there were others who had "confessed" and never again spoke an intelligible word. Their tortures were over. They knew nothing of their past; present and future had no meaning to them; they never stood trial—they escaped the prison, the penitentiary, the forced labor, in the country, or in the slave-labor camps in Siberia. It did not even take long for them to leave the dungeons of "Andrássy ut 60." They were taken, as speedily as could be arranged, to an insane asylum, to end life there. General Péter was known to dread insanity.

Very few ever managed to outwit the inquisitors, and they not for long. One or another reasoned intelligently that if he "confessed" at an early stage he would be spared further tortures and, when appearing for trial, would find justice. They were disappointed. The methods of the secret police adapted from the Soviet's are thorough. The public knew of only one man who reached trial in such a state that he was able to tell the judge that his confession was of no value, that it was extorted; but even his heroic stand did not succeed.

That was Valentine Arany, a defendant in the first of the "conspiracy" trials in Hungary; and the judge interrupted him, adjourning the trial.

Arany was taken away by the secret police for "corrective processing," part of which was administered by Soviet experts stationed at Budapest. They corrected the mistake committed at "Andrássy ut 60," and a week later the trial was resumed. The result astonished the public. In court the defendant "confessed" everything, stood by his confession, and did not deny any of the accusations.

Now he had been adequately "processed," and the prescribed results achieved.

"Processing" by the secret political police consists of three phases. In the first the prisoner is made to "confess." In the second, the most difficult, he is convinced of his deeds, is made to elaborate on his confession, and is taught to analyze, simply and logically, the details and the circumstances of his "crimes." This phase ends when the prisoner himself becomes absolutely convinced of his guilt and his mental and emotional reactions give conclusive proof of it. In the third and last phase he is prepared for the public trial, to be a witness against himself and others, to show remorse and indicate through words or behavior the wish to atone, and to accept the sentence passed upon him without argument. If his own trial or his appearance as a witness extends over a period of a day, this third phase is continued beyond the prisoner's last appearance in public.

The methods used during the three phases of "processing" varied with the individual prisoner, but the average personality could be made to succumb through brutality, terror, and fear. Drugs were used in the transitory stages.

In intellectual or complicated cases, where sheer brutality, exercise of terror, or threat would have little effect, a union of the sciences of neurology, chemistry, and psychiatry was employed. The prison physician called it the "biodynamical" treatment.

From the very beginning the Cardinal was treated as a complicated case.

The staff physician of the secret police—himself of "Muscovite" training—has held seminars for the "examiners" and the staff officers, explaining the "biodynamical" method.

In the first phase of the "processing," after the physical breakdown of the victim had been accomplished, a near-complete mental collapse had to be brought about.

He explained, that as drugs had been used by science to help along a mending in the brain of the human creature, they could be used to promote disruption. Actedron and Mescaline had been the tools of the "biodynamical" method for years.

* * *

The drug known as Actedron is synthetically manufactured and is described as phenylisopropylaminohydrophosphoricum. As a stimulant it is used in doses ranging from 0.15 grams to 0.50 grams; but it is known that both the Soviet and the Hungarian secret police have used doses of 3.0 grams at one time.

In small doses Actedron enlivens the physical functions of the subject, gives him a feeling of strength; as the doses are repeated and increased, the seemingly benevolent effect is overshadowed by dizziness, strong headaches, a sensation of turning in circles, and the incapability to relax. Mydriasis (the abnormal enlargement of the pupils) and tachycardia (an increased heartbeat) are the distinct signs noticeable on the victim.

Mescaline is the more dangerous of the two drugs, and is used only in the second and third phases. Today it is being manufactured in Russia as a synthetic compound, trimethoxyphenylethylamine. Its qualities were already known in the sixteenth century, for Hernández, the physician to Philip II of Spain, mentioned them in a report on the Indian tribes in Mexico; they swallowed them to produce hallucinations and trances during their rituals and religious ceremonies.

Mescaline, in natural form, is found in the peyotes or mescal buttons of a cactus known as Lophophora williamsii. For modern science its discovery was reported by Dr. Lewin in 1888. The use of the natural extract had been prohibited, in one form or another, as being harmful to the nervous system of the human being.

The psychological effects of the mescal buttons were investigated by Weir Mitchell (*British Medical Journal*, December, 1896), Havelock Ellis (*Lancet*, 1897, p. 1540), and Dixon (*Journal of Physiology*, vol. 25, p. 69, 1899). Among the effects they describe are astonishing color hallucinations and exhilaration; one states that "an indescribable feeling of dual existence" was produced.

Modern medical science has used the synthetic compound in the field of psychiatric research. Its potency can be gauged by an extract from the *Journal of Mental Science* (G. T. Stockings, 1940, b. 86): "It is important to realize that unless the dose is very large, that is, above 0.4 grams, the mental changes take place in a state of clear consciousness and without weakness of the intellectual faculties; this clearness of consciousness is all the more remarkable in view of the profound disorders of personality and thinking with which it is coexistent. . . . Mescaline produces no intellectual weakness unlike alcohol and other narcotic drugs. The characteristic change appears to be the peculiar divorcing of the intellectual part of the personality from the rest of the psyche, with disturbance of association, blocking of voluntary intellectual thought and extreme distractability. . . . Mescaline intoxication is a true schizophrenia, if we use the word in the literal sense of 'split mind,' for the characteristic effect of Mescaline is a molecular fragmentation of the entire personality exactly similar to that found in schizophrenic patients."

While Actedron was used by the Hungarian secret police to keep the prisoner awake and under tension for a prolonged period, beyond the limits of normal fatigue, Mescaline was administered to produce a weird psychological effect—found in morbid mental states—known to science as "depersonalization."

The first phase of the "processing" was the most dangerous, because it might bring an irreparable, complete physical, mental, and emotional breakdown of the prisoner endangering the entire process, and was always carefully supervised by expert officers. They determined the near-exhaustion stages, and also the time and size of the doses.

In the seminars the secret of the synapses was explained: Tiredness in the prisoner causes the poisonous products of metabolism to become more and more diffused through the tissues and the fluids of the body, acting on the synapses, the terminal arborizations of neurons, in the brain, so that the passage of the nervous current is impeded and, through the relative isolation of one neuron from another, the nervous system of the prisoner becomes partially disassociated.

The longer this period is continued without a regeneration, the more difficult it becomes for the prisoner to overcome fatigue and exhaustion. At the limit a general diffuse poisoning of the brain sets in.

At this stage the stimuli are administered and continued periodically until the desired results—"confessions"—are achieved. The drugs take control over the neurons and their synapses; the first link of the chain in the Satanic misuse of science has been created.

From then on the brain of the prisoner is kept near the exhaustion point, and through the use of both Actedron and Mescaline direction or even absolute control of the mental process of the victim is achieved.

Even in the most complicated cases, like that of the Cardinal, the integrated system of the psychic entity can easily be divided at this stage; as the psychiatrists say, the soul can be split!

The conscious mind has been separated from the coconscious and the subliminal self; the personality disintegrated.

A psychiatrist, with the use of drugs, may put the pieces together at his will; reintegrate a completely new personality, and triumphantly present the new "him" to the world. And thus the Satanic chain is completed.

Tediously pieced together, this is what happened to Joseph, Cardinal Mindszenty, stage by stage during the forty days between his arrest and his appearance at the trial.

*   *   *

While the Cardinal was still being processed at "Andrássy ut 60," the Hungarian government published on January 19 a pamphlet called the Yellow Book, which was to indict the Cardinal and prove to the world his guilt in advance of trial. It contained pages of photostats of the Cardinal's "confession" in his own handwriting. Published also in French, for foreign consumption, under the guise of factual reporting it carried commentaries of the government spokesman.

The strangest part of the pamphlet was set in bold type and read:

The Hungarian police authorities arrested Joseph Mindszenty . . . on a charge of having committed treason, espionage, crimes aimed at overthrowing the republic, and foreign-exchange speculation.

The above documents convincingly and undeniably justify the charges against Mindszenty, and the trial that is soon to begin will cast light on every aspect of Mindszenty's list of crimes. But even on the basis of the documents, every objective observer must recognize that there is no question of persecuting the Church or the priests, or of infringing the freedom of worship.

The documents themselves consisted of letters written to the Cardinal and three drafts of his own. To prove the letters genuine, they made the Cardinal countersign some of them on the margin. There were also photostats of the "confession" of the Cardinal's secretary.

To further prove the documents genuine, a photograph was included showing the Cardinal's private secretary, Father Andrew Zakár, and the archiepiscopal archivist, Father John Fábián, next to a metal container which had been "buried a yard deep in the cellar of the Archbishop's palace in Esztergom."

This was found necessary because obviously there were at least two forgeries among the documents.

Forgery seems to be indicated by an oversight on the part of the experts of the secret political police, who, in trying to present a proof of the complicity of the Cardinal, reproduced a photostatic copy of a letter of Archbishop Rohracher of Salzburg to Cardinal Spellman of New York which supposedly had been written at the behest of Cardinal Mindszenty. It is dated November 18, 1947, and contains the request to Cardinal Spellman to intervene with the United States Army to have the Holy Crown of Hungary delivered for safekeeping to the Vatican. To prove the complicity further, a photostatic copy of a letter from Cardinal Montini, papal undersecretary of state, to Cardinal Mindszenty is reproduced, transmitting a reaction to the request. The date of Cardinal Montini's letter is September 9, 1947. According to the documents, the answer had been written more than two months earlier than the request.

The letter of Cardinal Montini to Cardinal Mindszenty has all the characteristic earmarks of a forgery. In good faith it cannot be assumed that the undersecretary of state in the Vatican should not know his Latin; that his office would not know how to abbreviate Latin.

In the very first line of the letter, in addressing the Cardinal, the word "Eminentissime" is abbreviated. The abbreviation should be "Em.me.," but in the letter it is written as "Em.ne." In the first line of the address, at the bottom of the letter, the word "Eminentissimo" is abbreviated as "Em.o." but it should read "Em.mo.," if written correctly.

To go further: the second paragraph of the letter from the Vatican contains this sentence: "Heic adiunctum, id Tibi mittere studeo, cum de re agatur, quae Tibi cordi est." The word "Heic" is meaningless in Latin; the relation of "Heic adiunctum" makes no sense. It is inconceivable that the office of the undersecretary would have sent it.

There can be no question that Latin is known in the Vatican.

The reaction to the publication of the "proof of guilt" was an unpleasant surprise to the government.

The Hungarian papers were instructed to publish the "confession" and the proofs in installments; the government radio blared forth day by day, citing the contents of the Yellow Book. The people must be convinced.

In Budapest and in the towns, in Erdöd and in the villages, throughout the country, wherever people felt safe from the spies of the secret police, they commented on the Cardinal's confession:

"He confessed that he is a nobleman. Why then did he remain true to his peasant origin all his life, even when he assumed the highest offices? Why didn't he declare that he was a nobleman when this would have been an asset, during the regimes? Why now, when he is in the jail of the Communists?" It did not make sense to them.

" 'From my youth I opposed all democratic movements,' he confessed; he was an extreme rightist, he says. Then why did the extreme rightists put him in prison when they came into power?" It did not make sense.

"He was a monarchist, he confessed. Well, what of it? Everyone knew he was; so are a lot of others. That is not a crime."

"He did not want the Holy Crown to be brought back to Hungary.

Well enough. Let us thank the Lord that he did what he could, for the Russians would have taken it away and sold it somewhere; the same as they did with their own crown jewels."

No one in Hungary believed in the "confession" except the Communists; and they believed in it because they wanted to.

*   *   *

On January 21 the planning group assembled in full force. Professor Gerson and General Péter reported that the Cardinal was ready for trial. No unpleasant surprises were to be expected, because he had been fully "prepared" and would do in court as he was told to. Iván Boldizsár informed the group that the release of the documentary evidence had created the reaction expected; the Cardinal was in disfavor with the masses; the publication of the Yellow Book was convincing public opinion abroad.

One of the ministers countered that it seemed as if public opinion abroad was rallying to the defense of the Cardinal; that the tattling of the guards about the treatment of the Cardinal in prison had given rise to rumors. Colonel Kotlev asked him how he knew. The minister had answered that he read it in the foreign newspapers and heard it while listening to the Hungarian language broadcasts of the British and the Voice of America. His words caused an embarrassed silence, and General Péter and Colonel Kotlev raised their eyebrows and looked at each other.

Révai proposed that steps be taken to insure that reports of the trial in newspapers abroad should be favorable and to counteract the effect of the foreign broadcasts on the people of Hungary. Boldizsár answered that such arrangements had already been made; "traveling correspondents" would not be admitted before or during the trial because, even if they reported in a more or less acceptable manner while in the country, there was the risk that they would repudiate their own dispatches after leaving. Local representatives would attend the trial, and they could be "controlled," he said. The trial would be broadcast to the Hungarian people, and by short wave abroad. It would have all the earmarks of a "live broadcast" except that transmission would not be directly from the courtroom. Master discs would be cut while the trial was in progress, which would be edited to eliminate all undesirable matter, and a re-recording would then be made of the convincing high lights, with a commentary. This would suffice; no one could question an "original recording" made in the courtroom itself.

Then another member brought up the subject that was worrying most. Rumors were circulating, and reports had appeared in the foreign press, that the Cardinal before his arrest had written a note to the Bishops, which he had deposited with his suffragan in Esztergom, repudiating in advance any confession that he might make and declaring it void, as an eventual product of the "weakness of the flesh." When it was suggested that the Cardinal be required to repudiate this note in open court, Révai interjected that one repudiation does not offset another repudiation; that more positive signs of the Cardinal's confession of guilt must be produced.

It was suggested that a note from the Cardinal to one of the bishops asking for help to escape should be "smuggled out and caught." This would prove that he was fully conscious of what awaited him; would disprove that he was fearless; and last—but not least—would embarrass the bishop to whom it was addressed. (In execution the idea was modified, the note being addressed to the American Minister.) To further strengthen this point, it was suggested that the Cardinal be made to write a letter in his own hand to the Prime Minister, admitting his guilt and declaring that he was the obstacle to reconciliation between Church and state and expressing his readiness to disclaim all his rights of office. This would help politically, because the people would conclude that the Cardinal had accepted the supremacy of the government over the Church. (As this idea was worked out, the letter was addressed to the Minister of Justice with convincing embellishments to fit inner-political aims.)

The drafts of the letters were to be approved by Révai, and Professor Gerson was charged with having them executed by his ward.

One member questioned whether the issues raised in court would have strong enough legal basis to convince the average man. Révai answered that the simple truth would provide the groundwork of credibility to the minds of the public, in which the roots of conviction would sink; then if untruth was added it would immediately distort the original truth, and as lie was mounted on lie the original truth would lose its simple character and become the keystone holding the mosaic of lies together.

Then one of the ministers pointed out that the tattling of the guards had given rise to reports abroad that drugs had been used on the Cardinal, and that he was in a state of somnambulism.

First Professor Gerson, then Colonel Kotlev, explained that no one in a courtroom has ever been able to judge whether a subject is under hypnotic influence or not. Only a person who in close personal contact for an extended period of time would be able to tell; and as the guards were changed constantly no such person existed.

Furthermore, experience had proved that the public and even some scientists were doubtful that anyone could be kept long enough under hypnotic influence to confess and accept the consequences. Nevertheless, Gerson said, the Cardinal would stand up in court as expected; he would admit all he was told and deny all he was expected to deny, in a convincing manner. A long discussion ensued about what the Cardinal should deny. Gerson explained that he would have to deny a number of things; otherwise his attitude would appear as abnormal.

The manifestations of the newly reintegrated personality must at times resemble—mirror—the publicly expressed ideology of the past. By minute adjustments the Cardinal would appear to be in complete control of his senses.

To the question whether the Cardinal might regain his old composure in court, Kotlev gave the sardonic answer: "No man who has experienced such psychic battering could ever regain his old self." And he turned to two of the cabinet members, saying "Don't be doubtful. Believe me, if we ever took any of you into our hands, and if we wanted to go so far, your own mothers would not recognize a semblance of your souls."

As one of them said afterward, whenever he remembers Kotlev's words he shivers in his whole body.

A member of the planning group told afterward that when he

left this meeting he felt as if it had been a dress rehearsal conference before the opening night of a play.

Truly a great human drama was to reach its peripethy; staged by minds infested with the ideology of destruction; managed by puppets under the guise of Justice. The actors were helpless victims; voices emanating from bodies with broken souls.

Its purpose was to display Joseph, Cardinal Mindszenty in open court where, with the formal embellishment and outward show of judicial procedure, he would be divested of the cardinal's scarlet and would appear at the fall of the curtain garbed in the frieze of the criminal.

*   *   *

The day of the trial dawned.

During the night of February 2, Colonel Kotlev and General Péter themselves had supervised the cautionary measures and inspected all posts. The blocks surrounding the Criminal Courts building and the streets leading to it resembled an armed camp. Machine-gun crews had been placed in the courtyards, on the roofs, and in the doorways of all buildings of the surrounding area.

The ground floor and the cellars of the Criminal Courts building itself, containing the ill famed Markó Prison, teamed with the detachments of General Péter's secret police and those of the political police of the army. In addition to these multitudes of uniformed forces, there were numberless plainclothesmen dispersed throughout the entire building. Seventy-six of Kotlev's own men, whom he had brought from Moscow, were watching all the others.

During the preceding nights all the prisoners who were to stand trial had been transferred to the cells in the Criminal Court; the Cardinal was last. He had been brought from "Andrássy ut 60" by two of Kotlev's assistants, and an aid of General Péter, in one of the armor-plated limousines of the Soviet High Command, accompanied by eighteen officers and guards. Professor Gerson came with him to his new quarters, a completely segregated cell.

The transfer took place in the dark of night; hardly anyone could have noticed it. Only after the Cardinal had arrived at the prison had the precautionary measures in the surrounding neighborhood been taken.

A noticeable tension had existed in the capital for several days. Rumors were circulating that the Cardinal had died. On the previous Sunday plainclothesmen had been posted throughout the churches of Budapest, mingling with the crowds and arresting anyone who dared to make a fearless remark. On Tuesday the Communist mayor held it necessary to send a warning to the clergy of Budapest that they would be held personally accountable for any "disturbance of the peace"; that he regarded them individually as hostages.

The silent threat of a reign of terror overshadowed the thoughts of the people.

The trial was held in the largest courtroom on the third floor. It may have been selected with cynical forethought. For in that very room Mathias Rákosi, the people's commissar of the Communist terror regime of 1919, had stood trial. There a court of independent Hungarian judges had sentenced him to sixteen years' imprisonment. He had never spent this sentence behind bars, because the Soviet had agreed to take him in return for Hungarian hostages. In Soviet Russia, Rákosi had received high honors. When he returned in 1945 to "liberate" Hungary, he held the commission of a general in the Soviet armed forces. Now Rákosi, known popularly as "Little Potato Head," was the Deputy Premier in the puppet government and, as head of the Communist party and viceroy of Moscow in Hungary, the most powerful man in the country. The day of his revenge had come. The Prince of the Church he hated was to take his place in the prisoners' dock.

At seven o'clock in the morning the search of the entire building began. Every corner and closet was looked into. At eight-forty the press and the "public" began to arrive. No one could enter the building who did not have a personal pass issued in his own name and who could not prove with identification papers to be the person to whom it had been issued.

The "public" consisted of reliable members of the Communist

party, wives of party leaders, and high government officials. Despite this careful selection, each visitor was paired with a plainsclothesman from the secret police; they occupied half of the seats.

The press consisted of "the representatives of the public opinion of sixteen nations," as proclaimed by the government spokesman. With the exception of two persons of integrity, the group consisted of Communists, crypto-Communists, and "controlled" individuals. The two exceptions were correspondents who did not speak the language of the country. They had to rely on the translators they had employed, who later turned out to be agents of the government. These two restricted themselves to factual reporting of what actually transpired in the courtroom and what they could see. They were not permitted to go near the Cardinal or the other defendants or their families, and were told that, as guests of the country, they would be supplied with all information they desired. The government was fully at their service.

Visas were refused to the correspondents that the major news services and the leading daily papers of the world wanted to send, to cover the trial. The Foreign Office preferred that their "local representatives, familiar with the circumstances," report the trial.

These "local representatives," who were Hungarian citizens and residents of the country, if not in the pay of the government or the Communist party, were prepared to follow the suggestions of the Press Department of the government. Three of them had already spent weeks in the dungeons of "Andrássy ut 60," gaining experience with the "examiners" of the secret police, and had received their freedom only because the government needed "independent" local correspondents to report to the press of the world, while two colleagues still remained in prison for having sent "false and misleading" reports on conditions in the people's democracy. Under such conditions, trembling with fear that one little deviation from the information supplied by the government might bring down on themselves and their families the wrath of Rákosi and his cohorts, the three could not be expected even to attempt to report factually.

The majority of the correspondents and reporters were Communists or crypto-Communists, with a flaming hate for the clergy;

but even they were supervised, to see that their messages, telegrams, and mail on the trial and the background of the case were in accordance with the "Party line."

Thus the government spokesman could state to his own countrymen that the newspaper correspondents of sixteen nations reported on the trial.

Neither radio commentators nor news photographers were permitted to enter the country. Two "reliable" photographers took pictures in the courtroom. Identical prints of those that suited the government propaganda and had been passed by the censor were handed to all press services and newspaper correspondents.

At 8:59 A.M. the Cardinal was brought into the courtroom by two guards with revolvers in their holsters. He could hardly be recognized. He walked with short steps, dragging his body. He hardly lifted his eyes from the floor as one of his guards directed him to a seat in front, facing the bench. He wore a plain black suit with a long double-breasted coat, and a clerical collar. His garb displayed none of the distinctions of his rank or his exalted office.

Soon the codefendants followed him into the courtroom. They were escorted by policemen carrying carbines with bayonets fixed.

The counsel who was to defend the Cardinal approached him. He had been appointed by the court for the defense; later the Cardinal was told that he had selected him voluntarily.

The choice of defense counsel was a most peculiar one. Koloman Kiczkó had headed a group of radical lawyers in the early days of the 1918 revolution, and had been a judge in the Communist courts during the terrorist regime of 1919. Now he was to defend a man whose life work was opposed to his ideas, whose mentality he could not understand, and whose endeavors he had fought all his life. Thus he executed the farce of defending the Cardinal to the full satisfaction of his masters the Communists. Except for one feeble attempt to relieve the Cardinal of some minor issue of guilt, he echoed the words of the Prosecutor.

The Prosecutor, Julius Alapi, was not the man originally chosen to try the Cardinal. His predecessor had refused, reported sick, and was now languishing in prison. Alapi, a renegade Catholic with a shady past, wanted to throw a red veil over his fascist acts, and his ambition was to be regarded as the outstanding protector of the Communist "people's democracy."

At eight minutes past nine, the President of the "people's court" appeared, flanked by the lay judges, who had been chosen by the Communist party. William Olti, who had been selected by the planning group to prepare the case against the Cardinal, opened the proceedings, reading the official notice of trial.

As President Olti began to speak, the Cardinal suddenly raised his head, and looked up. His eyes opened very wide; their irises were pitch-black. He squinted a few times, as if he were trying to focus his eyes, and a second later his face went white. His head dropped, and he lethargically looked at the floor.

(The Cardinal had recognized the voice. It was the voice of William, the friend of Professor Gerson.)

The defendants were told to rise, and each in turn had to recite his personal history.

First, the Cardinal. His voice sounded mechanical, and no one could understand the words. The President interrupted him, told him to speak out clear and loud, and made him repeat the words already spoken. The other defendants followed.

After they had finished, the President examined the credentials of the Counsel. He declared that all defendants had their own choice of attorneys except Andrew Zakár, for whom the Court had appointed counsel.

The President then stated that regarding the summoning of witnesses, the Court would make arrangements at a later stage. Yes, the witnesses came from the dungeons of the secret police.

The defendants were made to rise again.

The President then read the Indictment.

"Joseph Mindszenty, Cardinal, Archbishop of Esztergom, is accused of having committed the crime of leading an organization aimed at the overthrow of the democratic order and of the Republic;

second, of having committed the crime of treason; third, of having committed the crime of failing to declare foreign currencies and of speculating . . ."

Then he read the Indictment against the codefendants.

Professor Justin Baranyai was accused of having committed the crime of directing an organization which aimed at the overthrow of the democratic order and of the Republic.

Dr. Andrew Zakár, archiepiscopal secretary, was accused of having committed the crime of active participation in an organization aimed at the overthrow of the democratic order and of the Republic; second, of having committed the crime of treason.

Prince Paul Eszterházy, house owner, was accused of having committed the crime of failing to declare foreign currencies and speculating.

Nicholas Nagy, secretary of Actio Catholica, was accused of having committed the crime of treason; second, of having committed the crime of failing to declare foreign currencies and speculating.

Dr. Béla Ispánky, dean of a college, was accused of having committed the crime of treason; second, of having committed the crime of failing to declare foreign currencies and speculating.

Leslie Tóth, journalist, was accused of having committed the crime of treason.

This Indictment was based on the following: (The official translation of the words of the President is reproduced verbatim.)

"First: Immediately after the liberation, Cardinal Archbishop Mindszenty began a campaign for the establishment of an organization aiming at the restoration of the Hapsburg regime in Hungary. After the enactment of Law VII:1946, for the protection of the republican state order, not only did he not stop this activity but, to the contrary, took steps toward formal organization. His idea was that after the overthrow of the republican form of state and of the democratic order, respectively, he, Joseph Mindszenty, as Prince Primate, would issue a manifesto by virtue of which he would seize power. . . .

"In June, 1947, under the pretext of visiting the Marian Congress at Ottawa, he traveled first to Canada and then to the United States, where Paul Zsámboki, an old acquaintance, the confessor of the Hapsburg house, arranged meetings with the widow of Charles Hapsburg, Zita, and with Otto Hapsburg. These meetings took place, and those present agreed how the overthrow of the Republic might best be organized. . . .

"As one can see from the documents seized, they well knew that the overthrow of the democratic Republic would be possible only through war. . . .

"One part of the action aimed at the overthrow of the Republic was the attempt to assure the retention of the Royal Crown of Hungary abroad. The Royal Crown of Hungary was of vital importance to the organization of which Mindszenty was the leader, for it was necessary for the crowning of the king of the kingdom which was to be reestablished after the overthrow of the Republic. . . .

"Mindszenty was well aware of the extreme importance of this matter. He therefore took it in hand himself and wrote a letter to Mr. Chapin, the United States Minister to Hungary, emphasizing the importance of the problem and underlining, 'as a consequence of a request for its return and of military advances the Holy Crown might meet a tragic fate.'

"A further act of Mindszenty aimed at the overthrow of the democratic order concerned the circular letters inciting against the secularization of the school. . . .

"The last, but not least, of the acts aimed at the overthrow of the democratic order was directed against the land reform, one of the most important achievements of our people's democracy. The course of this action of Mindszenty can be seen by one of the pieces of documentary evidence, a draft of a paper he wrote entitled, "There Is No End to Bolshevization in Hungary." . . .

"Second: Joseph Mindszenty, according to a number of pieces of documentary evidence, got in touch with the United States Ministers to Hungary, Arthur Schoenfeld and, after his departure, Selden Chapin, for the purpose of inducing the United States to commit hostile acts against Hungary, to influence the Hungarian government by threat of force, and to cause the realization of the aims of the Legitimists by forceful intervention. . . .

"On June 12, 1947, he addressed himself directly to President Truman and tried to persuade him, through false statements and distorted descriptions of measures taken by the democratic government, that the American government should put an end to the Hungarian Republic through intervention by force.

"At the time Chapin was appointed Minister to Hungary, Mindszenty knew from Otto Hapsburg that this minister favored a more forceful policy on the part of the American government. Soon after his arrival, therefore, he got in touch with him and in the course of several meetings informed him of the situation in Hungary, of the outlook for the Legitimists, and asked that American intervention should take place as soon as possible.

"His connections with Mr. Chapin reached a climax in February, 1948, when the minister, accompanied by Mr. Koczak, secretary to the legation, came to see him at Esztergom. They agreed that Mindszenty should forward to Mr. Chapin data coming to his knowledge, and forwarded by his priests, on the Hungarian political and economic situation and on the democratic parties. He instructed his secretary, Dr. Andrew Zakár, systematically to hand over material of this kind to Koczak. . . .

"By these acts, Joseph Mindszenty was in contact with the government of a foreign power and with a foreign organization to try and induce them to commit a hostile act against the Hungarian state and to get them to take aggressive measures against the said State.

"Third: Joseph Mindszenty brought back from his journeys American dollars and Swiss francs which he failed to register. . . ."

After finishing the reading of the indictment of the codefendants, the President announced that the Cardinal had written a letter to the Minister of Justice, which he now read (the official translation of the Court is reproduced verbatim):

DEAR SIR:

I beg the Minister of Justice to consider my announcement, or rather request. For some time, publicly and repeatedly, there has been raised against me the complaint that I stand in the way of an agreement between the State and Church, and that my attitude is hostile to the present order of the State. As for the former, it is a

fact that I always emphasized the prerequisites. Now I want to contribute to an improvement in the general situation. Before the trial,
which is soon to open, I voluntarily admit that I have committed the
acts I am charged with according to the penal code of the State. In
the future I shall always judge the external and internal affairs of the
State on the basis of the full sovereignty of the Hungarian Republic.

After this admission and declaration, the trial regarding my person
does not seem to be absolutely necessary. Therefore, not because of
my person, but considering my position, I ask that my case be ex-
empted from the trial on February 3rd. Such a decision, more than
anything else, would facilitate a solution, even more than the wisest
judgment of the Court.

After thirty-five days of constant meditation, I also declare that
apart from other reasons, it may have been due to me, to my attitude
as described above, that reconciliation has been delayed; and also
that I consider the establishment of true peace between the State and
Church necessary, as long as it has not been made. I, too, would take
part in the realization of this reconciliation, according to the teachings and laws of the Church, were there not complaints against me
just in this respect. But in order that I should not be an obstacle to
reconciliation and that all efforts should be concentrated on avoiding the usual material obstacles, I declare hereby, of my own accord,
without any compulsion, that I am ready to withdraw for a time
from exercising my office.

If the wisdom of the Bench of Bishops considers it best to make
peace, I do not wish to stand in the way at all. Even at the Apostolic
Holy See, which has the last word in the matter, I would not oppose
the materialization of the cause of peace. I make this statement in
the knowledge that a true state of peace can be only to the good of
both the State and the Church and without it the life of the country
is threatened by discord and decay.

Please accept my sincere respect.

(Signed) JOSEPH MINDSZENTY, *Cardinal*

PRESIDENT (*to the* CARDINAL): Is this written in your own handwriting? It contains your proposal to adjourn the trial in so far as
it concerns you. (*The* CARDINAL *does not answer.*) Has the Prosecutor any motion?

PROSECUTOR: The proposal of the first accused aims actually at the adjournment of the trial. However, no legal grounds for the adjournment are given. This proposal is in no way substantiated by the rules of procedure. The aim of the petition undoubtedly was that the defendant is to delay the trial. Therefore, I move that the Court reject it and order the trial to take place without delay.

PRESIDENT: The Counsel for the accused, please.

COUNSEL: Honorable People's Court! Your Honor! The proposal that the trial of the first accused be adjourned is certainly, in every respect, legal and other aspects, warranted, and so there is no obstacle to the adjournment of the trial on the basis of the letter of Prince Primate Mindszenty.

PRESIDENT: The Court will consider it now. Please keep your seats.

The Court retired for a short deliberation. Upon returning to the bench, the President announced that the plea was rejected.

Lunch recess was ordered. The Cardinal was led out as if in a daze, breathing hard, with his chin low. He walked as if his steps were impeded.

An hour later the trial continued. First, Professor Justin Baranyai was called to the stand. To the question of the President whether he felt guilty, he answered No. For a second the President was taken aback, surprised; then he picked up the thread again and continued to question him about his personal data.

During Baranyai's examination the Court was once more surprised. When asked to identify his signature, he at first replied Yes, then followed it up with a protest: "No, No." After a few seconds he corrected himself again with a Yes.

Professor Baranyai admitted everything the Court wanted him to admit; and after Counsel asked him a few formal questions, the trial was adjourned for fifteen minutes.

Each time the Cardinal was brought back to the courtroom, he seemed to be refreshed, to have gathered new energy.

After the short pause the Cardinal's secretary, Andrew Zakár, followed Baranyai on the stand. He qualified his answer to the question of guilt by stating that according to criminal law he felt guilty, but not ethically.

He stood by his "confession" and incriminated the Cardinal and all defendants. Questioning by the Prosecutor followed. Then Court recessed.

At 4:18 P.M. the Cardinal was told to step before the microphone placed in front of the bench.

PRESIDENT: Joseph Mindszenty, step forward. Did you understand the indictment?

CARDINAL: I did.

PRESIDENT: Do you plead guilty?

CARDINAL: To the extent that I did perform a considerable part of the activities charged to me in the indictment, or as I indicated in my letter to the Minister of Justice which you read this morning—to that extent, I feel guilty. What I have done, I do not wish to place in a favorable light. This does not mean that I accept the conclusions of the indictment. For example, with regard to the offenses mentioned, I do not deny a part of it; but I do not subscribe to the conclusion that I have been planning the overthrow of the democratic Republic, even less, as the indictment states, that I might have played the leading role.

PRESIDENT: We shall proceed. Where were you educated?

CARDINAL: At Szombathely.

PRESIDENT: Yes. In theology, wasn't it?

CARDINAL: Yes, theological seminary.

PRESIDENT: After finishing theology, what did you do?

CARDINAL: I was chaplain at Felsöpaty for a year and a half. Then for another year and a half I was a teacher of religion at the State Latin School of the County of Zala. Later I became priest at Zalaegerszeg.

PRESIDENT: When?

CARDINAL: Autumn, 1919. I was a priest there for twenty-six years and later became Bishop of Veszprém.

PRESIDENT: When?

CARDINAL: At the end of March, 1944. Then on October 8, 1945, I became the Prince Primate.

PRESIDENT (*interrupting*): Well, well, that is enough. The Prosecutor's Office has attached, among the exhibits, your article, "Beware of the Newspapers." This was published at Zalaegerszeg in September, 1919?

CARDINAL: Yes.

PRESIDENT: It contains your speech to a women's meeting. (*Sternly*) Do you recognize it?

CARDINAL: Yes.

PRESIDENT: You also remember its contents? This article, according to the Prosecutor, stirs up racial hatred. Do you deny this, or do you admit that there are parts of it which do stir up racial hatred?

CARDINAL: I had collected quotations from the press of the time. In any case, it was a pity that such quotations were published in newspapers. Today, however, I would not write that pamphlet in the way I wrote it then.

PRESIDENT: Today you no longer agree with this?

CARDINAL: I would not quote it like that now.

PRESIDENT: The Prosecutor charges you with having proposed at a meeting of the Municipal Council on November 18, 1938, that Imrédy—Béla Imrédy who has since been executed—be elected Freeman of Zalaegerszeg.

CARDINAL: This is correct. But, if you please, that does not mean that I agreed with Imrédy's policies. I did not.

PRESIDENT: Now, now—if a person formally proposes somebody as a Freeman, one cannot logically conclude from this that he disagrees with the policies of the man concerned. Were you arrested on November 21, 1944?

CARDINAL: Yes, I was.

PRESIDENT: Now listen. Was it for political reasons, or was it because of personal antagonisms—your disagreement with Francis Siberna, the so-called County Prefect of the Arrow Cross? Perhaps as a consequence of his irascibility?

CARDINAL: I was signator to a memorandum, along with the Transdanubian Bishops, which I took to Budapest on November 13 and

handed to Vice Premier Szöllösy. In that memorandum, I had protested against the continuation of the war and the destroying of the
towns and villages of Transdanubia as a consequence of the war.

PRESIDENT (*cynically*): Then how could Siberna, a local figure in
Veszprém, know of this?

CARDINAL: Because he had been notified by the Government.
When I delivered the memorandum, it had such an effect that I felt
I could not leave the Prime Minister's office, that I would be arrested
immediately.

PRESIDENT (*cynically*): But you did get out, and soon afterwards
you filed another petition to the same Szöllösy, in which you stated
that the circumstances surrounding your arrest were unlawful. Here
is a copy of that petition which you filed on January 12, 1945, addressed as follows: "Mr. Eugene Szöllösy, Royal Hungarian Deputy
Prime Minister, at Köszeg." It states the following: "I protest to the
Hungarian Government against Francis Siberna, County Prefect."
Did you consider the Arrow Cross people the Royal Hungarian
Government? This does not indicate that you were against them!
Then you state: "I bought eighteen hundred shirts and eighteen hundred pairs of underpants for 110,000 pengös in order to distribute
them among the needy wounded soldiers, refugees, and the poor.
Upon my arrest, he confiscated them without a court order, and thus
diverted them from their purpose." From that it can be concluded
that, for the clothing you had bought, he moved against you. Besides,
the petition as a whole indicates that you then—on January 12, 1945
—considered Siberna to have acted with antireligious motives. You
emphasize, for example, such things as: "He, with his antireligious
attitude, does not belong in a Government directed by a head of
State who attends religious services and lives the life of a fervent
Catholic . . . while members of the Government are emphasizing
more and more that they not only do not persecute religion but are
definitely against irreligious elements. . . . These are the occur-
rences [that is, that you and some other church people were ar-
rested] which convinced the common people of three counties that
it was the fault of Dr. Siberna that church and religion are persecuted
in our country. Because of this, our people's resistance against the

really irreligious Soviet system is obviously weakened . . ." You just stated that you had filed a petition with Szöllösy, stating: "We should discontinue this war because it has become purposeless."

CARDINAL: That is correct. Yes, yes, that (*exclaiming*) is correct.

PRESIDENT: And in this petition of January 12, 1945, you say the opposite: "Because of this, our people's resistance against the really irreligious Soviet system is obviously weakened . . ." From this it follows that you wished the resistance to be strengthened instead of weakened.

CARDINAL: If you please, Mr. President, it was *argumentum ad hominem*.

PRESIDENT: *Argumentum ad hominem* in debating is not the best of methods, as we once learned in rhetorics.

CARDINAL: Hear! Hear! The fact is, that I was commissioned by the Transdanubian Bishops to file such a memorandum.

PRESIDENT: But there is no doubt about the fact that you, in your individual petition of January 12, 1945, took a stand in favor of increasing resistance against the Soviet system. In the twenty-five years between the two wars did you declare yourself a Legitimist, an active Legitimist?

CARDINAL: Yes.

PRESIDENT: Since what time? When did you join the Legitimist movement?

CARDINAL: About 1920 or 1921.

PRESIDENT: So about 1921.

CARDINAL: Yes.

PRESIDENT: Were you then, in the twenty-five years between the two world wars, in direct touch with the former royal family of Hapsburg?

CARDINAL: Yes, I was, on one occasion.

PRESIDENT: Were you abroad?

CARDINAL: Yes.

PRESIDENT: Did you visit them?

CARDINAL: When I was in Lourdes, I spent half an hour in Lequeitio along with the pilgrimage which visited that place.

PRESIDENT: Did you make a special trip to visit the family?

CARDINAL: Lequeitio was on the way.

PRESIDENT: When was that?

CARDINAL: It might have been in 1924.

PRESIDENT: So in 1924. Afterward, was there any correspondence, exchange of messages? We are still speaking of the time of the Horthy era.

CARDINAL: Not until the beginning of 1946, I believe.

PRESIDENT: So, there was none until the beginning of 1946?

CARDINAL: None.

PRESIDENT: Did you consider that more favorable circumstances for your Legitimist ideas existed after 1946?

CARDINAL: No.

PRESIDENT: Did you consider that more favorable circumstances for your Legitimist ideas existed after the liberation than between the two world wars?

CARDINAL: At that time, in the spring of 1945, I could not form an opinion. I could not determine whether the relationship between the great powers would last or not.

PRESIDENT: Listen! At the end of 1945, in the autumn, there were legislative discussions in progress concerning the form of state, weren't there?

CARDINAL: Yes.

PRESIDENT: Concerning the founding of the Republic which later materialized in Law I: 1946. Is that true?

CARDINAL: Yes.

PRESIDENT: Did you take any steps against the establishment and the enactment of the Republic?

CARDINAL: No! Yes. No!

PRESIDENT (benignly): What steps? Tell us, please.

CARDINAL: I warned Béla Varga, I think in writing—that he should be careful. Then, as I remember, I also wrote to the Prime Minister.

PRESIDENT: I'm going to read your petition to the former Prime Minister, Zoltán Tildy. The petition, dated December 31, 1945, bearing the number 53/1946, reads as follows: "Mr. Prime Minister: Until now, I have received no official information, but because this report is being repeated in serious quarters, I am compelled to bring it up and, if it is substantiated, to protest against it for serious reasons. I understand that the National Assembly will soon place constitutional reforms upon the agenda, among them the question of the Republic, the plan to put an end to the thousand-year-old Hungarian Monarchy. If this is true, even though I have not received official confirmation of it, I protest against these plans on the basis of the legal rights exercised by Hungarian Primates for more than nine hundred years . . ." You sent a copy of this letter three days later, on January 3, 1946, to Canon Béla Varga, a member of the National Supreme Council?

CARDINAL: Yes.

PRESIDENT: Yes. This letter reads as follows: "I am sending to you, as a member of the National Supreme Council, the enclosed copy of the petition which I have sent to the Prime Minister in connection with rumors of projected constitutional reforms . . ." You sent it to him so that he too might protest and throw his political weight against the establishment of a Republic, did you not? Did you protest in a similar manner at the beginning of January? There is no date on this draft. Is this draft written in your own handwriting?

CARDINAL: Yes.

PRESIDENT (*reading*): "To Béla Varga (Confidential), the Very Reverend Canon, Member of the National Assembly: Your Honor has been asking instructions from me regarding the stand you should take in certain questions. I believe the time has come to give advice at this significant turning point. Your Honor has never pledged himself for a Republic but, to the contrary, has been entrusted by his Majesty, the King. Under such circumstances, Your Honor can take a stand only on the side of the Monarchy, openly, proclaiming its timeliness, lending definite support to its defending camp. As a matter of fact, this stand was taken by the Prime Minister in your presence on November 16 when you both visited me. The idea, which is now to be realized, is in opposition to the thousand-year-old Hungarian Constitution, endangering our independence. The list of candidates is disadvantageous for Catholicism. In this, no faithful Catholic and especially no Catholic priest may cooperate." Here you answer the letter of January 2. Béla Varga had written a long apologetic letter explaining that, faced by a stronger force, he must retreat?

CARDINAL: Yes.

PRESIDENT: And then you answered it. The letter substantially is this (*reading*): "The Very Reverend Canon: To your letter of January 2, I have the following comments to make: In the question of the form of Government, serious action should have been taken. I see none. Not only have the most competent failed to take the initiative, but, as I see, they have failed even to support the initiative taken by laymen. In public life one must take a strong stand on principles and not equivocate. I understood from Your Honor that you were directing the Party. But now I realize that the Party is sweeping the clergy along with it." These were the first steps you took against the proposal and proclamation of the Republic. Later, when the Republic was actually formed, did you stop your Legitimist activities then, or did you continue with them?

CARDINAL: In any case, I took into consideration the decision that a Republic should exist.

PRESIDENT: We shall examine this, too.

CARDINAL: Here and there deviations occurred, but it was my determined intention to respect the decision of Parliament.

PRESIDENT: Did you know George Pallavicini, Jr., personally?

CARDINAL: Yes.

PRESIDENT: Did George Pallavicini come to see you in 1945, informing you that he wished to make a journey to see Otto Hapsburg?

CARDINAL: He came to see me once.

PRESIDENT: Only on a single occasion?

CARDINAL: As I recall, he came to see me once.

PRESIDENT: What did Pallavicini tell you then?

CARDINAL: That he wished to go abroad. He said that it was possible that he would meet Otto Hapsburg, but he was not sure that he could.

PRESIDENT: And he did ask you what message you had for Otto Hapsburg?

CARDINAL: Yes, he did.

PRESIDENT: And what did you answer?

CARDINAL: I simply sent greetings.

PRESIDENT: Then did Pallavicini return in a few weeks?

CARDINAL: How long it was before he returned, I couldn't say, but after a certain period he returned.

PRESIDENT: And he did tell you that he had delivered your regards?

CARDINAL: Yes, and brought greetings in return.

PRESIDENT: Did he bring any concrete message on the subject of what you Legitimists should do, or whether there existed any possibility for the restoration of the Monarchy?

CARDINAL: What he brought was very little. It was only that we should stay in the background and be as quiet as possible since times were difficult and we could expect even more difficult times. As I remember, this was the substance.

PRESIDENT: So you were not organizing any political party as yet. When did you next contact Otto Hapsburg?

CARDINAL: It must have been in February, 1946. He addressed a letter to me in Rome when I was there to receive my Cardinal's hat. I answered this letter.

PRESIDENT: Did you send this answer through the Belgian Cardinal Van Roey?

CARDINAL: I don't remember whether I sent it through him.

PRESIDENT: You don't remember . . . (CARDINAL *seems tired, the* PRESIDENT *eyes him—motions with his hand*) Very well, in 1946, Joseph Közi-Horváth, Papal Chamberlain, former Member of Parliament, fled from Hungary.

CARDINAL: Yes.

PRESIDENT: Then Közi-Horváth sent a letter and a message to you through Father Stephen Borbély, a Jesuit, didn't he?

CARDINAL: Yes, on one occasion I received a letter. Yes.

PRESIDENT: What did Joseph Közi-Horváth say in this letter?

CARDINAL: He wrote that he had conferred with minority leaders of various former member states of the Monarchy, and that he had met Otto.

PRESIDENT: Yes. And what was Otto's message?

CARDINAL: I don't remember. Only that there was a message. But what it was, I cannot remember.

PRESIDENT (*angrily*): I shall read your testimony made during the investigation. (*Reading*) "At the conference Otto outlined his plans for the Restoration." He wrote to you and informed you of the prospects. Furthermore, he informed you of his extensive negotiations with Croatian, Slovenian, Slovakian, Ukrainian, and Austrian Legitimists. Furthermore, Közi-Horváth declared that the secret services were actively working at the preparation of a third world war, and were directing underground organizations against the Soviet Union and the People's Democracies. He emphasized that you could not leave everything to the great powers, but "we Christians must organize ourselves against Bolshevism." Was this the content of the letter?

CARDINAL: Yes, this was its content.

PRESIDENT: Well, this then was the third contact with Otto Hapsburg. The first time through George Pallavicini, the second time through Cardinal Van Roey, and the third time through Joseph Közi-Horváth. After the Liberation did Hungarian Legitimists—and I want to know whether you knew this—look upon you as their director and leader?

CARDINAL: I did not know this.

PRESIDENT: Did they consider you the most serious representative of the Legitimist idea?

CARDINAL: I did not know this, for I was not in direct contact with them.

PRESIDENT: Were you not in direct contact with the Legitimist group?

CARDINAL: I did meet Professor Baranyai. He visited me several times, and we discussed this question, but not with a group.

PRESIDENT: Did Baranyai repeatedly inform you that they were meeting at Csekonics's apartment? Did he inform you what was going on among the Legitimists?

CARDINAL: Yes, but I sent messages on two occasions that they should cease activities and should restrict themselves to social contacts.

PRESIDENT: All right, let us continue. "In the spring of 1947," so goes your testimony during the investigation, "we discussed the possibility and prospects of the restoration of the Hapsburgs with Justin Baranyai on several occasions." Is that true?

CARDINAL: Yes. Among the many possibilities this came up in the course of the conversation.

PRESIDENT: Well then, in the course of these talks, how did you see it? How could a de facto restoration come about here? The Republic had existed since the spring of 1946—for a year already—hadn't it?

CARDINAL: Yes.

PRESIDENT (*in a declamatory manner*): Economically too, it was constantly growing strong and more robust, wasn't it?

CARDINAL: Yes, yes! We didn't feel it was possible to realize our aim. Only in the event of a historic change could the thought and possibility of this arise at all. From the inside it could not arise by any means.

PRESIDENT: So you recognized clearly that the great mass of Hungarians did not desire the restoration of the Hapsburgs?

CARDINAL (*after a long silence*): What we did know, was that we did not want to start any kind of disorder. If something happened as a result of global events, that was another matter.

PRESIDENT: But you did start something! After all, during Baranyai's examination this morning we heard that the Legitimists met at Csekonics's apartment, divided the country among themselves, deciding who would carry out Legitimist activity in what section. They established cooperation among the Legitimists, distributing the various ministries among themselves in order to place Legitimists inside these as well. Understand! So, such a movement already existed here. What is more, even a list for the cabinet was introduced. These constitute positive indications of a certain trend—and this trend was the restoration.

CARDINAL: I did not take part in these detailed affairs. I received information from time to time, but was not informed of everything.

PRESIDENT: You couldn't know every little detail, but you knew essentially how the Legitimist organization was progressing?

CARDINAL: Yes.

PRESIDENT: We shall examine the points one by one and see just what you knew, what you approved of, and what you did not approve of. In the spring of 1947, you repeatedly discussed what role the Prince Primate might play in the event a change occurred.

CARDINAL: Yes, we discussed this.

PRESIDENT: And then the idea came up that you would become provisional Head of State until Otto came home and was crowned?

CARDINAL: Only in the form if—as it was strongly rumored all over Europe in 1947, that a third world war was on the threshold—the historic turn of events should create such a situation on the territory of Hungary that here too, as a result of war, a change might occur. And then, what should be and what could be done here then, should—as the Professor of Law expressed himself—a *vacuum juris* be created here. And he mentioned to me the example of Greece, where the Patriarch took over the role of provisional Head of State. I replied that for such a role as this no one would reach out.

PRESIDENT: But then later you made a statement to the effect that you would be willing to accept this position?

CARDINAL: Yes. But only in the event the necessity should arise. I stress, not through overthrowing anything.

PRESIDENT: But, after all, only by overthrowing the State could anything of the sort be imagined.

CARDINAL: Yes (*excitedly*), but not that we should overthrow something from the inside.

PRESIDENT: Hand in glove with outside forces then?

CARDINAL: No, this was not mentioned either.

PRESIDENT: The Prosecutor has enclosed a number of statements about it. Your letter, for instance, according to which intervention would serve the overthrow of internal forces.

CARDINAL: When the professor and I spoke together, we emphasized that we were not to take part in any overthrow of the State. If, however, it occurred through the action of external forces, in that case, in that *vacuum juris*, for the good of the nation we would not refuse.

PRESIDENT: Joseph Közi-Horváth seems to give voice to another point of view. As I have read already, he stresses that "we cannot leave everything to the great powers, but must organize." And here already certain organizing actions are evident, for example, the dividing of ministries among themselves, the rallying of Legitimists, establishing contacts, keeping the idea alive, and so forth.

CARDINAL: I do not know whether I received definite information on the discussions.

PRESIDENT: Well, when this group was dissolved, obviously the question arose among you how the Legitimists, in what kind of organization, or under what form, should stick together and keep in touch in order that they should not be dispersed?

CARDINAL: Yes.

PRESIDENT: And that is when it was suggested that contacts be kept up socially?

CARDINAL: Yes.

PRESIDENT: During these social gatherings at which you were not present, the territorial division and the distribution of ministries took place. According to evidence at this trial, there is no doubt about that. Did Justin Baranyai always report to you about these questions?

CARDINAL: How the division occurred, I do not remember, or whether he gave me any information about it.

PRESIDENT: Justin Baranyai made a plan for you, to which he later attached the list of proposed cabinet members, didn't he?

CARDINAL: Yes.

PRESIDENT: Well, please read this again.

CARDINAL (*reading with great difficulty, moving paper near and far from his eyes*): "If the great *vacuum juris* occurs, the very first, the most important, and the most difficult question will be to found a regime based on a moral foundation. It would be a political impossibility to base it directly on the defeated revolution. To restore the Horthy regime would create new and unpredictable complications. There is only one possibility of quiet evolution. The Prince Primate of the country, with the high rank of Prince Primate, is the only one in this land predestined by the traditions of centuries, of nearly a thousand years. According to the ancestral laws of our nation, in the absence of the King the ruling power deposes in the Prince Primate. His authority has never been questioned by public opinion in the country. In times of difficulty or catastrophe, the nation has always looked to him for the initiative. Today the extremely fortunate situation exists that the present bearer of this rank, Joseph, Cardinal Mindszenty, has raised in the last two years, in these particularly sad years of our national life, the prestige of the Prince Primate to extraordinary heights. For the first time, perhaps, in the recent history of the country it has occurred that all Protestants, Calvinists, and Lutherans, standing on a nationalist platform, also see him as the only true, predestined leader of the nation. Today the national aspirations of the whole nation are anchored in him. In politics too, only his words are heeded. Like the Metropolitan of Athens, he seems to be the only competent authority, and in the same way here, at the beginning of an American occupation, it would be his duty to appoint the new government."

PRESIDENT: Here is a list of cabinet members.

CARDINAL: Yes, and—

PRESIDENT: Were lists of government members submitted on other occasions as well?

CARDINAL: Yes.

PRESIDENT: Well then: you received this proposal. Did you read it?

CARDINAL: Yes.

PRESIDENT: You had spoken of this subject previously and again discussed it afterward? Were you in agreement with it?

CARDINAL: First he came, brought up the idea. Then a few weeks later—I couldn't say exactly when, perhaps over a month later—I received it. Events then seemed to indicate that the rumors which had been so widespread in Hungary, and I think in western Europe as well, had quieted down.

PRESIDENT: What were these rumors? (*Leaning forward, slowly and suggestively emphasizing each syllable*) That the third world war was upon us?

CARDINAL (*mechanically*): That the third world war was upon us. I considered the whole matter of the list of cabinet members and the manifesto as a legal case.

PRESIDENT: The project was sent to you after a month?

CARDINAL: Yes.

PRESIDENT: And did you talk it over then?

CARDINAL: Yes.

PRESIDENT: It seems, then, that the position you had taken was, after all, not completely negative, because afterward the defendant Justin Baranyai worked out the list of cabinet members, which he later brought to you. So this does not indicate that the project was considered unimportant by the time you received it, because if you had considered it unimportant you would have probably thrown it into the waste basket. Before Justin Baranyai prepared the cabinet list, you did discuss it in general, who should be in it, and whether the candidates should be taken from a large group or from as narrow a group as possible?

CARDINAL: It was mentioned that it was important that it should be a government of men of public standing.

PRESIDENT: When you discussed this, were any names mentioned?

CARDINAL: Only as examples.

PRESIDENT: Did you discuss them one by one—which one might be considered?

CARDINAL: I think, we merely referred to names as examples.

PRESIDENT: Essentially, would the cabinet have been formed according to the testimony you gave during the investigation? More specifically, the Prime Minister was to be either Leopold Baranyai or Charles Rassay? No? Yes?

CARDINAL (*with sudden eagerness*): Yes.

PRESIDENT: Did you receive that list, and did you put it away with instructions that it be treated as confidential?

CARDINAL: I put it away because there was nothing to be done about it.

PRESIDENT: If you receive a draft of a project that you regard as unrealizable, or not serious, and there is nothing you want to do about it, then you would throw it away. If we kept piling up all the papers that are sent us, then in one or two years' time our homes and our archives would be cluttered up.

CARDINAL: It was our custom at Esztergom that every paper that had been examined and was not to be kept inside, in the chancellery, was sent to the files. Documents were filed and not destroyed.

PRESIDENT: I asked defendant Andrew Zakár, your secretary,

whether there had been objects which he had considered of no further importance, which he had thrown away, destroyed.

CARDINAL (*astonished*): That was a personal letter.

PRESIDENT (*cynically*): This was not even a personal letter! (*In a matter-of-fact way*) Were there some things which were marked for the files and in addition confidential things which were handled separately?

CARDINAL: Yes.

PRESIDENT: And now the fact that neither the memorandum nor the list of members of government was thrown in the waste basket —did that not indicate that you had some plans for them after all, and that you did not consider them unimportant?

CARDINAL: I had no further plans concerning the matter.

PRESIDENT: Then why were they put in writing? It was done by responsible men!

CARDINAL: You see, for what it had been prepared—I may put it like this—they lost their topical significance.

PRESIDENT: Let us go on. Have you knowledge of a memorandum that Justin Baranyai wrote for the American Government, to be signed by four persons, in which the restoration of the Hapsburgs was advocated?

CARDINAL: I know of a memorandum, but I don't remember who was to sign it.

PRESIDENT (*loud*): Still you sent a message saying that Ullman also should sign it as fourth signatory.

CARDINAL: Yes.

PRESIDENT: So such a memorandum was drawn up. Did you discuss with Justin Baranyai what it was to contain?

CARDINAL: I don't remember its content any more.

PRESIDENT: You don't remember? (*Intensely*) When did Baron Ullman visit you for the first time? He was also a member of the Legitimists, wasn't he?

CARDINAL: I think he came to see me in Buda soon after my becoming Archbishop of Esztergom. He came to pay his respects, since my late predecessor had been fond of his family and he felt he should visit his successor.

PRESIDENT: Did he tell you at this first meeting that he too was an old Legitimist, and that he was happy to present himself to you in this capacity?

CARDINAL: Whether on the first or second occasion, I don't know. But it happened.

PRESIDENT: So it happened.

CARDINAL: Yes.

PRESIDENT: Did he also tell you that he was soon going abroad, to France, and there would get in touch with Otto?

CARDINAL (*showing signs of fatigue—at times closing his eyes*): I think he said this, too.

PRESIDENT: He did, in fact, leave and discussed matters with Otto abroad in 1947, and returning home in October, 1947, he visited you again?

CARDINAL: Whether in October (*irritatedly*), I don't know—it is unimportant. He visited me.

PRESIDENT: It is unimportant. It could have been in the autumn of 1947? The year before last?

CARDINAL: Yes, I think so.

PRESIDENT: Where did you meet? You will certainly remember the place.

CARDINAL: I think at the central seminary.

PRESIDENT: Did Ullman report what he had discussed with Otto?

CARDINAL: Yes. He sent his greetings.

PRESIDENT: Fine! Did you write to United States Minister Chapin on August 31, 1947, asking him that the Hungarian Holy Crown, which was in the possession of the American Army, should not be sent to Hungary but to Rome?

CARDINAL: Yes.

PRESIDENT: What was the reason for this? To whom does the Crown belong?

CARDINAL: Unquestionably to the Hungarian nation.

PRESIDENT (*fast*): Who is entitled to care for the Crown? And where should this be done?

CARDINAL: In any case, in normal times we all consider it natural that the Holy Crown be guarded in Budapest in the Castle of Buda. Nevertheless, in the given situation the matter did not appear to be so, since everybody believed the Holy Crown lost and was sorry about it.

PRESIDENT: It was known at that time that it was not lost. It survived the events of war and the excesses of the Arrow Cross.

CARDINAL: Yes.

PRESIDENT: Now I am going to review another letter (*showing it*). Is this your own handwriting?

CARDINAL: Yes.

PRESIDENT: Here is also Zakár's own English translation:

Your Excellency,

The United States returned, and her soldiers brought back the Sacred Right Hand of St. Stephen, our first king, which has remained preserved for nine hundred and nine years. His Holy Crown, our most valued constitutional historical relic, is also in the hands of the United States Army in Wiesbaden, Germany.

My request to you is to obtain an order from your Government, effecting the transportation of the Crown by the Army and its transfer to the same Apostolic Power, His Holiness the Pope, whose predecessor presented St. Stephen with the Holy Crown in the year 1000.

Since this cause is a very important one for our nation, and since demands for its return and military advances might be fatal for the Crown, only Rome could reassure us.

Please accept my sincere. . . .

(*A slight hush goes through the courtroom as the* CARDINAL's *body becomes unsteady. He seems ready to collapse.*)

DEFENSE COUNSEL: I beg the People's Court to permit the Prince Primate to sit down.

PRESIDENT: Tell me if you are tired, then of course. Are you? A chair!

(*Attendant brings a chair,* CARDINAL *sits down.*)

(*Looking at him with piercing eyes*) If you are mentally tired, tell me, and I shall order a recess. Should we go on with the trial?

CARDINAL (*unusually loud*): Yes!

PRESIDENT: So here is the original letter from Selden Chapin, dated September 2, 1947. It reads as follows:

Legation of the United States of America

Budapest, Hungary, September 2, 1947

My dear Cardinal Mindszenty:

I have received your letter of August 31 with regard to the disposition of the Holy Crown of St. Stephen that you state is now in
the hands of the United States Army in Wiesbaden. Permit me to
assure you, my dear Cardinal, that your suggestion will be given
due consideration at such time as the disposition of this relic is
brought to the attention of this Legation.

Sincerely yours,
(Signed) SELDEN CHAPIN,
American Minister

To: His Eminence Joseph, Cardinal Mindszenty
Arch Primate of Hungary, Archbishop of Esztergom
Esztergom, Hungary

Did Zoltán Csáky visit you in September, 1947? Did you know
him formerly?

CARDINAL: No, never.

PRESIDENT: How did he happen to come to you? Who recom-
mended him to you?

CARDINAL: I think he came with a letter from Professor Baranyai.

PRESIDENT: Here is the letter written to you by Baranyai on
August 26, 1947.

Most High and Very Reverend Prince Primate,
Your Eminence,

Ernest Sigmond (Strecke) presented to me his spiritual child,
Count Zoltán Csáky, who is a nephew to General Ernest Pajtás, Commander of the Crown Guard. He not only has very interesting first-
hand information on the Crown, but is also a person suited to take
directions concerning the further fate of this our greatest treasure.
In my humble opinion the following procedure would be necessary
for the sake of the absolute security of the Crown: Your Eminence,
as the only person to be considered competent in the present situation, should persuade the American authorities to give instructions
to the competent American authorities in Germany to have the

Crown transported from Wiesbaden to Rome and handed over for safe-keeping to the One it came from, His Holiness the Pope of Rome.

Considering the extraordinary importance of the matter, I asked Ernest Sigmond (Strecke) to visit your Eminence in Esztergom along with Count Csáky. I beg you to receive them graciously.

Kissing the Holy Purple of your Robe, I remain ever

> Your obedient servant,
> JUSTIN BARANYAI

Baranyai considers you alone competent to deal with the matter of the Crown. This also shows that you considered this matter from the Legitimists' viewpoint. Isn't it so? You said just now that only the Hungarian Government was competent.

CARDINAL: In any case, I thought that on the religious side I had some competence in this respect.

PRESIDENT: Did you report to any official of the Hungarian Government in what danger the Crown was, and that it would be a good idea to get it to Rome for the time being, and later, after the international tension had ceased, we could bring it home? Did you suggest this to anybody?

CARDINAL: No, I did not report this to anybody because I was told meanwhile that the American Government was already beginning to be reluctant about returning certain Hungarian property. I was told this right here in Hungary by the Minister of Finance. (Sits with eyes closed.)

PRESIDENT: All the more reason! If you had wanted to save the Crown for the Hungarian nation and not to make use of it against the existing State, then you would have cooperated with the Government officials. We had an organization abroad searching for looted property, until its work was made impossible. This would have been the natural course to follow.

CARDINAL (opens his eyes): It never entered my mind.

PRESIDENT: This would have been legal and natural, wouldn't it?

CARDINAL: I didn't think of such steps.

PRESIDENT: You didn't. Listen! Did Zoltán Csáky visit you later on with the above-mentioned letter? What did he report?

CARDINAL: I think he referred to his relationship with Ernest Pajtás and said that he no longer doubted that the Holy Crown was in Wiesbaden. He said he could perhaps cooperate in bringing the Holy Crown to Rome. Then I gave a note to Csáky, wrote a letter for him, that he might intervene with the authorities concerned. If I remember well, the Archbishop of Vienna and then the Archbishop of Salzburg were mentioned.

PRESIDENT: You actually wrote the letter of recommendation. Is this your own writing? *(He holds up two sheets of paper.)*

CARDINAL *(looking at the* PRESIDENT*)*: Yes.

PRESIDENT: Did you send the letters of recommendation to the above-mentioned Archbishops?

CARDINAL: Yes. Then Csáky turned to other people whose names I had not expressly mentioned.

PRESIDENT: Did you know that Csáky returned home from the West illegally?

CARDINAL: This I only knew when he returned the following year. If I remember correctly, it was in the middle of January, and he showed me the replies. I asked him why these letters had come so late, though they were addressed to me. He answered: "I didn't want to send them any other way. I wanted to bring them personally, and I was not able to pass the frontier." Then I knew that he used to go illegally.

PRESIDENT: Csáky asked you for financial support for these trips on his first visit. Did he get it? Did you give him any financial support?

CARDINAL: Yes, I did. I couldn't say exactly how much. I had four to five thousand forints given to him.

PRESIDENT: You gave him four to five thousand forints.

CARDINAL: That's right.

PRESIDENT: The money you dealt with was given you for Catholic Church purposes, wasn't it?

CARDINAL: Yes.

PRESIDENT: It is not a small sum, five thousand forints. If you wanted to insure that the Hungarian nation received the Crown back, if you were in agreement with the State and acted according to the interests of the State, then nothing would be more natural than the legal way which was at hand.

CARDINAL: Yes.

PRESIDENT: It shows again, that this was an illegal method and illegal activity against the State. Wasn't it?

CARDINAL: I'm sorry that I did not think at that time to turn to the Government for assistance.

PRESIDENT: Csáky left. He sojourned abroad, and when he returned in January he gave a long report on his activity.

CARDINAL: When he brought letters, the replies.

PRESIDENT: He brought letters. One of them, for example, the number A/13 of November 18, 1947, was the letter Archbishop Rohracher wrote to Cardinal Spellman. Did Rohracher send you the copy of this letter through Csáky, signed by his own hand?

CARDINAL: Yes.

PRESIDENT (*reading*):

"Your Eminence,

"His Eminence, the Most Reverend Primate of Hungary, Cardinal Mindszenty, has just sent to me an authorized courier who submitted the following request.

"The Crown of St. Stephen of Hungary, which was received over one thousand years ago from the Apostolic See, is to be found in Wiesbaden, Germany, in the American zone. Ever since that time all legal decisions in Hungary have been made in the name of this Crown. It embodies both the power of the State and the sovereignty of Hungary. So it is a holy relic and an invaluable treasure, not only in the eyes of Catholics, but also in those of people of other religions of Hungary."

(*Here, where the letter was about to state the significance of delivery of the crown to Hungary in the current political situation, the* PRESIDENT *stopped his reading. The letter continued, as follows:*

(*"Now our concern is to save this Holy Crown for the Hungarian nation. There seems to be a danger that it will soon be handed over to Hungary, which under the present political situation in Hungary would mean literally the loss of this holy object.*

("Therefore the courier sent to me by His Eminence the Cardinal asks me to request the following from Your Eminence:

("1. To make measures against the surrender of the Holy Crown to Hungary under any circumstances, and for its transfer to the Holy Father in Rome.

("2. The Crown should be handed over to the Holy Father by the American authorities, either officially, or at least under their unofficial protection.

("3. At this transfer the Guardian of the Holy Crown, Colonel Count Ernest Pajtás (at present at Grabenstött, 32, Upper Bavaria), and his escort, Count John Csáky, should be present.

("To fulfill this request of the Hungarian Catholics, it seems necessary to get in touch directly with the President of the United States. A separate letter of recommendation, written by Your Eminence to General Kloyes, would surely make this effort successful and engender the greatest joy among the Hungarian faithful.

("Permit me to express my special esteem.

("Yours most faithfully,

("ANDR. ROHRACHER, Archbishop

("To His Eminence
The Most Reverend Cardinal Spellman.")

PRESIDENT (*continuing*): Here the political importance of the action and its political character are to be seen directly. This letter reveals that Csáky instructed Rohracher. And Csáky was your messenger. This is obvious from your letter of commission. To Archbishop Rohracher, it was obviously a reflection of your intentions. This is the only logical conclusion. And Rohracher's letter reveals that there was no question of the Crown being endangered by a possible war, but that it would be lost for Mindszenty and his followers forever in case our Government received the Crown. This is obvious from the letter.

CARDINAL: Please, Mr. President, Zoltán Csáky was certainly not my emissary! I talked with Zoltán Csáky. What use he made of my expressions of opinion and what he did not, I could not tell.

PRESIDENT: It is inconceivable that Csáky, who did not even possess three or four thousand forints for the trip, would have followed an independent political line. Rohracher in his letter to the Holy Father asks the American military authorities, if not officially at least unofficially, to take the Crown under their protection to the Pope. Csáky would have been afraid of being made responsible if he had acted differently from your instructions. Did you take him to task? Did you ask, "What sort of policy is this?" and say, "I do not want to deprive the Hungarian Government of the Crown, but I am afraid that it will get lost because of a war"? Why does this letter show intent against the State? Why did you advise Rohracher in this way? You didn't take him to task, did you? You certainly wrote it because you were interested in the fate of the Crown. Here, I am afraid, there is a contradiction between the defense and the facts reflected by the letter. I have to underline this to show these matters in their right light.

CARDINAL: Obviously it shows that we wanted the Holy Crown to be taken to Rome and not to Budapest.

PRESIDENT: Yes, but this is only a fraction of the whole. He is asking furthermore that (*he reads*) "the guardian of the Holy Crown, Colonel Pajtás, resident in Upper Bavaria, and his companion, Count John Csáky, also participate. In the interest of this petition of the Hungarian Catholics, it would be necessary to get directly in touch with the President of the United States. The line of action which I was to recommend to General Clay, and which would have caused great joy to the Hungarian faithful, would certainly succeed." (*After reading*) This is Rohracher's part in it. Cardinal Faulhaber also wrote a letter to Cardinal Spellman. A copy of it was brought to you also by Csáky. (*He reads:*)

Munich, November 21, 1947

Dear Cardinal:

It was important and also agreeable for me that your Eminence wrote a letter to me about the appointment of Wagner, new Governor of Bavaria. I am grateful to you for this information, and I am ready to cooperate with the new Governor. Walter Muller, who leaves Bavaria in a few weeks, will be so good as to deliver this letter to your Eminence. The name of your Eminence is honored and admired here also. This letter contains the humble request to help us save the Crown of St. Stephen. Your Eminence knows about the matter already and the intention to deliver this relic legally to the Holy Father for the duration of the present critical times. Colonel Walter Muller, as an officer, enjoyed very great prestige in Bavaria. On Sundays, when he appeared in Church with his soldiers, he did a great service. He also brought the gifts of the Holy Father from the Vatican to Munich under his protection. For this, the Holy Father Pius XII decorated him with the Order of Saint Sylvester.

(*After reading*) Csáky also gave you an account of the situation regarding the Holy Crown and the steps taken in this respect. He expressly writes that with the American military authorities in Germany the right hand does not know what the left hand is doing, so there are some who promise not to deliver the Crown to the Hungarians, but other American organizations, which have no knowledge of this, might deliver the Crown to the Restitution Commission. You, according to your defense, did not give instructions to Csáky to deprive the Hungarian State of the Crown, but from this letter, from this account, it is obvious that he did just that. But you did not disagree with Csáky. You remained in contact with him, and he left once again on your instructions to continue the activities. What do you say?

CARDINAL: I acknowledge having left the Government officials out of this matter.

PRESIDENT: Now, it is not this that matters. But here was an action aimed directly at the Hungarian State. Please look here. The report of Csáky contains, for instance, this (*he reads*): "I could prevent the delivery of the Holy Crown to the Hungarian Government by remaining in close touch with the American Army in Germany." Here it can be read in parenthesis: Alas, I consider this work very necessary, because sad experience with the American services proves that the right hand really does not know what the left is doing. And then he writes in this letter of "the complete secrecy as far as my person is concerned." This makes it obvious that this was an illegal act. But you also wrote letters to the Holy See, to the Pope. Obviously the letter of Montini, the Undersecretary of State, dated September 9, 1947, was the answer to this letter, wasn't it?

CARDINAL: Yes, it was.

PRESIDENT: The letter which Montini, Undersecretary of State, wrote to you, enclosing the answer of the American Secretary of War to the intervention of Archbishop Spellman; where Kenneth C. Royall notifies Spellman of having transmitted the request to the State Department for careful consideration, if the request could be complied with—

CARDINAL: Yes, but—

PRESIDENT: The Prosecutor charges you with having called for American intervention in the interest of overthrowing the State and also for wanton interference by the Government of the United States in Hungarian internal affairs. You turned to the Government of the United States through the accredited American Minister in Budapest with several petitions, asking the United States Government to intervene in Hungarian internal affairs. So you sent memoranda through the accredited American Minister to Hungary asking for intervention by the United States Government.

CARDINAL: Yes.

PRESIDENT (*in a declamatory manner*): Every state, every people, may shape its life and the form of its government according to its desires and needs. (*Motions with his hand at the* CARDINAL.)

CARDINAL: That is so. Unfortunately, I overlooked these principles, and that is why I asked for this intervention.

PRESIDENT: Do you think this act of yours regrettable?

CARDINAL (*in a clear voice*): I do.

PRESIDENT: The first letter in the files before us, asking for intervention, was drafted in connection with the trial against the conspirators. (*He reads the draft of the letter.*)

CARDINAL (*excitedly*): May I make a statement?

PRESIDENT: Go ahead!

CARDINAL: As announced before, I accept the evidence before the Court and regret having dispatched these documents. The documents should be divided into three parts. A small portion of the first group, although completed and addressed, was never sent, but retained; these are among the documents. Not each and every one of those letters was sent.

PRESIDENT: Will you state if any of them were not sent.

CARDINAL: The majority were sent. The aim of these letters was not to expose faults or to do harm to people. My intention was to help, but I chose the wrong way to do the right thing. (*Excitedly*) At any rate, it would have been better not to have dispatched those letters. (*Sighing*) I regret having sent them, and in the future I shall never depart from my basic principle—pointed out in my letter to the Minister of Justice—to observe the external and internal policy of the Hungarian state in the light of its sovereignty.

PRESIDENT: Yes.

CARDINAL: Kindly accept my statement.

PRESIDENT: We shall put it on record, and shall consider its worth. Let us proceed. We have to treat every note individually, according to the rules of the court procedure, and we shall only be able to estimate their worth if we discuss them in Court and you make a statement concerning each of them. Will you, please, take particular care as to which document was actually sent, and which were only drafts?

CARDINAL (*with eyes closed*): I would be unable to state that here and now.

PRESIDENT: The receipt of most of them was confirmed. There is no doubt in such cases, is there?

CARDINAL: No. (*Looks to the side.*) At the police interrogation, letters were produced to which there was no answer: these may not have been dispatched.

PRESIDENT: The Prosecution does not maintain that all memoranda, applications, or requests written by you are criminal. We only examine those which are stated to be criminal. We shall discuss these and decide whether or not they are actually criminal. Listen!

CARDINAL: Yes.

PRESIDENT: Was there a Conference of Bishops with reference to the elections of 1947?

CARDINAL: Yes.

PRESIDENT: Did it deal with the elections?

CARDINAL: Yes.

PRESIDENT: Was a resolution adopted?

CARDINAL: Yes.

PRESIDENT: Was that resolution ever published?

CARDINAL: It was.

PRESIDENT: The *Magyar Kurir*—

CARDINAL: Yes!

PRESIDENT: —printed it, and so did the newspapers. What was the official standpoint adopted?

CARDINAL: That the conference did not take any stand for any of the political parties, but left it up to the faithful what to do.

PRESIDENT: They should not interfere with the elections.

CARDINAL: Correct.

PRESIDENT: That was the official point of view. But was there any other decision in the background under the cover of the official point of view?

CARDINAL: Individually, certain dioceses gave their support to the Women's Camp, or to the Barankovics Party which was launched at that time, others to Zoltán Pfeiffer, others again to the Small-holders. This was jointly discussed at the conference.

PRESIDENT: Wasn't there a decision that you were not to back any of the parties openly, but actually you advised the dioceses to tell the congregations, through the priests attached to the various chapters, to support the Christian Women's Camp wherever it was taking part—

CARDINAL: Yes.

PRESIDENT: —and where not, to support Pfeiffer, and where the latter had no candidates or no chance of election, to vote for Barankovics's party, and in the last place for the Smallholders.

CARDINAL: There was such an idea.

PRESIDENT (*sternly*): There was such a clause! Listen!

CARDINAL: Yes, there was.

PRESIDENT: In that case, this meant interfering with the elections, didn't it?

CARDINAL: Yes.

PRESIDENT (*sternly*): So it meant interfering with the elections! You gave two thousand forints to support the Schlachta Party. Is that so?

CARDINAL: I gave some financial support, but I could not tell you whether it was exactly that amount, more or less.

PRESIDENT: In the summer of 1948, in connection with the Mihalovics case, we tried one Ödön Lénárd, who was sentenced to six years by the People's Court for the spreading of inciting leaflets. At that time we suspected that these leaflets had emanated from you. This has not been confirmed by the investigation. Do you recall that? It was in connection with the nationalization of schools.

CARDINAL: I drafted some of those. I did not draft them all, but I drafted many leaflets.

PRESIDENT: I see.

CARDINAL: Or, if someone else had drafted them, I edited them.

PRESIDENT: Then, the leaflets were secretly and illegally multigraphed on the two machines that you had ordered to be purchased.

CARDINAL: They had asked for my approval, when buying the machines.

PRESIDENT: Yes. Did they also ask you for money?

CARDINAL: Yes, they did, and they got some. As to how they prepared the leaflets, I had no knowledge.

PRESIDENT: Another example of interventionist activities is your memorandum of May 4, 1946, addressed to the American and British Ministers, asking them to send British and American military forces into Hungary. Did you send such a memorandum?

CARDINAL: I did.

PRESIDENT: You did. Well, this is another gesture which is anything but friendly toward the Hungarian State—

CARDINAL (interrupting): This is a matter about which I have already made a statement.

PRESIDENT: Yes. I am going to read your memorandum No. A/21 to the American Minister, forwarded to him on December 12, 1946. Here is the confirmation in your own handwriting—that is, a copy of your letter. (He reads the letter in which the CARDINAL urged American intervention for public officials, discharged because of their political views.) On December 16, 1946, you again urged American intervention in a long memorandum. It is at the end that you request intervention. (He reads)

. . . I request the help of America, which is fighting for freedom and justice, to put an end to the tremendous pressure and rotting, so that the unfortunate Hungarian people can be preserved for Western civilization. A solution is possible with outside help. I could point out the ways and means of this. The evidence supporting my statement is in my possession.

To these letters asking for intervention Minister Arthur Schoenfeld replied to you on December 27, 1946. The original of this letter is here on file.

Legation of the United States of America

Budapest, Hungary, December 27, 1946

Your Eminence:

I have the honor to acknowledge receipt of your letter of November 22, concerning certain actions taken by the Czechoslovak Government affecting the Hungarian minority in Slovakia, as well as your letter of December 12, concerning the program for retrenchment of the Hungarian civil service, and your letter of December 16 containing observations on general matters of political interest in Hungary at the present time.

Copies of your letters have been forwarded to the Department of State.

It is noted that your letters of December 12 and December 16, touching on internal political problems of Hungary, requested the assistance of the United States Government in altering certain conditions which Your Eminence deplores. In this connection you are of course aware of my Government's long standing policy of non-interference in the internal affairs of other nations. This policy has proven over a long period of time and through many trying situations the best guarantee of spontaneous, vigorous and genuine democratic development. It will be clear to Your Eminence that it necessarily precludes action by this Legation which could properly be construed as interference in Hungarian domestic affairs or which lies outside the normal functions of diplomatic missions.

I should like to take this opportunity to assure Your Eminence that I shall continue to welcome the expression of your views on any matters to which you may desire to draw my attention.

In conveying to Your Eminence my best wishes for the holiday

season, I take the opportunity to renew the assurance of my highest
consideration.

(Signed) H. F. ARTHUR SCHOENFELD
American Minister

His Eminence Joseph, Cardinal Mindszenty
Prince Primate of Hungary
Esztergom, Hungary

PRESIDENT: Wasn't it unpleasant for you that the American Minister gave you such a lesson?

CARDINAL: It was.

PRESIDENT: I am going to produce another letter addressed to
Schoenfeld in which you informed him that if his waiver of the
requested intervention was merely a demonstrative, official gesture,
you took note of it trusting that he would do everything to prevent
the developments in progress here. Is this correct? Did you write
such a statement?

CARDINAL: I did.

(At this point the PRESIDENT *ordered a short recess.)*

PRESIDENT: You made another statement, and submitted another
request directly to President Truman through the American Legation. Is that so?

CARDINAL: Yes.

PRESIDENT: Did you ask him also to intervene in the domestic
affairs of the country?

CARDINAL *(shaking his head as if he wanted to indicate a "no")*:
Yes.

PRESIDENT: You close your letter with the following request:
"We are asking for aid to get rid of this unbearable oppression,
mendacity and cruelty."

CARDINAL: Yes, I did *(excitedly)*. But—

PRESIDENT *(interrupting)*: With this you were asking for intervention. Well, your priests were sending you reports from various
parts of the country, weren't they?

CARDINAL: Not regularly. It did happen sometimes. And it happened also that I asked for reports.

PRESIDENT: You forwarded these reports to the American Legation, didn't you?

CARDINAL: Not the reports as far as I know; summaries were made of them.

PRESIDENT: The data were extracted?

CARDINAL: Yes, in some cases.

PRESIDENT: What kind of data were these? Just give us a few examples. On the political and economic situation of the country?

CARDINAL: I think there were some referring to the drought. And then some atrocities occurred in the country; data were given about these too.

PRESIDENT (*cynically—staring at the* CARDINAL): For instance, about military forces, the supplies for the military forces, and their budget?

CARDINAL: As I remember there was only once a reference to the supplies, for a few months, for the occupation forces in Esztergom and Komárom counties. But—

PRESIDENT (*interrupting*): Now let us talk about your journey to America. Until now we have discussed the fact that you were in contact with Otto Hapsburg through various persons, through messages and exchanges of correspondence.

CARDINAL: Yes.

PRESIDENT: Did Otto Hapsburg know of you? Did he know that you were loyal to him? Did he know that you were one of the leading figures of the Hapsburg restoration movement here in Hungary? Did he?

CARDINAL: Probably he knew of me.

PRESIDENT: When did you leave for America?

CARDINAL: About June 17, 1947.

PRESIDENT: Together with your Secretary, the defendant Andrew Zakár?

CARDINAL: Yes, we went together.

PRESIDENT: Did you go to Vienna by a British military plane? and from there by a scheduled airliner?

CARDINAL: I went by regular service.

PRESIDENT: Between Vienna and Budapest there was no scheduled passenger plane. Listen! Did you travel by a British military plane?

CARDINAL: Yes.

PRESIDENT: Upon arriving at Ottawa did you attend the Marian Congress there?

CARDINAL: Yes. (*Leans back and closes his eyes.*)

PRESIDENT: Was Paul Zsámboki attached to you?

CARDINAL: Yes, the bishops and the cardinals from the United States detailed Monsignore Zsámboki to assist me.

PRESIDENT: Paul Zsámboki was also a Legitimist, an old friend of the Hapsburg family, their confessor, and loyal to them, wasn't he?

CARDINAL: Whether he was their confessor, I do not know; but it is true that at one time he had been in their service.

PRESIDENT: He was detailed to you. When did he mention to you that he would like to put you in touch with Zita and Otto Hapsburg?

CARDINAL: We were in Ottawa toward the end of the Congress, and then he reported that the widowed Queen had arrived at Ottawa and a meeting was desired.

PRESIDENT: Then you visited her. The meeting was held at a convent?

CARDINAL: Yes.

PRESIDENT: Were you accompanied by Zsámboki and Zakár?

CARDINAL: Yes.

PRESIDENT: Did you talk at this meeting about the chances of Legitimism and about Legitimists in Hungary?

CARDINAL: Well, it is possible that we touched on this matter.

PRESIDENT: Was there any mention that her son, Otto Hapsburg, would also like to meet you, and did she ask you for such a meeting?

CARDINAL: She might have.

PRESIDENT (*shouting*): You mean Yes?

CARDINAL (*eagerly*): Yes.

PRESIDENT: Zsámboki appeared one day, asking whether you could meet Otto in Chicago, didn't he?

CARDINAL: He did. The previous year I had not seen him in Rome. I did not want to be impolite this time and I said, "All right, let there be a meeting."

PRESIDENT: Well, then, Zsámboki arranged the meeting. Where did this take place? In Chicago?

CARDINAL: Yes!

PRESIDENT: It came about in a convent. Who took part?

CARDINAL: Only the two of us.

PRESIDENT: You were alone, and the two escorts remained outside?

CARDINAL: Yes.

PRESIDENT: This conference lasted about an hour?

CARDINAL: Yes.

PRESIDENT: What did he ask, whether the movement for the Hapsburg restoration had many followers? Whether you could get help and support from the United States of America? Did he, or did he not have a favorable opinion about the chances of a Hapsburg restoration with the existing international tension?

CARDINAL: Well, he was not too optimistic in this matter; or rather let us say, he had some hopes, but he was not too optimistic.

PRESIDENT: Did he say that he had contacts with the American Department of State and with leading American personalities?

CARDINAL: He mentioned something of the sort.

PRESIDENT: Did he say that he was in constant contact with these?

CARDINAL: Yes, he said that too.

PRESIDENT: And that there was a possibility for the restoration of the Hapsburg throne? Listen! That certain American leading circles saw that it was a wrong policy on their part to have—

CARDINAL (*automatically*): To have liquidated the monarchy.

PRESIDENT: They admitted it and were inclined to its reconstruction under a certain given international situation?

CARDINAL: Yes.

PRESIDENT: Did he tell you what his plan was, what sort of setup?

CARDINAL: Well, if you please, he mentioned as much; that he considers Austria and Hungary separately. This is how he said it.

PRESIDENT: Yes. In a personal union?

CARDINAL: He could visualize it as a personal union.

PRESIDENT: Is such a setup in line with certain intentions of American power politics?

CARDINAL: He mentioned—

PRESIDENT (*interrupting and yelling*): And you, as the highest priest in the Hungarian Republic, did not get up right away, saying: Excuse me, please, I am the highest priest of the Hungarian Catholic Church in the Hungarian Republic; I no longer wish to take part in a matter of this sort, since there is a republic here; my country is a republic, and therefore I cannot take a stand against—

CARDINAL: This did not arise. These were not tasks for tomorrow or the day after tomorrow; these were only theories, and so I listened to them as such; but there was nothing in this which would have been directed against the present order in Hungary.

PRESIDENT: Then why did you wish to keep this, as well as the conversation with Zita, a secret, and treated as a secret, if there was nothing to it?

CARDINAL: Because the matter could be misinterpreted. This was just an act of courtesy at a meeting already requested for the second time. The first time I did not fulfill the request, but the second time—

PRESIDENT: Well, this was not just a simple meeting. A courtesy call may last for eight to ten minutes. This lasted an hour—more in the nature of a conference. At a courtesy call there would have been no objection to other people having been present.

CARDINAL (*raising his head high*): Well, Mr. President, our talk did not follow such a course or direction that I should have felt obliged to act in such a way as you have suggested.

PRESIDENT: Did he ask your support, that you should stand at his side, that the Legitimists should hold out at home in hard times? Did he say that there would be hard times in the future, but the outcome of the issue was approaching?

CARDINAL: Well, he went as far as to say that the followers of the Hungarian Legitimists should not be in the limelight too much, no sacrifices should be made for the ideals, and not even a single person should get into trouble or inconvenience because of the cause; that the people should restrict themselves to social activities only. This is what he touched on.

PRESIDENT: You stated that you were an old supporter of his and would do everything you could to strengthen further the Legitimist cause here, and that in favorable circumstances they would be ready.

CARDINAL: He had no doubts that I—

PRESIDENT (*interrupting*): But did you bring out the point that you were an old follower of his?

CARDINAL: I think—

PRESIDENT (*interrupting*): Did Otto ask you who were the leading personalities of the Legitimist cause here today?

CARDINAL: Yes, he did.

PRESIDENT: Who were these persons? Whom did you name?

CARDINAL: I mentioned Professor Baranyai, Joseph Cziráky, and then I don't know whom as third and fourth.

PRESIDENT: Three or four persons?

CARDINAL: Three or four persons.

PRESIDENT: Those who are playing a role at this trial? That they used to meet with each other?

CARDINAL: Yes.

PRESIDENT: Well, then, afterward you took leave of each other. The conference lasted for an hour. Then you went to New York, where you were a guest of Cardinal Spellman.

CARDINAL: Yes.

PRESIDENT: When you conferred with Spellman, did you tell him of your conference with Otto?

CARDINAL: Yes, I did. *(He closes his eyes.)*

PRESIDENT: Yes. Listen! There is no doubt that you really conferred and talked with Otto.

CARDINAL (*lethargically*): I do not deny it.

PRESIDENT: Well, that's all very well; but then Otto makes a statement for the world press. Here it is: the *Osservatore Romano* reports it. It said things like this: As far as the expressed accusations of the Budapest Government are concerned, according to which, Otto had met Mindszenty in Chicago during the Cardinal's American journey, Otto declares that the first knowledge he had of this was when he read it in the newspapers recently. . . . This is what Otto Hapsburg states. Here it is in the *Osservatore Romano*. Well, then, you talked in New York with Cardinal Spellman about your conference with Otto.

CARDINAL (*with closed eyes*): Yes.

PRESIDENT: Did you inform him of the situation, the activities, and the strength of the Hungarian Legitimists? Was he interested?

CARDINAL: I spoke of that.

PRESIDENT: Was he interested in what sort of chances there were for this Legitimist movement, what strength it had here?

CARDINAL: I said already that I did not think the idea was timely now.

PRESIDENT: But this is not the idea shown by the drawing up of the cabinet list. In thinking of a regency, of becoming provisional head of the state; in planning the whole setup in the one-hour conference with Otto. In a matter which one considers untimely, one does not negotiate, one does not plan.

CARDINAL: At that time it was still strongly rumored—there are waves of this kind of rumor—that a historic change might come about.

PRESIDENT: A third world war?

CARDINAL: A third world war is what was talked about.

PRESIDENT: Now, you were thinking of a third world war. That they would establish a system of government here which would suit you, instead of concentrating all your strength here and abroad to prevent the outbreak of such a third world war.

CARDINAL (*excitedly*): I beg your pardon, Mr. President, I was not working for a third world war.

PRESIDENT: This premise, this desire was the condition *sine qua non*.

CARDINAL: In any case, I, as a Hungarian, dread a third world war —any war.

PRESIDENT: But the whole plan was based on this. You thought of a new sea of blood. The war would break out and the Anglo-Saxon powers would win.

CARDINAL: These ideas had gained ground among the people.

PRESIDENT: The war was the condition *sine qua non*. Without war you well knew that in two or three months such a change, the overthrowing of the state order, could not be imagined.

CARDINAL: Yes. However, public opinion then took a war almost for granted.

PRESIDENT: But, if you please, was there any step taken, was there even one stroke of the pen made against the outbreak of war, for the lessening of international tension?

CARDINAL (*emphatically*): We did so, for we always prayed for peace.

PRESIDENT: Listen! At the same time you drafted a whole series of petitions aimed at making the international situation worse. Isn't that so?

CARDINAL: Yes. I—

PRESIDENT (*interrupting*): There seems to be a big contradiction here with your outward actions. You based everything on international tension. Wasn't that your presupposition? And then you say that you were praying for peace. In any case, your actions are listed here in the court, in documents which cannot possibly be interpreted otherwise than as manifest expectation of an approaching war. Right to the end, the whole series of conferences, the cabinet list, all was for this.

CARDINAL (*showing extreme fatigue*): Indeed.

PRESIDENT: This was the starting point. Can a cardinal, a Catholic priest, make a sea of blood, a new war, a starting point? You should have fought tooth and nail, with all your power in every continent, to prevent another war.

CARDINAL: I did not desire war.

PRESIDENT: These documents indicate otherwise.

CARDINAL (*in a tired voice*): At the most I considered it as a possibility.

PRESIDENT: All these actions tended to drive things to the extreme It seems that you wanted to make relations with the Americans worse. All reports had a certain tendency. They all showed the country and the developments in an unfavorable light.

CARDINAL (*very tired*): Yes, but Mr. President, I have already expressed my regrets.

PRESIDENT: That is very nice, but now it is for me to establish logical connection between these questions, for this is how they were connected in reality. Listen! Once more we are going back to your conversation with Otto. Otto called attention to the fact that Selden Chapin, a new American Minister, was to come to Budapest.

How did he characterize Chapin for you in comparison with Schoenfeld?

CARDINAL: He said he was a more positive person than his predecessor.

PRESIDENT: Did he say that he had already spoken with him? That he knew him?

CARDINAL: He said that they had met.

PRESIDENT: Did he say that it would be good if you could contact him while you were still in America?

CARDINAL: I do not know whether he said this, for, as I remember, by the time we got there, Minister Chapin had already left for Hungary. *(He seems near exhaustion.)*

PRESIDENT: Did you speak with Spellman about Otto? Did Spellman know Otto?

CARDINAL: Yes, he knew him.

PRESIDENT: How did he speak of him?

CARDINAL: As I recall, he spoke of him favorably.

PRESIDENT: How did you come to discuss the matter of your giving an authorization to Otto? Was it Cardinal Spellman's idea?

CARDINAL: It seems it was that of Cardinal Spellman.

PRESIDENT: What reasons did he give? Why was this authorization needed?

CARDINAL: We were discussing the fact that the Slovak and Czech peoples were getting support, and that it would be useful for some one representative to have the authority to do something for Hungarians along this line.

PRESIDENT: What kind of support?

CARDINAL *(weary)*: In American circles.

PRESIDENT: But what right did you have to give such an authorization? It was not appointing a priest as representative, although in America you would not have had the authority to do even that. This was a political authorization, and in such matters Hungarians are represented by our Hungarian legation in Washington and by the Hungarian consulate general in New York. By what right did you do it? Listen! Was this not a Legitimist authorization?

CARDINAL *(staring at the court)*: No.

PRESIDENT: What kind of authorization was this?

CARDINAL: I think it was a brief two-line note, something like, "I authorize ———, in case I am prevented"—because I did not give this unconditionally but with certain conditions—"in case I am prevented, to represent the Hungarian Catholics."

PRESIDENT: But what do you mean by being prevented? You mention that he as a representative should secure help for Hungary since you were not in the States, that he should have authorization empowering him to deal in such matters.

CARDINAL: First of all, I had in mind that he should urge the American Catholic relief organization to send relief.

PRESIDENT: All right. But then why this proviso, "in case I am prevented"? Wasn't he supposed to urge them whenever he could?

CARDINAL: I thought that while I could keep in touch by mail and otherwise, I could do this myself.

PRESIDENT (cynically): If there was no mail, no relief could come!

CARDINAL: Then, please understand, they could support Hungarians who were outside the mutilated country, for instance, the displaced Hungarians abroad and so on. We considered them to be the same as our people here, in matters of relief.

PREIDENT: So you gave this, drafting it in Hungarian, to Cardinal Spellman?

CARDINAL: Yes, I gave it to him. I wanted to do this, because Cardinal Spellman is a great benefactor and supporter of the Hungarian people; but I gave it only in conditional form.

PRESIDENT: When you arrived home, you gave a report to the other Legitimists, to the leaders of Legitimist circles, on what you discussed with Otto, what your impressions were in America. Was that so?

CARDINAL: Yes.

PRESIDENT: To whom, tell us?

CARDINAL: Well, I know surely that I told Professor Baranyai. Who the others were I'm not quite certain.

PRESIDENT: Tell us who? Mention a few names.

CARDINAL: I imagine Joseph Cziráky and then Professor Gruber. I'm not quite sure whether Margaret Schlachta was one.

PRESIDENT: You told them that you had spoken with Otto and what you spoke about, as you mentioned a short time ago?

CARDINAL: To each, I said—*(He wants to continue but is interrupted.)*

PRESIDENT: Listen! This had an inspiring effect on the Legitimists here; it gave them strength and confidence, didn't it?

CARDINAL: If you please, I do not know what this means. I do not know about their behavior in the outside world. Professor Baranyai was glad to hear that Otto sent him greetings.

PRESIDENT: No! Listen! That is not what I want you to talk about. I am talking about the plans of the Hapsburg restoration, which were told to you by Otto—the aid that could be expected from American circles, a possible change in American power politics, the fact that increasingly more people were believing that their policy in Central Europe liquidating the Austro-Hungarian Monarchy was wrong!

CARDINAL: Because of their views, of course, they would like to hear this. *(PRESIDENT of court shows annoyance.)*

PRESIDENT: When you returned from your American journey, you were visited in Esztergom by Chapin, the newly appointed American Minister?

CARDINAL: Yes.

PRESIDENT: For how long did it last, approximately?

CARDINAL: Perhaps for half an hour.

PRESIDENT: Listen! For half or three-quarters of an hour. Did political questions come up during this conversation?

CARDINAL: I think very briefly.

PRESIDENT: You returned this visit in two or three weeks, going to the American legation?

CARDINAL: In two or three weeks.

PRESIDENT: Accompanied by your secretary?

CARDINAL: Yes.

PRESIDENT: Here again this meeting took approximately the same time?

CARDINAL: Yes, approximately as long.

PRESIDENT: You were discussing concrete issues, weren't you?

CARDINAL: Yes.

PRESIDENT: You did talk, for instance, about fighting against developments here, through pastoral letters?

CARDINAL: The pastoral letters were mentioned and he asked how the flock received them and how the clergy reacted; and he said that he regretted that he only knew them from translations.

PRESIDENT: He did say that he approved very much of the aggressive tone, and that resistance against the development should be continued further?

CARDINAL: He may have said so, but I do not remember it. *(He slumps, closes his eyes.)*

PRESIDENT *(loudly)*: The third meeting occurred then on February 16, 1948, at Esztergom. Chapin came with Koczak, his wife, and two other women employees of the legation?

CARDINAL *(with eyes still closed)*: Yes.

PRESIDENT: During this visit did you, Chapin and Koczak withdraw for a talk?

CARDINAL: Yes.

PRESIDENT: What did Chapin tell you then? How you should keep in touch in the future? How you should get your information to him, and through whom? Listen!

CARDINAL *(opens eyes)*: Through my secretary and his secretary.

PRESIDENT: Why was this necessary?

CARDINAL: He said that we live far from each other.

PRESIDENT: Well . . .

CARDINAL: Well, he said so.

PRESIDENT: There are automobiles; there is telephone, mail; there is no distance today.

CARDINAL: I do not live in Budapest, as Your Honor knows. This is what he was referring to.

PRESIDENT: Wasn't it in order that this contact should not get too obvious and it would be better if you kept in touch through your secretaries, secretly?

CARDINAL: If you please, our meetings had been infrequent. Up to then—

PRESIDENT *(interrupting)*: Listen! You were to meet through your secretaries. Then, according to this, you instructed Zakár that in the future when Koczak came, he should always give him material. Was it so?

CARDINAL: I said that he could supply the right kind—

PRESIDENT (*interrupting*): What right kind of material—(*shouting*) what data were those? Those which praise the developments here, the results achieved? Material should be given to help the Americans see what fine fruits the efforts of the Hungarian people yield? What data? What data do you mean?

CARDINAL: I— *(He is again near exhaustion.)*

PRESIDENT: Yes!

CARDINAL: —that Church—Church data were concerned.

PRESIDENT (*shouting*): I asked whether the data were favorable! When one is in touch with foreigners, after all, one likes to show the advantages, the results, the cultural, artistic, scientific results, economic results, political results, proudly. You know this too. Was this the kind of results you indicated?

CARDINAL (*raising his eyes toward the ceiling*): Rather negative— *(He is interrupted.)*

PRESIDENT (*ironically*): Rather negative results. What was the purpose of giving negative results! What was the aim? Make a statement! Listen! To get the American government to adopt an unfriendly attitude against the present regime. Isn't that the truth?

CARDINAL: That was not the aim.

PRESIDENT: At any rate, that could have come of it. Now then, this was not an isolated act on your part. You did inform in this manner not only the foreign legations, but other organizations. Such false information was sent abroad through Actio Catholica and Sigmund Mihalovics. He reported to you several times what information he did send abroad, for instance, through the representatives of the Danish Red Cross?

CARDINAL: Yes.

PRESIDENT: Until now we have spoken of three conferences and meetings with Chapin; then a fourth one came. For the fourth time you went to see him. Where to?

CARDINAL: I think to his house.

PRESIDENT: What made this talk timely?

CARDINAL: As a matter of fact, I had been informed at this time that a great change in Yugoslavia was taking place as far as Hungary was concerned. They said that it was not impossible that something would start in Yugoslavia, from Tito's side, which would not remain an isolated phenomenon.

PRESIDENT: Then you thought right away that if there was a re-actionary step taken in Yugoslavia, that is, a step against progress, then you should quickly size up the situation to investigate the possibilities for a similar regressive step in Hungary. This was what you thought! Why didn't you ask the Hungarian foreign ministry if you were in want of information? Why did you get in touch with the minister of a foreign power and his adviser? Who took part at this conference? Chapin, Koczak, and from Yugoslavia—

CARDINAL: An American, the Southeastern European adviser.

PRESIDENT: There was talk of actions and steps that the Legitimists should take in case we should be on the verge of a change!

CARDINAL (*staring at the* PRESIDENT): By political circles I was advised to keep my eyes open, but whether this was from Legitimists or others I do not remember.

PRESIDENT: Listen! The fifth meeting came about in the middle of November, 1948. Then you asked that Chapin should come to see you. He visited you together with Koczak. Between these two meetings, the meeting in the summer and this meeting, Koczak had been in Esztergom several times, always collecting material from Zakár!

CARDINAL: I beg you, I do not know how many times he was there. In most cases I did not even know of it.

PRESIDENT: He came at night, around eleven o'clock, to your house.

CARDINAL: I occasionally learned about it in the morning, when my secretary mentioned it.

PRESIDENT: It seems strange that a representative of the legation kept coming to the palace of the Primate at night! Once you, too, met him at night, didn't you?

CARDINAL: Yes, once I did.

PRESIDENT: After all, this is rather strange. Diplomats don't usually call at night.

CARDINAL: I thought that he had more time to make visits.

PRESIDENT: At night? Well, this is a very naïve plea. Obviously he went at night in order not to be seen, not to call attention to himself; but he did call attention to himself.

CARDINAL: Yes.

PRESIDENT: Let us go on. In November, 1948, Chapin came to see you at your request, at Esztergom, in the company of Koczak. What did you talk about then? You conferred again for about three quarters of an hour. Listen! You discussed—

CARDINAL: I mentioned how strong the campaign was getting against me, in the press and in other ways. Then we discussed—

PRESIDENT (*interrupting*): And what sort of statement did Chapin make? That he too had noticed this?

CARDINAL: He had noticed, he had seen it and—he brought up the proposal that—that I should go abroad—

PRESIDENT (*interrupting*): And that he would help you in this!

CARDINAL: I had the impression that he would not refuse help.

PRESIDENT (*shouting*): Listen! Don't give diplomatic answers! Answer straight! Did he offer that in case you decided to take this step, he would help you, or did he say that he would not help you?

CARDINAL: Why is it necessary that I give such an answer?

PRESIDENT (*nervously wiping sweat from forehead, after a pause*): No, you do not have to answer a single question. Court procedure permits your not answering, but perhaps you deny yourself a point of defense. It is my duty to call it to your attention. (*Benignly*) You are not obliged to answer, if there is any question you do not wish to answer. Simply say, "I do not wish to answer this." Listen! During the interrogation you did answer this question.

CARDINAL: Yes.

PRESIDENT: You do wish to answer now!

CARDINAL: Yes.

PRESIDENT: Then go ahead. He did offer to help to get you out of the country!

CARDINAL: He did not offer to get me out, but that he would help me anyway, I—

PRESIDENT (*interrupting*): That he would help getting you abroad!

CARDINAL: Yes.

PRESIDENT: And you answered to this—

CARDINAL: I said to this—

PRESIDENT: Speak louder.

CARDINAL (*with eyes closed*): —that I would remain at home.

PRESIDENT: After this, did you not consider flight at all? *(Stares intently at* CARDINAL.*)*

CARDINAL (*after a pause, with a changed tone of voice*): Please, your Honor, permit me not to answer.

PRESIDENT: Listen! You are not obliged to answer. The Prosecution charges you with having always been in touch, both during your travels abroad and at home, with emigrants, sworn enemies of the regime, with people condemned, political criminals, for whose arrests warrants had been issued; and in some miraculous fashion, or perhaps very understandably, these all sought you out. So, for instance, at the time of your journey to Rome in February, 1946, Nicholas Kállay approached you. Nicholas Horthy, Jr., sent his secretary to you, saying he wished to meet you. Then Nicholas Horthy sent Aladár Kovács in 1947 or 1948—you said that you did not remember accurately—with a message to you. Correct?

CARDINAL: Yes.

PRESIDENT: Then Desider Sulyok, who had left the country, sent a letter to you on December 28, 1947?

CARDINAL: Yes.

PRESIDENT: He addressed the letter to you, offered his services. He asked you to give him political instructions, because he wished to act as directed by you. Correct?

CARDINAL: Yes.

PRESIDENT: This letter, too, is here among the documents. It was written to you. All these people are organizing abroad along the Legitimist lines. Is that right?

CARDINAL: Yes.

PRESIDENT: They are busy trying to set up a Central European Catholic kingdom. Is that right?

CARDINAL: How many of them stand for this cause—

PRESIDENT: Sulyok stands for it. They live together; they form a group. Is that right?

CARDINAL: But as far as I know, they do not all live together. The letters did not show it.

PRESIDENT: Sigmund Mihalovics fled abroad, didn't he?

CARDINAL: Yes.

PRESIDENT: He sent you three letters. Correct?

CARDINAL: I recall a long letter—

PRESIDENT: The third one is a long letter. This is a long, type-written letter, stating that he got in touch with the CIC abroad.

CARDINAL: Yes.

PRESIDENT: The CIC provided him with forged papers. Is that correct?

CARDINAL: Yes.

PRESIDENT: With these forged papers, he wanted to get to Rome and to establish an office abroad, an information bureau. Is that right?

CARDINAL: Yes.

PRESIDENT: He asked for data, confidential information; he could use it, and it would be paid for, and so forth. Is that so?

CARDINAL: Yes.

PRESIDENT: His intention was to work in two ways: partly to spread the data communicated to him, which was intended to make Hungary appear in an unfavorable light in the foreign press, and partly to obtain confidential information, as he explicitly stated. This was spying. Does this hold good?

CARDINAL: Yes, it does. He asked for data, but I never sent him any.

PRESIDENT: You suspected that the letter in which he had asked for data had gone through the hands of our political police!

CARDINAL: I had heard something—

PRESIDENT (*interrupting*): If you had not suspected that, in that case, the Mihalovics group would have obtained the same kind of information that the American minister did obtain? Isn't that so? (*The* CARDINAL *suddenly slumps forward. Pause.*) Let us consider the foreign currency offenses. Upon your first trip to Rome in 1945, how many dollars did you get from Undersecretary of State Montini?

CARDINAL (*automatically*): Thirty thousand—

PRESIDENT: $30,000?

CARDINAL (*near collapse*): If I remember correctly—

PRESIDENT: Do you need a rest or would you rather we continued the hearing? You can follow! Listen! Can you?

CARDINAL (*slowly, staring at* PRESIDENT): I can. I shall answer . . . as I can remember. . . .

PRESIDENT: If you feel too tired we shall stop to give you a rest. Listen! For the moment you seem to be fresh enough to reply!

CARDINAL: I am at your disposal, willingly! (*Stares at* PRESIDENT.)

PRESIDENT: Let us proceed. Your second trip to Rome in 1946. On that occasion you received $10,000 in one sum from the Holy See.

CARDINAL: Yes.

PRESIDENT: There is an item of $3,000 from Spellman, another for $1,000 from Gigan, one of $5,000 from donations, according to Zakár. That is about right?

CARDINAL: This would be about right.

PRESIDENT: You bought three motorcars, for $3,000 or $4,000.

CARDINAL: Yes.

PRESIDENT: You brought home with you $12,000. That is correct! Did you report this to the National Bank?

CARDINAL: I do not know.

PRESIDENT: You don't know?

CARDINAL: I don't know. I did not handle the money.

PRESIDENT: Well, then, how did you distribute the money? You gave $4,000 to whom? To the bishops?

CARDINAL: Yes, for the dioceses.

PRESIDENT: All right. Mihalovics got $2,000. That is correct.

CARDINAL: Yes.

PRESIDENT: $2,000 you kept. You gave it to Bóka.

CARDINAL: Yes.

PRESIDENT: I see. What did Bóka do with the money? Obviously, he changed it into forints. That is so!

CARDINAL: That is so.

PRESIDENT: You were aware of the regulations concerning the dealings in dollars, as a foreign currency? I do not mean any recent regulations.

CARDINAL: Yes, I was.

PRESIDENT: This regulation has existed for about a decade. Did you know about it?

CARDINAL: I did.

PRESIDENT: You also knew that the dollars were exchanged at a black-market rate higher than the official quotation, didn't you?

CARDINAL: I only knew of a single item, of $5,000; I believe it was a check, that was exchanged that way.

PRESIDENT: Yes.

CARDINAL: In November of last year I asked about this at the time we were attacked for this reason.

PRESIDENT: Yes.

CARDINAL: I think it was on November 27. I was then reassured I need have no fear on account of the foreign currency because—

PRESIDENT (*interrupting*): Did you receive statements of account weekly?

CARDINAL: Yes.

PRESIDENT: You received weekly statements. Those statements showed receipts and disbursements, didn't they?

CARDINAL: Yes.

PRESIDENT: No doubt, you always examined them carefully. You saw there, for instance, the sale of $1,000 or $2,000. It is not important whether you received 11,000 forints from the sale of $1,000, or 45,000 or 50,000 forints, or is it? Whenever you needed some cash, and you had dollars, you gave instructions to sell so and so many.

CARDINAL: Sometimes—

PRESIDENT: Can you imagine that they would have sold a part of the foreign currency without your permission? Could Bóka have done so, for instance? Was he authorized to do so? Would he have dared do it?

CARDINAL: I do not know what he dared do, but, if you please, I realize the mistakes and feel that—

PRESIDENT (*interrupting*): Listen! First answer the question, then I shall listen to where you see the mistakes. Answer me! Was Bóka authorized to trade or sell any of the foreign currency in your possession without your knowledge?

CARDINAL (*ready to rise*): Please, I am the accused.

PRESIDENT: That is a fact, but we cannot check your responsibility unless you answer these questions. Of course, it isn't Bóka who is accused. Listen! Answer!

CARDINAL: Naturally, from time to time, I gave instructions to sell.

PRESIDENT: You knew that he did not deliver and sell the dollars to the National Bank, that these dollars were not even registered at the Bank?

CARDINAL: In any case, I take the blame for all that happened. I have written to the People's Court concerning reparations. Kindly separate the dollars that I personally handled from the foreign currency charges against the others, and the damages caused to the state.

PRESIDENT: Whatever you did not handle shall not be held against you. Listen!

CARDINAL: I shall make it good with my best efforts.

PRESIDENT: That is not the point. The problem of reparations and damages is another problem. We are now examining whether or not there was in your case a criminal offense committed with foreign currency or not! We have to deal with this matter. Listen! You did know that you were not supposed to keep foreign currency at home, that it had to be surrendered to the National Bank?

CARDINAL: I knew it.

PRESIDENT: Were you aware that in spite of that, you were keeping foreign currency?

CARDINAL: Yes, but—

PRESIDENT (*interrupting*): You obviously knew that you were violating the laws. Do you feel guilty?

CARDINAL: I did not give direct instructions, yet in the face of the situation, I take the responsibility for it in the same manner as if I had given direct instructions.

PRESIDENT: Listen! Do you feel guilty of these acts?

CARDINAL: I do.

PRESIDENT: Over a period of two to three years, you carried out a series of foreign currency deals. In my experience, the special court handling financial crimes has passed sentences of one or two years' penal servitude for amounts ranging from $100 to $5. We never dreamed that there were dollar manipulations of this size somewhere in the background and that these should be perpetrated by the Archbishop of Esztergom! It is unprecedented in Hungarian jurisdiction that such enormous dollar amounts should be involved in speculation. Is this permissible according to Catholic ethics? Whom were the foreign currency laws meant to serve?

CARDINAL: In any case I regret and—

PRESIDENT (*interrupting*): Yes, you have said so. Tell me: Whom were the foreign currency laws meant to serve?

CARDINAL: The country's economy.

PRESIDENT (*in a declamatory manner*): The country's economic welfare, a stable currency, the stable forint?

CARDINAL: Yes.

PRESIDENT (*triumphantly*): And of all people, you, the Archbishop of Esztergom, violated them. Are there any questions, members of the court?

ASSOCIATE JUSTICE: You collected the documents of the present case, and you gave them to your secretary to safeguard in a confidential place.

CARDINAL (*relaxed*): Yes.

MEMBER OF THE COURT: When did you instruct him to hide them underground?

CARDINAL: I think it was early last autumn.

MEMBER OF THE COURT: What made you issue the order? Why did you wish to hide them? Did you have the feeling that this was criminal material?

CARDINAL: No, their contents were just of a delicate nature.

ASSOCIATE JUSTICE: Will you please tell us: Did you feel that they were criminal actions, or did you feel that they were not criminal actions but just confidential documents?

CARDINAL: I had an uneasy feeling about them, but I never reckoned with their being regarded criminal; as they are looked upon here in court—

PRESIDENT (*interrupting*): Yes. Yes.

CARDINAL: This is why it was decided to bury them underground.

PRESIDENT: Listen! Did you instruct Zakár and Fabian—

CARDINAL: I did.

PRESIDENT: —to hide this? *(Showing a metal container.)*

CARDINAL: Yes.

PRESIDENT: Take a look. Is this the identical thing?

CARDINAL: Please, I did not see it before it was buried.

PRESIDENT: When did you see it?

CARDINAL: When it was produced at the hearing. It was there that I first saw it.

PRESIDENT: Open it and see whether it is the same. Was that it? Look at it!

CARDINAL: This is what they produced at the hearing.

PRESIDENT: Defendant Andrew Zakár, look at it. Who made this?

ZAKÁR: This was in our archives, as we have had such document cases for many years. We took one of them and put the documents into it.

PRESIDENT: When you decided to hide it in the cellar, did you report it first to the defendant Joseph Mindszenty?

ZAKÁR: Yes, we reported it.

PRESIDENT: Did he approve of the scheme?

ZAKÁR: I told him that it seemed best to bury them underground. He did not ask about details, but merely said: "See that they are in a safe place."

PRESIDENT: I see. And then you put in the documents. Did you choose what to put in, and what not?

ZAKÁR: The Prince Primate handed the documents over to me.

PRESIDENT: In order that they should be put away?

ZAKÁR: In order that they should be put away.

PRESIDENT: Then it was not you who made the selection, who chose the papers?

ZAKÁR: Part of them, those which had been safeguarded by us, we put in; another part the Prince Primate—

PRESIDENT *(interrupting)*: Mr. Prosecutor!

PROSECUTOR *(addressing the* CARDINAL*)*: You said here in court that this whole affair which has been unrolled before us, with the list of the cabinet, the vacuum, and the rest of it, was just one of many possibilities. You, as good Hungarians, thought of this possibility, among others.

CARDINAL: Yes.

PROSECUTOR: Well then, you thought of many possibilities. Why didn't you work out a scheme for other eventualities? Why did you draw up a memorandum and prepare a list of the cabinet, and so forth, for just this eventuality?

CARDINAL: Well, I dare say, obviously to those who thought about this idea—

PROSECUTOR (*interrupting*): This scheme was the one they insisted on.

CARDINAL: This issue was closer.

PROSECUTOR: This issue was closer to them.

CARDINAL: Yes. This was the—

PROSECUTOR (*interrupting*): This was the objective.

CARDINAL: Yes.

PROSECUTOR: Next, it is characteristic that the list of the proposed cabinet is made up of men of an advanced age. I ask, didn't you think that some trouble might befall these men, or did you think that the change was so imminent that the list was already due?

CARDINAL: Please, MR. PROSECUTOR, this was not a deliberate plan. It was based on sudden rumor, and—as you may recall—the matter was dropped there and was not pursued further.

PROSECUTOR: Indeed, indeed, for the preliminaries did not come about.

CARDINAL: If I had considered the matter earnestly, then, I repeat, I would have prepared a second and third set too, but since I did not really consider it—

PROSECUTOR (*interrupting*): All right, all right; that is not the point. This proposed list of a cabinet was preserved in a tin box, in this tin tube, in which it was buried in the ground, evidently in the hope for better times. Had you dropped the idea—all the more, as it had passed through your mind that the contents of the documents were of a delicate nature, and as a rule citizens do not usually busy themselves with setting up lists of cabinets on paper, you decided to hide it—I repeat, had you definitely dropped the idea, you would have destroyed the list and thrown it into the fire.

CARDINAL: Mr. Prosecutor, when I looked at some of the documents before they were placed—

PROSECUTOR (*interrupting*): Buried.

CARDINAL: —in the tube to be buried, I did not check the documents, and this document was not in my hand at that time. I did not check everything.

PROSECUTOR: Still, what an amazing coincidence. Even if I accept your statements, the contents of this tin tube compromise you. I cannot accept this as a mere coincidence.

CARDINAL: Before hiding these documents, we kept in the office in a separate place those which were not strictly clerical.

PROSECUTOR: Yes, and these were kept in a separate place too.

CARDINAL: These may have been among the clerical papers.

PROSECUTOR: Very few of these papers have any clerical character. I am sufficiently familiar with them.

CARDINAL: Yes, and—

PROSECUTOR (*interrupting*): Among these, the letters to and from foreign legations, copies of reports to foreign legations, the letters of Mihalovics and their copies, the list of the cabinet, the petitions, the legal and historic setup of the taking over of power and the reasons thereof: these are not clerical, but political matters. So, our point of departure is the cabinet list, and we have arrived again at this point.

CARDINAL: Yes, and—

PROSECUTOR (*interrupting*): From the composition of the cabinet list, one might assume that in 1947 you considered that the chances for a war were so imminent that the list of a new government was topical. Did you think a war was so close at hand?

CARDINAL (*wearily*): At that time there were such strong rumors —you may remember yourself—that people reckoned with this possibility.

PROSECUTOR: Did you reckon with it too?

CARDINAL: Well, if you please, I was one of the general public—

PROSECUTOR (*interrupting*): My next question refers to something that was not yet precisely answered: if that certain *vacuum juris* that you referred to, had occurred—

CARDINAL: Yes, but—

PROSECUTOR (*interrupting*): With one word: If the Hungarian Republic and her sovereignty did not exist. This is what you meant by vacuum.

CARDINAL: If world conditions should eliminate something without the incentive of inside forces—

PROSECUTOR (*interrupting*): Yes, yes. Well, what part did you—

PRESIDENT (*interrupting*): I beg your pardon, inside forces were not to be passive; they were to be active, in order to make the outside force take action. (*To the* CARDINAL) I refer to what you said yourself: the aim of the negative reports was also to bring matters to a head.

CARDINAL: I beg your pardon, any action taken on this side would have been too modest to bring about a decisive step, so to speak. Compared to the aim ascribed to them or charged against them—

PROSECUTOR (*interrupting*): You stated that the projected government would have been a cabinet of officials, so to speak. That is what you said, if I remember well.

CARDINAL: Yes, and—

PROSECUTOR (*interrupting*): Well, then, if I look through the list, I see names like Peyer, Rassay, Keresztes-Fischer, Julius, Mór, Valentiny, Apor; not one of these are active officials. They are all men against whom proceedings have been started for high treason. Some already escaped. So, this is not a government of officials. These men are enemies of the Republic.

CARDINAL: It appears that the list was modified while we were—

PROSECUTOR (*interrupting*): If you please, you stated that you had been an old follower of Otto and that you had said so in Chicago to him personally. Are you faithful to the Republic?

CARDINAL (*looking at the* PRESIDENT): If you please, as I stated, I wish to be an obedient subject of the Republic and of the present Hungarian system of government and its laws—

PROSECUTOR (*interrupting*): It will be hard to reconcile that someone should be the adherent of a popular democratic republic and at the same time of Otto Hapsburg. The two are opposed to each other; there is an antagonism between them. We have heard about a conversation with Mr. Chapin when you declared that you wish to stay in the country. Would you recognize your own handwriting in a letter which I am going to read to you?

Mr. Minister, you must take action by Thursday and I request you to do so, for a death sentence is likely and the trial will be pointed against America. They want to prove that I was paid by America for secret information. Please send a car and a plane; there is no other way out.

With warmest regards,
MINDSZENTY

January 23

P.S. Please instruct Koczak immediately to meet the bearer of this letter today to discuss every detail. MINDSZENTY

P.S. Please promise the pilot $4,000 in the interest of the cause. I shall refund it. MINDSZENTY

Did you write such a letter?

CARDINAL (*still looking at the* PRESIDENT): Yes.

PRESIDENT: Any other questions? Defense counsel, please ask questions.

KOLOMAN KICZKÓ (*counsel for the* CARDINAL): Your Eminence, do you identify yourself with the scheme of Justin Baranyai so completely that you clearly understood every single phrase of it—that you studied it—or did you simply accept it as a finished plan?

CARDINAL: If you please, by the fact that in the end I did not follow up the matter—

COUNSEL: Yes.

CARDINAL: —and provided no printing paper, it may be concluded that I did not identify myself with it.

PRESIDENT (*in a raised voice*): You did not say so awhile ago. You just said that before the scheme was worked out, you had discussed it with Baranyai; then after a few weeks, perhaps after a month, that he had come to see you and handed it to you. You studied it together and discussed it again. You agreed with him. Then Baranyai set up the list of the projected cabinet after previously discussing it with you; you agreed that Baranyai was to make up a list for a cabinet of officials. Certain names were mentioned, too. Baranyai prepared the list and sent it to you, and you more or less agreed with it. Listen! This is what you said here two hours ago. That is correct?

CARDINAL (*wearily*): Yes.

COUNSEL: Although you studied the matter, you did not fully grasp its meaning.

PRESIDENT: That he did not say.

COUNSEL: He does say it now.

PRESIDENT: That is exactly why I remind him of his statement made to the Court.

These words were spoken on Thursday, February 3, 1949, at twenty minutes past eleven o'clock at night.

The President then adjourned court until the following morning at nine.

The Cardinal was led back to his cell. One could see that he was in a distinct state of excitement.

On Friday morning he looked exactly as he did when he came to court the first time, except with a more hunted look, with his chin drawn even closer to his chest.

The next defendant to be examined was Prince Paul Eszterházy; he was followed by Nicholas Nagy and Béla Ispánky. At the end of the latter's examination the President turned to the Cardinal and asked him what his reaction was. The Cardinal answered, "It fills me with sorrow."

Ispánky was followed by the last defendant, Leslie Tóth, an old man, half deaf, who had to use a hearing aid. Nevertheless, he was the only one who spoke up and admitted his guilt with a clear voice and in no way resembling the automaton characteristics displayed in the declarations and answers of the other defendants. He had only been arrested on January 25th and, despite his age, looked fresher and more natural than the other defendants. His counsel also went through the motions of asking a few questions, which in no way helped his case.

After a recess President Olti reopened the court at two-thirty in the afternoon. He turned to the Cardinal and asked him whether he had written the note disavowing any confession that he might make. The Cardinal answered in the affirmative. To further questions he answered that he had written it before his arrest, in November, to be delivered in case he should be arrested. Conforming to the statements he had made in his letter to the Minister of Justice that had been read in court the previous day, he now retracted this note.

Then the witnesses were paraded, trembling men and women who had been in the hands of the secret police for weeks. Their demeanor was as strange as that of the defendants who had preceded them.

To the observer they all seemed alike, whether old or young, whether lean or fat; whether basically sedate or temperamental. They all spoke practically in the same tone of voice, used practically the same set of words, the same grammar, the same syntax. The entire structure of thought of each individual seemed to have been adjusted to one governing formula.

That Friday night, as the testimony ended, the onlooker could not help wondering why none of the defendants for even a split second betrayed the diabolic scheme; why none of them had the thought of acting in self-preservation; why none of them could muster the mental strength to cry out to the world the shame that had befallen them. None of them could.

These tortured defendants were not conscious of the fact that they had anything to defend. They had been divested of their free will —of their self-confidence, of their self-determination, of their pride and dignity and, above all, their self-control.

The contradiction between the personality of the Cardinal before his arrest and his appearance at the trial is the textbook example of how ruthlessness combined with the achievements of modern science has been able to reduce the personality, the soul, to complete disintegration; and that it is possible, from such a state, to reintegrate within the familiar frame—but with a strange mind—a new personality in accordance with satanic designs.

On Saturday morning court opened late. A physician had been called to examine Prince Eszterházy. After an hour's delay, the Prosecutor rose at ten o'clock and began to speak.

PROSECUTOR: There is no doubt that those who followed the trial and listened to the evidence of the accusation and the defense could see that the rules of criminal procedure were carefully observed in the course of the trial, and that the accused and their defense counsels were allowed to make their pleas in perfect freedom.

Is there anyone who, seeing the defendants, would dare maintain that they were intimidated, harassed, or influenced in any way? Is there anyone who would dare to say that we did not grant perfectly free access to the defendants, to the documentary evidence, and who would dare to state that the defendants were not allowed to speak in utter freedom and frankness on the subject of the letters and documents produced? . . .

In order to attain their purpose, the defendant and his accomplices got into touch with imperialist politicians who hate popular democracies, with certain officials and agents of the United States. They wanted to make them believe that the Hungarian people would welcome the outbreak of a new war. They were deliberately scheming with the objective of making the imperialists of the United States start a war against our country. . . .

Anyone knowing the evidence produced here could not presume that in performing his deeds Joseph Mindszenty was guided by the idea of defending religion. There is no need for defending religion in the Hungarian people's democracy, for the simple reason that nobody wants to harm it. Should anyone wish to do so, it would be, in the first place, the Hungarian people's democracy, its organs, and, not last, the Prosecutor who would stand up in its defense. . . .

[Then the prosecutor reviewed the offenses supposedly committed by the Cardinal's codefendants. Justin Baranyai worked out and planned the details of the organization, and outlined the manner in which power would be taken over.

[The prosecutor asserted that Andrew Zakár's activities were connected with those of Mindszenty; that he was Mindszenty's interpreter at his conferences with foreign officials, transmitted Mindszenty's instructions, and executed Mindszenty's orders in hiding the archives, and that he buried the metal case later seized as part of the evidence;

[That Paul Eszterházy wished to smuggle his fortune out of the country, and at the same time wished to support the plot which was headed by Joseph Mindszenty and which aimed at the restoration of the Hapsburgs;

[That Paul Eszterházy's foreign-currency offenses had the purpose, by their very nature, of giving substantial financial support to the plot which aimed at overthrowing the democratic republic and, after the end of the expected third world war, placing the Hapsburgs on the throne;

[That Nicholas Nagy sent out information to Mihalovics, who had fled abroad, through the cooperation of Béla Ispánky and Leslie Tóth.]

PROSECUTOR (*concluding*): I ask the People's Court to declare Joseph Mindszenty and his associates guilty as charged. The irrefutable papers, letters, and documents before the Court, the authenticity of which the defendants did not even attempt to deny, are sufficient in themselves to establish the facts.

The open trial by the honorable People's Court, the whole verdict, should be a historic confirmation of the truth that Joseph Mindszenty and his accomplices have committed treason as part of the imperialist plan which endeavors to permeate the whole world and in which the destruction of the liberty of the Hungarian people would have been only a small episode.

The People's Court should present the truth to the Hungarian people and to everybody in search of truth all over the world. The correspondents sitting here should write the truth. They have seen with their own eyes that in this trial the People's Court, on the basis of democratic laws, brings in a verdict in fullest compliance with legal criminal proceedings. Let this verdict be a proof that the Hungarian people can protect the liberty it has received. Let this verdict brand everything that the defendants have committed; let the verdict be a hard and uncompromising defense of the cause of the people. Let it be to the service of all who are oppressed in the fight against tyranny, exploitation, and special privilege. Let the verdict proclaim the brotherhood of the nations, the solidarity of the forces fighting for freedom, the indivisibility of world peace.

Then, at the direction of the Court, the Counsel for the Defense rose and spoke. (The following are excerpts from the official translation.)

DEFENSE COUNSEL: Esteemed People's Court, Honorable President! First of all, I should like to declare that I am here as an attorney selected by the defendant, a circumstance which testifies to the fact that the defendants, according to law, have been free to defend themselves. In this I completely share the view taken by the Prosecutor.

My defendant, as the Prosecutor has also stated, has admitted committing offenses outlined in the indictment. He has declared here, as befits a man, as especially befits his dignity in the Church, that he is repentant for what he has done that has clashed with the laws of the state, and he has proclaimed that he is infinitely sorry for what has happened. . . .

My defendant, in his dignity as Primate, lived, one might say, in an ivory tower, and he was not aware of the inevitable path of progress in history. . . .

Prince Primate Mindszenty was not aware of the progress of the people's democracy, the immense reconstruction accomplished by the working people of the country, the clearing up of the ruins of the last war brought about by fascism.

Prince Primate Joseph Mindszenty held the conviction that the secularization of the schools might subject the Catholic Church and the principles of the Catholic faith to grave danger. This was my defendant's most serious error. . . .

As you have seen during the trial, he has answered all questions precisely, and when he could not answer, he said so. . . .

As the highly esteemed Prosecutor has mentioned already, Mindszenty, Prince Primate of Hungary, has been tried only for criminal deeds, with reference to religious questions avoided. I think this was a correct stand, and therefore I wish to express the appreciation of the Defense to the Prosecution for accusing the Prince Primate only of deeds which have nothing to do with his priestly functions. But it is difficult to draw a line here. . . .

In Hungary the Church is particularly responsible for peace, but there can only be peace if the Church and the people's democracy are able to understand each other.

In conclusion I wish to state that my task was a hard one, but I tried to fulfill it in spite of my advanced age and to the full strength of my honor and integrity as a lawyer in the interest of my client, to help him in his situation after having pleaded guilty. I therefore request the esteemed People's Court to pass a wise judgment, for the esteemed Prosecutor is correct in stating that this trial, and the persons who have been involved in it, will be remembered in world history; and they may be called to account, after thousands of years, for the sentences passed here.

I appeal to you to pass an adequately lenient judgment in conjunction with your best conscience and wisdom.

These were the words spoken in defense of the Cardinal.

In the late afternoon, after several recesses, the Cardinal was called upon to speak on his own behalf. The circle had to be completed, the world convinced that Joseph, Cardinal Mindszenty "knew" what was happening, and was "pleading."

He delivered his words in a monotone, like a well learned but not understood lesson. Not an iota was left of the great preacher in the man who now stepped to the microphone.

PRESIDENT: Joseph Mindszenty! You wish to avail yourself of the opportunity to make a final plea!

CARDINAL: I do.

PRESIDENT: Will you stand here?

CARDINAL (*with a wavering voice*): Honorable People's Court! Availing himself of the right to make a final statement, a man is facing the Hungarian People's Court, the bearer of a high office, burdened with accusations. It took half a century to make me what I am, by a strict, determined education and principles. This education, these basic principles are built into a man's life as firmly as rails are built on the ground. These rails carry you along the track, and this accounts for many things. Basic principles built like rails into a man's life must be accepted for what they are.

We, and that includes myself, have been facing the police authorities and the Court for forty days. They question, and I answer. Questions and answer do not merely concern the interrogators, but all the while you are replying to your own soul.

In the answers I give to myself, alongside the answers I give the Court, I can see that I never abandoned good intentions throughout my life, and for this I am thankful to God.

I never meant to violate the laws of the country. If, for reasons of environment or for reasons beyond me, this occurred on one or two occasions, I confessed to it here without embellishing the facts. I regretted it and still regret it, and I think that in honest loyalty to the basic principles referred to above, I might take a different stand in certain matters if I were again in a similar situation.

Secondly, I may state that, thank God, according to my conscience I have never been and am not now an enemy of the Hungarian people. I have never had, have not now, any trouble with the Hungarian working classes, with the Hungarian farmers, to which class I and my family belong. I do not want to take from any class of society the rights due them. But, after the breakdown which followed the Second World War, my role was a difficult, historic role: to proclaim the all-embracing light and love of the Gospel.

Permit me to make a light deviation here, but what I wish to say logically belongs here. We have repeatedly spoken about the land reform in relation to the Hungarian Catholic Church. Therefore I feel it is my duty to make a statement in parenthesis—a statement important enough to override the parenthesis. In its circular letter of May, 1945, the Bench of Bishops sent their blessing to those who had obtained land. Later, they issued statements at home and abroad, on four occasions, to the effect that the Church has not claimed and does not claim the restitution of the land that had been given to deserving, hard-working simple people who are attached to the Hungarian soil. This attitude of the Bench of Bishops was never disapproved by the Vatican.

To continue with my final plea: I thank God also that, having strictly searched my mind, I cannot find myself guilty of being an enemy of peace. When the time came for the Church to make peace with the state, I was not against peace; I merely strictly outlined the preconditions therefor, and I sincerely meant that if we make peace, it should be a permanent one.

My attitude was made manifest in my letter addressed to the Minister of Justice on January 29, which the President of the Court read at the opening of my trial. I do not need to quote any part of it; it is still fresh in your memory.

As concerns my unintentional and unpremeditated violation of certain laws of the state, I confessed and admitted whatever had happened. I also offered to give material compensation. And I mean it.

This morning, the following prayer came to my lips: "Da pacem Domine, in diebus nostris, in diebus istis!" (Lord, give us peace in our time!) Not in the near or distant future, this ancient prayer beseeches, but, strangely enough, in our time.

And this peace I have asked for my Church, the love of which I brought with me here. This peace I asked for the Hungarian state, to which I have proved my obedience. This peace I ask also for my soul.

May the Lord of Heavens bestow upon the People's Court wisdom to pass such judgment as may be the token of the hope for a happy solution of our involvements both at home and abroad.

The pleas of the codefendants followed, Andrew Zakár saying: "I am sorry that in the course of my activities I acted counter to the laws of the Hungarian Republic. I also want to ask forgiveness of all those to whom I caused loss or pain, because of my activities. . . ."

Béla Ispánky stated: "I accept responsibility and shall willingly subject myself to the sanctions of the law. Your Honor, President of the Court! Honorable People's Court! Being a Hungarian, it is very hard for me to plead for mercy, to ask clemency. All I ask for is a fair judgment."

Justin Baranyai stated that although he wished to clear himself of the charges, he did not deny the facts.

Leslie Tóth made reference to his advanced age, his family status, and his infirmity.

Prince Eszterházy and Nicholas Nagy made no final plea.

On Saturday evening at eight-thirty the session of the People's Court adjourned. The Cardinal was led back to his prison cell to await the verdict.

*   *   *

At the very time President Olti adjourned court the government radio station began to transmit the radio transcript of the trial.

Cut to fit the plan to present the Cardinal in the role of an arch-criminal, it was saturated with propaganda commentary. The very introduction left no doubt that the broadcast was designed to convince the listener that the Cardinal was guilty of outrageous crimes not only against the state, the nation, and the people, but even against humanity. According to the Communist propaganda rule, the "people themselves" should pass sentence in advance of the verdict of the court; "popular demand" should be created for the "heaviest punishment of criminals."

Wherever Communist units operated, mass assemblies were staged. Everyone was ordered to attend the meetings to listen to the broadcasts.

Special "speaker kits" had been distributed throughout the country by the central office of the Communist Party; folders instructing the speakers just what to say before and after the broadcast, with slogans and outcries for a body of "representatives of popular indignation"—slogans not only against the Cardinal, but slandering the Pope, the Vatican, and the American Government. Also included were prepared forms of protest telegrams, to be sent in the name of the assembly to various official bodies and persons, including the president of the republic and the president of the court, in which it was suggested that the criminals who had "conspired against the security of the common man" be done away with.

Provisions had been made for all who for one reason or another could not attend the meetings; the broadcast and the meetings were repeated on Sunday at four in the afternoon.

The tenor of the meetings was the same everywhere! No spiritual power was permitted to block the progress of the people's democracy. Any priest, any dignitary, any bishop who might resist would find himself in the Cardinal's predicament.

It was obvious that these threats were intended to frighten the local clergy and the steadfast flock. The suggestion was obvious: "See, we do not even stop before the scarlet of the Cardinal. You small fry, behave!"

Following these meetings the zealous Communist Party functionaries spread themselves through the country, visiting the smaller communities where meetings could not be organized, and gathering people wherever they could find an audience.

But the government and the Communists found one reaction they had never expected.

The city people argued that, even if all was true that had been said in court, they could see no crime in it. Nothing had been proved. The Cardinal had not been permitted to call any witness of his own; he had not been given the opportunity to defend himself; he was being crucified because he had defended the interests of the common man, because he had stood in the way of the Communists, because he had fought the Antichrist.

Some went even further. The simple people said: "That was not our Cardinal who spoke at the trial; we have heard his voice over the radio so many times—we know it. The Communists put an actor into court to look and behave like the Primate. They have killed the Cardinal!" In spite of all the proof the Communists produced, that was their belief.

All churches were overflowing, and the faithful knelt in the streets; but the sermons of that Sunday bore no fighting words. One single thought filled the minds and hearts of all: the fate of Joseph, the Cardinal.

Never were there more candles lit in front of the altars. Never were there more fervent prayers said for the soul of a man.

*   *   *

On Tuesday morning the 8th of February, President William Olti announced the verdict, in the name of the Republic of Hungary: "Joseph Mindszenty, the first accused, is sentenced herewith . . . to accumulative penalty of: penal servitude for life as main penalty, to ten years' loss of office and ten years' suspension of political rights; further, to the confiscation of all his property as supplementary punishment."

Of the codefendants, Dr. Justin Baranyai received a sentence of fifteen years' penal servitude; Dr. Andrew Zakár, six years' penal servitude; Prince Eszterházy, fifteen years' penal servitude; Nicholas Nagy, three years' penal servitude; Béla Ispánky, penal servitude for life; Leslie Tóth, ten years' penal servitude. All codefendants were also sentenced to loss of office, ten years' suspension of political rights, and confiscation of all real property as supplementary penalty.

The Prosecutor and the Defense announced that an appeal would be made.

The President addressed the Cardinal:

"You, too, want to appeal, don't you? . . ."

"Yes . . ." answered the Cardinal.

"You do want to appeal to the Supreme Council of the People's Courts. . . ?"

"Yes . . ." came the hardly audible answer.

These were the last words heard from a man who had known no fear.

It was his voice, but the words were not his own; they expressed thoughts implanted by strangers, the men who had destroyed his soul.

A fortnight after the Cardinal's trial ended, Christine and Elizabeth succeeded in passing over the border into Austria. Walking by day, hiding at night in the mountains or forests and occasionally finding food and shelter with friendly God-fearing peasants they passed through the territory still occupied by the Russians. With bleeding feet and aching bodies, ragged and penniless, they reached sanctuary at Salzburg in the American Zone of Austria.

Their feet would heal, the pain in their bodies would pass, but their hearts would continue to ache.

They had left, like so many thousands before them, seeking peace and tranquillity to heal their ever wounded souls.

They had left when they saw their spiritual leader, the great shepherd, imprisoned; the last fearless spokesman of their rights and freedoms silenced. With him their last hope vanished. They had left because they were unable to live in constant fear and trembling; because they did not want to become slaves to the state and prey to terror. Wise old Barbara, Christine's mother, had told them to go.

Like the untold thousands before them and after, they had taken to the road in search of freedom from fear on foreign soil.

They left behind them Erdöd, the village, with its tiny church and the throng of faithful. They left behind them a once happy land, full of light and sunshine, now living in dark shadows of a crimson cloud. They left behind them a subjugated, terrorized nation—but a nation of brave men ready to defend their heritage with their last drop of blood; a nation of men imbued with the spirit of resistance, ready to rise when the day should dawn, to join hands with other brave men, to establish a world in which all the peoples could enjoy in freedom the fruitfulness of Mother Earth.

In the shadow of the ancient walls of the Mönchsberg two women kneel in prayer—praying, like so many men and women all over the world, for the soul of Joseph, the true Shepherd; for Joseph the Cardinal, Prince Primate of the Hungarian lands.

✠

BOOK III

✛

NO FEAR BUT COURAGE

Excerpts from His Notes, Letters, Addresses, and Sermons

THE CARDINAL'S PAPERS

ROME AND MY COUNTRY

(From the first message of the Cardinal upon becoming Primate of Hungary; spoken at the basilica of Esztergom, October 7, 1945.)

As your most graciously designated new shepherd, I shall, first of all, travel in spirit to Rome, to the Father of the Church, Pope Pius XII, who reigns in glory even though in suffering. At his feet our tortured, faithful Hungarian souls come to rest.

The world did not understand the efforts toward peace made by our Holy Father in fulfillment of his apostolic mission. Not only did the world not understand, but it took affront at the words of peace he spoke. Today, from the ruins of a shattered world, humanity, with repentance and hope, turns eyes heavy with weariness toward the Rock of St. Peter. Only the eternal truth enunciated there can heal the mortal wounds humanity and the nation suffered on the road to Jericho. At a time when mankind, the world over, is battling under the banner of the Reign of Falsehood, it is comforting to turn to faith and to know that there is a Power on earth—and the gates of hell shall not prevail against it.

I descend in spirit to the grave of Archbishop Justin, who, while he lived, showed the way, defended the holy truth, protected man, and advised meditation. Because of the blindness of a few and the paralyzing outrage perpetrated against many, we did not listen to him. His was the voice of one crying in the wilderness, and when the fruits were ripe, following the great collapse, he fell himself. I place over his grave the banner of the true Crusaders and the branch of palm of the awakening nation, as he was indeed *Homo Dei, Homo Patriae, Homo Ecclesiae.*

I come to you, brethren, from the ageless rock and the grave of yesterday to bring you in this sad year of peacelessness the message of the Eternal Shepherd: "Peace be to you."

At this point I ask myself the question, as did St. Bernard in the quiet of the monastery: Whence did you come? I shall now speak the answer.

According to the incomplete data of history, I came as the seventy-ninth shepherd from the City of Queens to the City of Kings. Martyrius led the way. I was preceded by Archbishop Robert, who lashed out even against the sinful leaders of the country with the lightning whip of the Church. There was also Francis Forgách, the standard-bearer of the renaissance of Catholicism, the great fighter of worthy causes who took to arms himself to defend the fort of Nyitra. I can see the immensly rich George Széchenyi arrive here at the age of ninety-three. He was the miracle man of good deeds; using his ecclesiastic and family fortune, he became the financial supporter of the war of liberation. I can also see Count Emery Eszterházy, who helped the brilliant triumph of the constitution by bringing about the Pragmatic Sanction which gave our weakened nation an invigorating respite of two hundred years, leading it to the marvelous glory of the Millennium. I think with reverence of that other Archbishop, Joseph Kopácsy, who, more than a century ago, with great constructive zeal, built this shrine of our nation upon the ruins of the past, making it possible for us to pray, here, for a better national future.

I do not come to you with the severity of Archbishop Robert; I wish to be your father; I wish to be a father even to those prodigal sons who have let themselves be led astray by the great temptations rising out of hardship.

I cannot, as yet, enter the ranks of the defenders of the constitution, since we now live in a constitutional whirlpool in which all the solid threads and the more delicate arteries in the continuity of the law seem to have been broken.

We are still missing more than one of the nation's constitutional elements, but the country's Primate has already occupied the place vacated by the ancestors. If, with the end of our misfortune, the wisdom of this nation will build a bridge across this whirlpool, then, as Pontifex, as bridgebuilder, and, on the basis of a nine-hundred-year-old tradition, the premier banner-bearer of the country, your Archbishop, the Primate of this land, will take part in the rehabilitation and promotion of your country's constitutional life.

I do not come to you with the immense wealth of a Széchenyi or a Kopácsy, however useful such wealth would be to the Hungarian nation, more destitute and more vanquished than in the time of the Turks. This I say without shedding undue tears over worldly goods, but without condoning, either, what was done without legal rounds. The purpose of these goods was not a worldly one; they were meant to provide comfort and relief and service to the souls in need. . . . These souls, therefore, were the ones to suffer most by the losses, they and important ecclesiastic and cultural programs. In other times the Church had been always able to satisfy generously the inborn needs of the Hungarian people; this is eloquently confirmed by the messages of gratitude engraved upon the stones of history and by the wonderful roll call of the aforementioned ancestors.

Were all the greatness of this roll inherent in one of the descendants, as it is not in this year of 1945, even this would be too little, oh, much too little!

There is before us today a blind, alarming, whirling abyss; the bleeding country, Hungary, is gasping for breath in the greatest moral, constitutional, and economic torrent of its history. Our psalm is the De Profundis, our prayer the Miserere, our prophet the lamenting Jeremiah, our world the Apocalypse. We sit by the waters of Babylon, and they want to teach us alien songs on harp strings which have broken.

The greatest disaster is not that the war burned the king's house and the houses of the people; that the land is stripped of man and cattle; that our gathered grapes are being ravaged, and our garden land is all bereft of joy and gladness. The greatest disaster is reflected in the report of the civilian medical staff of our helpless Capital city: more than 50 per cent of the dysentery cases reported this summer were, because of malnutrition, mortal to infants and the aged. Infant mortality and pulmonary diseases have doubled since before the war.

The bugle has not yet sounded in this land to lament the passing of the country. We seek in vain and do not find the place where the Hungarian hides his sorrow, but the gypsy's fiddle has struck its note of carousing gaiety. Indeed, in this year of 1945 the music gives the lie to the truth on the soil of Hungary, because it overlooks the unforgettable truth: the Hungarian pauper beggary, the moans of the slaves dispersed over the continents, the outer and the inner prisons, the homeless, dejected Hungarians and those who no longer soak with tears their headrest of snow, but the last shreds of rags that cover their shattered bodies.

A frivolous, pleasure-seeking, entirely new type of educational method which is foreign to our hearts and minds has been innovated in our country.

Sad is the youth which can celebrate with dance and song the death watch of its land. The blood of these young people, their tongue, even their names might be Hungarian, but there are oceans between the unhappy land and the ones who are rejoicing; it is in the valley of blood and tears, it is over sighs and ruins that those who do not know what they are doing rejoice and celebrate.

Instead of the shores we lost from sight, now, more than ever, we must keep a spiritual watch over our souls. Wherever the law of nature and the law laid down by men falter in the hearts of the people, deeply felt faith is as essential as is the factor that will dam the loosened mores of society.

For over a quarter of a century I have exercised spiritual care. I am striving to be a good shepherd; should it become necessary, I would lay down my life for my sheep, for my Church, for my Country.

My dear brethren! For five hundred years this nation was a glorious nation; for two centuries it was a struggling, bleeding people; and this twentieth century has again transformed our world into a valley of blood and sorrow.

Let us now be a nation of prayer! If we can learn anew how to pray, we shall have the source whence to draw strength and hope. I too place confi   in the prayer crusade of the millions and in the rosary o'   ther, which I am holding onto more securely than   ose your confidence. Let us hold fast to our '   ig. Thus we shall have strength for the strv

With tl   the Almighty and our Mother Mary I shall b   of my people. I am knocking at the door o   the guardian of your souls, and instead of ej   ll communicate the eternal truth to my peo'   on. I am delicately awakening the conse- cr   r land, without which individuals might live
h   .

          ountry, you shall be the guiding stars and goals
          ness shall come to me if we can spend our lives
          s thought, if these two virtues will rejuvenate the
col   Iungarian soil and will guide us safely across to the happy ha.   of eternal life.

✠

WHITHER, YOUNG PEOPLE?

(From an address delivered at an open-air meeting of the youth of Budapest, October 14, 1945.)

During the last decade of the oppression, Cardinal Faulhaber asked the mothers of Munich to bring their young children to the cathedral so that they might be blessed by him. Six thousand mothers came, bearing in their arms six thousand budding lives babbling with charm, and, like the Savior, the stern shepherd gave his blessing to the favorites of the Lord.

I too look over a human forest; before my eyes is a forest of mothers, fathers, guardians, educators, and children. The youth which now stands before me here has already left behind it the carefree bliss of childhood; it already senses the gathering storm of reality. This youth is the Maylike spring of life, the pride of the mothers and fathers, the deeply felt responsibility of the educators and the anxiously guarded hope of Church and country.

You came to greet your shepherd whom the Holy Father sent to you. Your shepherd is greatly pleased by your welcome and your greetings, but he is especially pleased by the demonstration of faith now performed before so many of us by the youth of the city and of the provinces, by young men and women, intellectuals and workers.

I welcome you too with warmly felt words of greeting, both you, young people of the Capital city, and you, young men and women of the land. I feel like the farmer who, with the advent of spring, goes forth to the fields and surveys with loving eyes the swaying golden crop; or like the pearl fisher who sinks his eyes and thoughts into the depth of the seas—I feel like them, indeed, when I contemplate those of my dear children who form here, before me, a human forest, or those who, the country over, are united in the name of the two inspiring thoughts: Church and country.

Welcome to you, youth of our land, promise-bringing spring on our darkening horizon!

But I can hear a question ringing as an echo of your greeting: "Whither shall we turn?"

Whither, indeed, young people of Hungary?

Into dereliction? Into destruction? Oh, no! *Vae soli—gloria multis*. Woe to the one who stands by himself! The glory of victory belongs to those who strive to unite under the auspices of heavenly love.

Or should we, as a whole, fuse with those masses who cannot be said to have, or not to have, any religion? That would be neither fowl nor fish, neither warm nor cold; that would not correspond to our ideological conceptions. The Lord Jesus himself despises this middle-of-the-road attitude. He would more easily tolerate unvarnished coldness. Besides, the status of one who cannot be said to have some religion or to have no religion does not exist in reality. No sooner have I pronounced the word "nonreligious," than the barometer of my heart points to, and stops at, the concept "godlessness."

Or should we enter the ranks of those who swear that they will cleanly sweep out the past? Wield slowly that nimble broom! It would do a better job if applied to trash and corruption.

We shall not let the sacred authority of the mother and the father be swept from the consciousness of future generations. Times might be hard on us, but in our hearts still sings the ancient folk song: "I also had a mother who raised me with great hardship."

The most cherished image of our past is that of our mother; we might approach it with reverence but certainly not with a broom! We shall not let them sweep out the doctrines and the spirit of our teachers; these we need as guides for the future. That broom shall also prove to be too weak for the two stone tablets of the Ten Commandments; and we shall not let anyone wield a broom against our two-thousand-year-old mother, the Church, or against our one-thousand-year-old mother, our Hungarian nation.

We live surrounded by the common national misfortune that cannot ever be forgotten by any of us; we live surrounded by the Hungarian pauper beggary, by the moans of the slaves of the continents, by the Hungarian graveyards that stretch over miles and miles of land, by the outer and inner prisons, by the homeless exiles, by the endless throngs of mourning mothers and widows.

Well, then, where, where should you go, youth of our land?

Once the Savior enunciated such hard truths to his audience that even his intimate friends tried to take to the road. Whereupon He turned to his disciples: So you would leave me too? It was the Apostle Peter who answered: My Lord, where would we go? You alone behold the Word of eternal life!

That is where your place is, too, Hungarian youth! With the Word of eternal life. Was there ever anyone setting foot on this earth who alone could say of himself, I am the way, and the truth, and the life, and whoever follows me does not step into darkness?

Have faith! The One you are following has convinced the world! The abyss of hatred might be frightening, but I believe in the ultimate victory of Love! And I declare with deep belief that our ideal is a Hungary built on religion and morality, a nation supported by love of country, a land whose sons and daughters are faithful and true Hungarians!

✝

NEW YEAR'S EVE, 1945

(From the notes of the Cardinal: excerpts from a broadcast delivered over the Hungarian radio December 31, 1945.)

On the last night of the year, at thanksgiving Mass, in thousands of churches, hundreds of thousands give voice to the ancient prayer which moves us anew: "O Lord, Almighty Creator of all things existing, in a few seconds another year will have passed. It will be gone with all its hardships and all its joys."

The hardships in 1945 were endless, and there was little joy indeed. The western part of our country, the Dunántul, also became the path of armies. It became, this year, a world of blood and tears. There is still no statistical data available on the exact number of those who were buried in graves, of those who were deported and became homeless, of those taken prisoner, of the refugees and slaves all over the land; but we know that hundreds of thousands are destitute and there is not one family which could watch in unbroken unity the last sunset of the year. At the meager table of each family there are empty places; on each heart, burning scars. The magnitude of destruction is unimaginable. The tragic facts of destruction in our Capital city, known the world over for its beauty, are already compiled. In 1945 its population decreased by 332,163 souls; there live in Budapest 28.5 per cent less people than in 1941. Of the buildings, 13,538 were completely destroyed, 18,785 houses were badly damaged but can be rebuilt, and 47,322 are damaged but can still be used. Among the destroyed buildings and monuments, the most outstanding was the historically, artistically, and internationally renowned castle of Buda. During the month of November, when the situation turned again for the worse, there were 822 births and 2,188 deaths in Budapest. The tragic, all-effacing suicides are becoming ever more frequent. In all cases of disease, the lack of calories and vitamins in the food supplies plays a major and constantly increasing part. Aside from the cold, the shortages are responsible for the many cases of chilblain. The shortage of food and its poor quality have already begun to contribute to the cause of death.

Before the war the population of the city had a daily supply of 350,000 liters of milk; today it only receives 30,000 liters daily, or 8.5 per cent of the old supply. Because of the reduced quantity and poor quality of the food supplies, public health in the Capital is seriously endangered. Operating and delivery rooms, wards and nurseries of the hospitals are unheated. Our hearts ache for the poor Hungarian life buds, the poor Hungarian mothers!

It has also become known that the Holy Apostolic Crown has been taken to foreign land; the end of the war tore the limbs of the nation from its already crippled body.

To add to the balance of hardships, there are also the great masses of the population who are being driven like cattle from the four corners of the land into regions unknown; there are, too, the prisoners of war, the near and distant prisons, the captives of the internment camps, the heatless, empty homesteads, the empty schools, the bomb-mutilated churches, the ravaged graveyards, the lifeless, empty pastures.

> My heart aches and my eyes fill with tears
> When I think of the sad fate of Hungary.

We would sin against God's Providence and against the truth if we omitted to mention the joy inherent in this tragic year. Man can no more live without joy than without sunshine. The hand that tries you, lifts you, too.

What were our joys?

That we remained in our land. Despite the fear-inspiring, tempting slogans we did not leave our country but made the famous words of the poet come true: "Here you will live and die!" Had we left, today we would have no homes; we would live as beggars in foreign lands, as do so many millions. The unheated and empty home is still better than cold and foreign regions. The hero of Kalevala spoke the truth when he said:

Far better tastes at home
Clear water from my wooden shoes
Than would in foreign land
Pure honey from golden goblets.

Wherever we would have gone after leaving our homes, our lot would not have been pure honey, either.

The sacred relic of St. Stephen's Holy Right Hand was returned to us from exile. This brought, in our sorrow, the first real joy to our religious and national life. This Hand, which showed us the way for over a thousand years, is home again; it is light in the darkness; it shows again the right path, if only the nation will heed its summons.

Oh, if the strength given by religion had not been present in the heart of our people, this blessed land would have become the realm of madmen and of candidates for suicide!

On this last night of the year, each soul has to account for its sins and for the good it failed to do. I should like to unite the entire nation for a common test of its conscience.

Since the year 1945 was one lived and formed by men, it was not, of course, a year without sin and crimes against the nation. We saw the glorious birth of human rights; but what is left of the freedom from want, of the freedom from fear? What have we done to reduce the fear and misery in this country and to increase the means by which to combat them? What did we do to counteract the freedom-restricting measures and what did we do to further the freedom of the individual, the freedom of speech, the freedom of the press? What did we do to develop our sense of responsibility? How many of the Ten Commandments did we apply to God, to our fellow man and to his physical and material well-being? How much effort did we make on behalf of the realm of justice and of peace? To what extent did we fight our ego and help the reign of the common good? To what extent did we dam the foaming lava of hatred and vengeance and to what extent did we feed the feeble stream of brotherly love and humane understanding?

Did we not, according to St. Paul, spend our days living in malice and envy, hateful and hating one another? Did we want to build with our fists, heal with hearts glowing with hatred? Did we not gloat over the crimes we reproached in others? To what extent did we lend an ear to the swelling tide of sighs reaching us from the four cardinal points of the land? How deeply were we afflicted by the plight of the Hungarian infants, by the wilted Hungarian youth, by the absence of our men, by the untold agony of the mothers, by the splitting up of so many families? How much did we care about the father being deported or captive in the West or in the East, about the enslaved mother, about the abandoned children who shifted from doorstep to doorstep? There is no greater ambition today in this unhappy land than the one expressed by the words of the poet: "Each human cry should find its answer!"

When 1946 brings us new crosses and new sufferings, at the horizon, where the earth and sky meet, there will rise a Cross, traced in capital letters, which will be our haven, our salvation, our glorious banner. This Cross brings us the message: Men of Hungary, fight and hope with trust.

Salute them that love us in the faith. The grace of God be with you all.

✠

PENITENCE

(From an address on the lessons of the past, delivered in the Church of the Dominican Brothers in Budapest.)

Today in the churches of little Hungary, hundreds of thousands and millions celebrate the feast of our flower, St. Margaret of Hungary, pearl of our past. We have also assembled here in the church of that venerable order of Dominicans, which created this gem out of Hungarian blood and sufferings.

My imagination carries me away from here to places which she made holy. To the city of Trau, over which I flew en route to Rome. I was moved, thinking of the vows made by the distressed royal family. To Veszprém, where, within the walls of the Convent of St. Catherine, which lie in ruins now, the little girl of not quite four started on her way toward the heights of the religious life. To the ruins of the Isle of Hares, on which she lived most of the eighteen years of her short life.

We all fly from the present to the past of seven hundred years ago. We see that nothing is new under the sun, not even the sufferings of Hungary; and we fervently pray: Just as then a pearl was created out of blood and tears, so may now the visitations of the present, by the grace of God, turn into pearls of salvation.

I am going to recall to you briefly the year 1241, the gloomy year of storms, terrifying events, sins, and expiation. Mohi was the first large cemetery of Hungarian Catholics. On the road to the cemetery, while Tatars rushed toward the Carpathian passes, throughout the whole country Carnival was being celebrated. Virtue was diminishing, bodily desires were strong, the eyes were covetous, life was shallow. People adorned themselves with jewelry; man craved luxuries, joys. There were clashes between rich and poor, noble and commoner, Hungarian and Kuman. The Tatar danger was minimized and many rejoiced over the king's defeat. Lent came, but the nation was not moved by the sufferings of Jesus, by his sacrifices. "Thou hast not known the time of thy visitation." And with the passing of Lent, fifty thousand Hungarians and a hundred thousand heathens faced each other. The latter were enraged because the Hungarians had killed their emissaries instead of guarding their Eastern frontiers. Over mountains of dead the East marched toward the West.

After an initial success at Mohi, on that portentous April night the Hungarians found themselves comfortable camps. Only Archbishop Ugrin and Prince Coloman stood guard.

Amid a rain of spears, stones, and flames the dawn rose, and the rays of the rising sun shone on a large cemetery. On the ground lay dead half of the army, among them the head of the ever valiant Church, the archbishops of Esztergom and Kalocsa, three other bishops, abbots, canons, templars, the palatine himself, the chief justice, and other dignitaries.

The land became prey to the Tatars. Swamps, fire, swords took their toll. Aged people, men, women, children, boys and girls died like lambs in the holocaust.

It is strange that this people who before had not sought churches and monasteries now had trust in them; but they were mistaken in the times and in the enemy.

In the Cathedral of Várad thousands perished in the flames. In the churches of Várad countless women fell victims to the lust of the Orient. Ten thousand crowded the quarters of the Dominicans in Pest. Had they only come in such numbers during Lent, God could have been more merciful, the Tatars less cruel, for religious people can more easily help themselves and, likewise, are more easily helped by God. But it was too late: they were mistaken about the times. Old Father Paul at the altar and all ten thousand of the faithful were killed. They were united in death. If only they had been united before, in the Christian spirit!

If a Christian indulges in sin without afterward bending his head under the ashes of penance, the scourge of God is felt: the Tatar carnival with a dance of death. Wherever the Tatars went, corpses paved their way. In Várad, as Master Roger wrote in his chronicle, they burned homes, robbed people, raped women until they were compelled to flee by the stench of burning corpses.

They left. Their last act was to raid the places where Hungarians had found refuge; at the frontiers of the land they killed some of their prisoners and drove the rest along into slavery.

In their wake remained ruins, bare walls, uncultivated land. For days the wanderer could see few human beings, only wild beasts, adventurers, robbers, and petty thieves, in this cemeterylike land.

They left and famine came. Happy were those who could sate their hunger with the meat of dogs or cats, bread made of powdered tree roots or wild berries.

And somewhere, in the depth of swamps and forests, the Hungarian prayer issued forth from heart to heart, from marrow to marrow:

"Merciful God! If after this hell on earth you let us just once more lead a Christian life, enjoy our home as promised by the two stone tablets, we would understand that compared to human beings, your yoke is sweet, your burden light."

Did this prayer resound in the desert? As far as the West was concerned, yes.

The prayer flew southward too, far away from the land of horrors; it flew to Trau, where the fleeing king of Hungary, the queen, and eight children found refuge. I was mistaken about the number of their children: the ninth was already growing beneath the queen's heart. The queen cried, prayed, and hardly ever smiled. And now in her distress, in her homelessness, amid noise caused by Tatar arms persecuting them, she vowed the pearl of her womb to God.

That was her sacrifice for you and me. The Hungarian blood flowing on dirty roads became sacred through this new life which had been conceived in a pure home so that it would never again anger the Creator and Lord of the Ten Commandments against our nation. On the firmament of our nation, she would be the rainbow of a flood of blood and tears, St. Margaret, the holy Joan of Arc of Hungary.

The Tatars had reached the fortress of Trau and wanted the royal family. It seemed as if they might achieve their aim. The opposite happened. The city refused to extradite the king, who had been disliked because of his strictness in his own country. An attack by the Tatars was expected. It did not materialize, however; they left quietly and the king remained. We honor him as the second founder of this country. His daughter was born and grew up and became like a lightning rod and expiation in time of wrath.

The Tatars left Hungary after one frightful year. They did not depart with a light heart. Never had they had such a good life, so much liberty in their native Karakorum, where—living by the rules of Genghis Khan—they never washed or changed their clothes. They left because the khan died and the selfish interests of the powerful generals proved to have more weight than the selfish little interests of the masses. The khan might have lived on, but God ordained otherwise; and we believe the great vow of Trau was also instrumental in bringing on his end.

His demise was the beginning of Hungary's resurrection.

The quarrels in Mongolia lasted a decade and a half. If that period of time had not been spent in quarrels, our nation would have been swept away for the second time.

After this decade and a half, a deterioration of the world-shaking empire of Genghis Khan began. Sin does not cause the ruin of one nation only. History tells us that everything on this earth is transitory, be it the work of Genghis Khan or Napoleon or Hitler. God sends to peoples and worlds a lash and many sufferings; but when the cold hands of death touch them, millions of peoples and nations sigh in relief.

The hands of God touch the keys of the organ of world history; earthly powers are nothing but registers of it.

The Hungarian nation recovered after uncertainty and misery. Villages, towns, and cities were rebuilt. The wild weed growths, savage animals, evil people, petty thieves and robbers all disappeared. Through industry, Hungarian bread grew again; there were order, laws, lawful authority, peace, and decency.

God multiplied his people; the veins of the nation refilled with blood. And after a quarter of a century, the envoy of Charles Anjou reported: "No one can tell how many soldiers has the King of Hungary."

First in the work of restoration was the king himself, with his exceptional energy, sense of responsibility, and his conscientiousness founded on deep religious convictions. There was love, too. The erstwhile rigid king discarded all prejudices, disregarded personal hurts and bitterness; he had learned to forgive his enemies. And the people, who had complained about the yoke though they did not appreciate liberty, now listened to him. Inwardly flourishing, outwardly powerful, and free became the Hungarians; they now lived in security under inviolable rights. When the king breathed his last in his palace near the convent of his daughter, he could honestly say that he had not only restored, but even aggrandized his country.

In this result and before it, in the marvelous change of king and nation, there was the penitence and sacrifice of St. Margaret, securing supernatural aid for the country.

My dear brethren! Do not expect me to draw a parallel between time and time.

It will suffice to point out with St. Paul that "for what things soever were written, were written for our learning: that through patience and the comfort of the scriptures, we might have hope."

✛

THE TABLETS

(From a sermon at St. Stephen's basilica in Budapest, calling for moral reconstruction.)

Ten years ago the leading slogan of every people and every nation was: "Strong, invincible armies! For these we are ready to make every sacrifice, until the final victory!" These words died down on the lips of the vanquished and the victors. Indeed, today a new—I admit—a necessary slogan pierces the air over the heads of two billions of people: "Reconstruction!"

There should be as much flame and power in this slogan as there was strength in the old one. We need reconstruction. The one thing to be feared is that indispensable, essential items and factors might be left out of this reconstruction. Constructing requires bricks, tiles, lime and cement, steel and lumber; it needs man power and the will to work; beyond the muscles and the pillars it demands intellectual elements such as architectural planning, technical supervision; but it also needs prayer so that assistance from above and grace shall not lack.

Thousands of years ago the Psalmist gave voice to the words still valid for our times: "Unless the Lord build the house, they labor in vain that build it."

Only a praying humanity can hope to build a better world. We have to rebuild not only the outside world, the houses, bridges, roads, and communications, but also our inner world. The latter was also shaken to its very foundation, whence all this talk about the fundamental human rights. To be truthful, we believers in God would like to hear the fundamental human duties and responsibilities mentioned along with human rights. Right and duty are twins. No sooner has the right made its appearance than duty follows in its wake. The fundamental duties of man are: duty to your God, duty to yourself, and duty to your fellow man.

Much has been shattered during the past few years, but the two stone tablets of faith have remained whole and intact, their contents engraved into human nature by the very fact that we exist as human beings.

It still stands today: Love the Lord thy God with thy whole heart. No foreign gods—blood, gold, race, or class—shall come before Him. "Thou shalt not take the name of the Lord thy God in vain." Keep thou the Sabbath day; it is the day of the Lord.

Whole also is the second tablet: "Honor thy father and thy mother." Our Heavenly Father and the Mother of God watch over them; but there are also the duties of the parents toward their children. "Thou shalt not kill. Thou shalt not commit adultery. Thou shalt not steal. Thou shalt not bear false witness against thy neighbor"—remember!

Thou shalt not defraud; thou shalt not cheat; thou shalt not slander; thou shalt not lie: these all are elements, cornerstones of "reconstruction."

✠

THE MESSAGE OF THE PALL

(From the Cardinal's notes: excerpts from a charge delivered at the Cathedral of Vác.)

I am presenting the head of your diocese with the *pallium* from the tomb of St. Peter, a pall made of the wool of little lambs especially reared for this purpose. And I have come to see more than your bishop and his priests, for not only the priests form part of the Mystical Body of Christ, but all the faithful as well.

If you ask me what I have brought for you, my answer is: I have brought you my never failing reverence for St. Stephen the King, my love for him, because it was he that nearly one thousand years ago founded this bishopric for your ancestors.

To my reverence for the saintly king I add my ardent desire for the rebuilding of our native land, a desire that I feel compelled to emphasize particularly in this region which has undergone so many sufferings; no other part of our country has ever suffered as much as this very heart of the land.

It was ravaged by Tatar hordes, by the remnants of the Black Army, by the crusaders of Nagybotu Lörincz. For a century and a half the Turks occupied this region. Nor was it spared by the Labanc and Kuruc armies. The consequence of these visitations was an almost total annihilation of the population. The yellowing pages of historical records reveal that in 1675 the bishopric counted fourteen parishes and thirteen thousand faithful. With the passing of time, the fourteen parishes grew into two hundred; and two hundred and fifty years later these faithful grew to 1,100,000. The moral strength of our nation revitalized this region.

We, the Hungarians of today, should learn a lesson from the past. When speaking about reconstruction, we must not lose sight of the fact that, in order to rebuild this country, more is needed

[232]

than a material and economic framework. Nor will it suffice merely to show our people the star of liberty. The world needs time-tested moral values, particularly if the new world order comes to us in the sign of democracy, the rule by the people.

The concept of democracy imposes claims on leaders as well as on those led by them. Leaders and followers must create a world order better than the old one. Above all, this new order needs faith and morals, decency and loyalty, order and discipline, justice and love, unselfishness. Our hands, our thoughts, our purposes must be clean, and we must see to it that our hands carry out what our words promise.

Thus, there are important obligations to be fulfilled, and even in a new world these are old obligations. They never become outdated, just as their mother, our faith, is also ever young.

This faith appears to us as our Church. The Latins called it "Sancta Mater Ecclesia"; we call it fully Holy Mother Church. Despite the fact that this Church is maligned in these trying times, there are certain aspects of the Church which everybody can clearly see: the first is that in the course of two thousand years the Church has never fallen victim to anarchy from within; she has never failed to defend human dignity; never did she betray the truth; like a real mother, she has never ceased to spread love through her teachings, and her actions as well.

Yes, she preaches love. Today, as well as throughout two thousand years, like a loving mother, she helps the frail; she defends the child, she defends women.

Child protection and dignity of womanhood have been inseparable from the history and concept of the Church. In the Middle Ages, when the slave market emerged as a profitable business, Pope Zachary sent his priests to the slave mart in Venice, where, for heavy pieces of gold, they bought men and women destined to be sold and freed them.

Pope Adrian I, exasperated by what he had seen, ordered the arrest and execution of slave traders and the burning of slave ships. The same Church established at the time of the Turks two religious orders. One of them, the Trinitarians, spent in the course of time five and a half billion francs to liberate a million prisoners. More than once the blood of the monks was part of the ransom; 7,115 monks died as martyrs for the prisoners. Of their own accord these monks sold themselves, using the money to free their fellow sufferers. Their hero, St. Peter of Nolasco, sold himself as a slave and freed in the course of his life over 64,000 captives. St. Vincent de Paul, the confidant and friend of two French statesmen, went out to the seashores, searched out married galley slaves, removed their chains, and sent them back to their families. Putting the chains on his own hands, taking the place of one of the galley slaves, he labored in his stead until freed by royal decree.

This Church—and you all must know it—waged a valiant fight for human dignity; and you are well aware that during the tumultuous war years your priests have remained with you, shared your lot because of their love for you.

This Church has always loved the sick; this Mother is responsible for the training of nurses, for hospitals established through St. Vincent de Paul and St. Charles of Borromeo. Anyone familiar with the activities of the Samaritan Sisters, their day and night vigils, their ceaseless work in hospitals, asylums, and orphanages, their self-sacrifice, their renunciation of all earthly goods, should recognize in these frail women the love of the Mother toward her suffering children.

Still, if the Church came to you only with the banners of goodness, her activities, indeed, would not be complete. Besides being merciful, she is also the "strength and pillar of justice." This Church speaks firmly, gives strict commands, asks for an account of the sins. She urges pure, indissoluble marriages and clean youth. For two thousand years this Church has fought against "bodily desires, the desires of our eyes, the haughtiness of life." In the course of history there can be found not a single fashionable, but evil, movement against which the Church has not fought. She told Herodes, she told the Roman emperors, Napoleon and Hitler what St. John the Baptist said: "Non licet tibi!" (You must not do this!) Yes, that is what the Church maintained, because the Church has always known that she is the repository of Christ's teachings. By Jesus Christ she is assured that not even the forces of hell can crush her gates.

It is a motherly feature of the Church that just as the simplest washerwoman has a right to tell her grown-up son what is right and what is wrong, the Church has a right to tell anyone, regardless of the rank or position he holds, whether his ambitions are opposed to moral laws or in conformity with them. This accounts for the steadfastness of St. John, who wrote from his exile in Constantinople: The waves are murmuring, a storm rages over the sea of life, but we do not fear anything because we stand on a rock. Why be afraid of death? Life to me is Christ, my death would be a gain. Why fear exile? I find God wherever they take me. Why fear loss of my earthly goods? We were born poor and we leave this world poor. I despise what this world likes and laugh at what she tempts me with. I fear not poverty, do not seek wealth. I do not fear death and do not seek life except for you, my flock, for your salvation.

Yes, indeed, such is the steadfastness of the Church.

This kindness which she manifests, this justice which she never ceases to preach, are the basis of her educational theories; and she teaches individuals, families, in churches among peoples and nations.

For two thousand years this Church has been teaching children to fear God, men to be honest, from kindergarten to the highest universities. She educates children in the family by molding mothers after the Holy Virgin and their fathers after St. Joseph. From them the child learns dignity, loyalty, and righteousness.

The Church has educated peoples and nations. Can anyone point out a single European nation which has not been educated by the Church? Wherever missions have gone, even in South America, the schools of this Church are a strong educational factor.

This Church has taught barbarians and taught our own ancestors, right here, to give up their nomadic, semibarbarian traditions and taught them how to keep their souls clean. And she taught them to say Our Father and taught us to call our fellow man dear brother, instead of killing him. That is what the Church has accomplished.

Unfortunately, when children grow up, when peoples emancipate themselves, they sometimes treat their mother as if aware of their own strength; but we, faithful Catholics, wish that when thinking of our mother we may say with the poet: "Bless, my Lord, the house where my mother lives, the street on which she walks. Bless her hands that rocked our crib, her lips which taught us our first prayer."

Strange to say, there are people who do not love, nay, they even hate their Mother. I find their ideals on the pages of history. King John Lackland did not hate, nay, he loathed the Church. His life was a never ending chain of murder and immorality. He killed with his own hand his cousin who was the rightful heir to the throne; and he killed the children of the mothers of Wales. He had twenty-eight hanged at one time and forced their mothers to witness the execution of their own offspring. And when he saw the mortal sufferings of the children and their mothers, he looked at them without concealing his malicious joy.

He hated his own mother too. And while he did all this, his country shrank to ever smaller size. Still he would not give up his evil practices; he arrested the most prominent in the land and extorted £100,000 from each victim. Whoever was unable to pay underwent, at royal decree, the jerking out of his teeth; but the life of John Lackland came to an end because the enemies of the Church are not eternal. His gravestone bears these words: "Here lies a King whose name was John. His whole life was a chain of evil deeds. When he arrived in hell, he besmirched even that place."

During the war we have become bloody and dirty from head to foot. Only the Church can cleanse and bathe us; only our Mother, the Church, can revitalize us. And just as when meeting my own mother, I kiss her hands with reverence, I kiss the hands of this Mother, the Church, and say: Beloved Mother, cleanse me and elevate me to human dignity as you did my ancestors. Give me inner peace and let me hope for a better life.

To be a Catholic means to regard God as a father, to regard the Holy Virgin and the Church as our beloved mother. To be a Catholic means to cherish her, to love her, to admire her. It also means to follow the Ten Commandments from the cradle to the grave. It

also means to die in peace and to throw oneself on the heart of
Jesus and the arms of the Holy Virgin. We hope that living truly
Catholic lives, imbued with the teachings of Christ, we can tell you,
our nation, our land imbued in Catholic spirit like a pallium: We
paid all that we owed thee.

This is what I have brought you with the *pallium* for your bishop.
Be faithful, be loyal, be guardians of rock, and praise the Lord for
having invited you to His community and thus to eternity.

✠

THE LIFE UNBORN

(From the Cardinal's notes: excerpts from a letter, dealing with the decline of morals in married life, to the congregations of the Archdiocese of Esztergom.)

The tribulations and the anguish of the war disrupted our lives, and these tribulations lay heavy upon our souls. Which of our wounds shall we heal first? Whom shall we mourn? Whom shall we pray for? For what? Should we bewail the fate of those resting in their graves or the plight of prisoners in foreign lands? Should we bemoan the lack of necessities or worry over the insecurity of our existence? What should we deplore: our moral or material losses? Should we look beyond our frontiers or concentrate on the problems within our borders?

At any rate, to heap sin upon sin is to make our lot even more difficult; to widen the ever deepening whirlpool engulfing us, our families, our nation. I am speaking of marital transgressions.

Up to 1900 the birth rate in the Capital was, with some exceptions, on the increase. Then, until 1939, it followed a downward trend (again with some exceptions). Beginning in 1940, our birth rate soared again, reaching its peak in 1943. Between April, 1944, and February, 1946, with the exception of September, 1944, no one month showed natural increase. The number of deaths exceeded the number of births. In the last fourteen months the population of the capital has decreased by 32,332 persons.

This most disheartening phenomenon manifests, in part, painful but natural causes: moving, bombing raids, sieges, epidemics, lack of hospitals, and so forth. Still, the decline in the number of births and its constant low point are attributable primarily to what an official report called "fear and avoidance of pregnancy and the fact that many women tolerate undergoing abortion." "Tolerate" seems

[238]

to be an understatement of what is going on, in hitherto unheard-of degree of mass murder, in more than one clinic and elsewhere. Guilty hands cooperate in the abortion of large, grown, healthy fetuses; godless women lacking every trace of femininity stay the hand of God by criminal force because they do not want to become mothers.

Whoever practices birth control clashes with God's very implicit law clearly laid down by both nature and revelation. "And God created man to his own image; male and female he created them." Nothing in life lacks aim and purpose. The mother's body is no exception, its aim and purpose being to give birth to children. It is for this reason that the human body is equipped with organs that serve this very purpose. The difference in the sexes would be senseless if the concept of procreation were discarded. The principal aim of marriage is the procreation of the race, thus relaying the torch of life. Just as God has given life, through their ancestors, to the parents of today, they in turn must give life to those children whom God wants to bear.

In the Garden of Eden God created man to his image; male and female he created them. Immediately after the creation of the first man and woman, God proclaimed the institution of marriage, pronounced the great eternal law: "Increase and multiply, and fill the earth, and subdue it." Not only once was this law proclaimed; it recurs almost continually in the New Testament. With more forcible motivation and new aims, the Apostle, and through him the Lord, require that: "Now therefore you are no more strangers and foreigners; but you are fellow citizens with the Saints, and the domestics of God." Men of different vocations can attain their salvation in countless ways but, according to the Apostle, for women the road to salvation leads through giving birth. "Yet she shall be saved through childbearing." According to the exegetes, procreation of life and rearing are correlated. Those married persons who do not want to give birth do not want to attain salvation either.

The position of the Church, based on the laws of nature, revelation, and the Saint Fathers of the Church, is clear and simple: True marriage means avoiding any and all birth control. Consequently, so-called "caution," any measure directed toward the prevention of conception, is a grave sin against God and nature.

Either we assume the responsibility for the consequences of marital life, in this instance the child, or we heroically abstain temporarily or entirely from marital life. Where one claims a right, one has an obligation. There is no other moral alternative. The only thing distinguishing marriage, in which procreative contact is allowed and sanctified by law, from mere lust, is the procreation of the species. If a married couple excludes the aim of procreation either continually or temporarily, marriage degenerates into a vulgar, guilty association, the home becoming a den of sin and the married couple a pair of accomplices.

According to the laws of the Church, marriage has three aims, the first of which is the most important: to procreate and rear children. Mutual assistance of the married parties is only a secondary aim, and to satisfy one's instincts is the third and the last only.

Those who are "cautious," that is, those who violate the laws of nature by taking precautions that their union should not bear fruit, sin gravely, even though they use no guilty measures or preventives. They rebel against the manifest will of the Creator. They injure the body, the nervous system, and the soul of their spouse. They create a guilt-laden atmosphere in which they bring up the children they already have. Perhaps they give diabolical "well meant advice" to others, make derogatory remarks about good mothers who remained true to God and nature. Those people are guilty of harming society; they are guilty of not fulfilling their duty toward their homeland.

Even the intent to control birth is a crime which, in the case of repeaters, cannot be absolved.

The Church, in spreading by divine authority the revealed truth to man, is implicit in her laws concerning the protection of life that has been conceived and that, in fact, is already breeding. The very intention of killing the sperm, even though the killing actually has not taken place, already constitutes grave sin. The case is even graver if the evil intent is successful. Anyone assisting, persuading, giving money or help of any kind to one seeking abortion, anyone participating in abortion or operations for abortive purposes, excludes himself from the community of the Church. Anyone who "disposes" of the embryo or makes someone else do so, ceases to be a Catholic; by this very act he ceases to be a living member of the Catholic Church.

This is the sin of sins, and more than that, several sins: sins against nature, God, the unborn child, the mother; sins against the family and your homeland.

Anyone with a conscience must realize that it does not matter at what stage the attack is undertaken, at the time of conception or near it, or in the last months of pregnancy. The stand of the Church is that there is no difference between the living and the "not-yet-living" child. The Church does not distinguish even between the fetus and the infant in his crib. Both are human; both are personalities. To harm the fetus under any pretext, be it medical, social, or eugenic, is equivalent to murder. If man intends or acts in order to make life cease to exist, he is a killer; and if he plans that no life should result from a union ordained by God for the creation of life, in other words, if he unites defying the aims set by God and prevents conception, he interferes with God's plans and thus disturbs the clear fountains of life. Thus he sins against the sixth commandment. The words of St. Paul will apply to him: "For know you this and understand, that no fornicator, or unclean, or covetous person hath inheritance in the kingdom of Christ and of God."

A great number of world-famous Catholic and non-Catholic physicians share the views of the Church. They claim that nothing is as "unmedical" as the killing of the fetus. It is not admissible in the ethics of either physician or midwife. The physician's task is to protect life, not to destroy it. Serious medical men have stated also that "caution" ruins the female body.

This may be true, contend many who have progressed far on the way of sin, but one must not forget that we live in unusual times. We are too poor to feed, clothe, and school even the children who have been already given to us. Shall we give birth to more and let the child starve?

The Church does not argue with anyone. Still, I must point out that the Church is fully aware of the misery and sufferings a family today must experience. The Church suffers with you and deeply respects the cares and anxieties that have beset the families of Hungary. However, the Church is not preaching temporal but eternal principles. The passing of time does not lessen the validity of the Ten Commandments.

Nor do the laws of life change. Let me point out, besides, that these black sins have not just begun in these black days; they flourished in the years of our greatest prosperity. There have always been people who enjoyed their wealth and who hated and exiled the child from their families. Still, even today we meet heroic mothers, who bear new lives and who are not guilty of having killed their unborn. The high prices for abortion are not paid, even in our days, by the poor.

As one of our eminent prelates stated long ago: "It is indeed cause for mourning when the cemetery is not on the outskirts of the village or town but, instead, starts at the very bosom and womb of married women. It is tragic for a woman to become a murderer instead of a parent; if instead of giving life she takes it away; if instead of rocking a crib she digs a grave."

Let us not rely in everything upon our own strength. Let us remember that Providence guides our paths. "Commit thy way to the Lord, and trust in him, and he will do it." If we oppose the divine law, what can we build upon? But living by his law, we can count on his help.

✛

THE STAR OF THE SEA

(From an address to a pilgrimage of men of Budapest to the shrine of Máriaremete.)

The world-famous sculptor Achtermann, once a lowly shepherd boy, was commissioned to create a memorial in Münster to the much maligned martyr Droste-Vischering, Archbishop of Cologne, imprisoned after a campaign of calumny. The memorial represented the Descent from the Cross and the Mater Dolorosa. The transportation of the massive and splendid group of marble statues from Rome to Münster caused no little worry. Hoisted with rope and pully onto a boat, they nearly crushed the ship. The irreligious captain raged in anger against "superstition and idol."

The artist had traveled on land from Rome to Rotterdam. While awaiting the arrival of his masterpiece, he was greatly shocked by the news that two of the three boats that had left Leghorn had sunk during a sea storm and the third could not be located. Worrying over the greatest work of his life, the artist suffered melancholy.

At last he found solace in prayer. A week later the vessel docked in the port. Our unbelieving captain warmly embraced the happy artist and exclaimed: "To your statues I owe my boat and the lives of my passengers. When waves that nearly reached the sky rocked our ship, your statues kept the boat continually in equilibrium. The Holy Virgin thus became our savior. And now I am going to do what I promised Mary when we all faced death: I am going to join the Catholic faith, because God's Mother is at home there."

We who have survived the terrible ravages of war feel that until death we are obligated to the guiding Star of all the Seas. I take it, brethren, that most of you were brought here by the same faith as the captain's; that is why you have come to this place consecrated to the Virgin Mary.

On March 4, 1944, I experienced in a bunker the most devastating

[243]

bombardment in the company of six hundred other terrified Hungarians. When the shadow of death covered us all, the three-story building above us started tottering like a leaf. Those with me thronged desperately around my hand which gave absolution.

I gave the absolution. With one of my arms I held a weeping little girl; the other I extended in benediction over the crowd. Then there arose from the crowd of men, women and children, laborers and tradesmen, a wave of prayer, "Pray help us, Mary merciful Virgin!" growing like the murmur of the sea.

Who is the Star of the Sea? It is God's Mother, with her imposing dignity and power. Her dignity is without any doubt such that nothing more dignified could be created. "Blessed art thou amongst women; and blessed is the fruit of thy womb: Jesus." The sanctity of the Virgin, her sinlessness, her mercy, her purity are the object of our faith.

This is our Mother, with all her goodness. This is not mere poetry, no mere imagination; it is as true and real as the love of our earthly mother.

My own mother is at this very moment praying for me and you in the little church of my native village, praying that I may spread the grace of God and that you too may prove faithful; you, good sheep of your Good Shepherd.

The Virgin Mary means incomparably more to me and to you. She is the Mother of Mercy and Omnipotence. These two features of hers keep the ship of our lives in equilibrium.

At the Elevation of the Host, age-old fields and forests, venerable centuries of the past talk to us like great educators and not like lying finger posts. And we know what our cemeteries, our beloved ones, so honorable, so peerless despite their simplicity, teach us.

We cannot and we do not wish to live without the teachings of our honored dead. The living may speak untruths, but not the dead. We shall fearlessly follow their warnings and teachings.

We shall be faithful to the Holy Virgin, to the Church, to her institutions, to our country, to the faith and morals of our ancestors.

In this repose our strength, our hope and consolation.

✝

THE PATRONESS OF HUNGARY

(From an address to the students of the school of the Cistercian Brothers, recalling the historical development of the Hungarian Marian cult.)

Even if someone had lost his belief in the supernatural and viewed Hungarian history in retrospect through the lens of historical materialism, he still would be impressed by certain powerful waves, rising at the very inception of our existence, accompanying our nation throughout vicissitudes of light and darkness, prosperity and depression.

The thousand-year existence of our country is an enigma; our nation did not collapse despite many crises. Despite tremendous blows, she has recovered. At her sickbed a good mother kept vigil: the Patroness. Our Lady of Hungary. If anything can console the Hungarians of today, it can only be this thought of our historic past.

The essence of this thought is that God's Mother is the Protectress, the Patroness of Hungary. The country is her gift, and by St. Stephen's legacy, her heritage, her possession. Because she has helped us on innumerable occasions, we brotherless, orphaned Hungarians expect her to help us perpetually.

Our age-old reverence for her is symbolized in many national treasures: the Holy Crown, the coronation mantle, the oath of coronation and the national flag. Indeed, on the flag of our country, the image of the Virgin is older than the three colors of the flag.

Our seals, stamps, documents, coins commemorate her. Our bishoprics, sixty-two abbeys, and our military commands mention her. Our prayers before starting our daily work invoke her. Our university, according to Pázmány, is her hall.

Out of the light of the past and the travail of the present, out of hope for the future, they wove a song which burst forth many times from the lips of millions and has not since died away:

> Our Mother Patroness,
> In our great need
> We implore you:
> Do not forget our country,
> And us poor Hungarians!

It might be questioned whether this thought cuts a wedge into much desired national unity. We reply that the mother in the family, the Immaculate Mother of God is no wedge in the life of the nation but, on the contrary, a blessed, all-uniting tie of love.

Our Transylvanian Protestant princes, Bocskay, Bethlen, and the two George Rákóczis, had their coins adorned with the image of the Virgin, as did the Catholic Francis Rákóczi II. When the latter set forth with his armies from the Carpathian Mountains *pro Deo et libertate*, there flew aloft banners bearing Mary's image, even though the majority—according to Alexander Márki, nine tenths—of the Kuruc soldiers were non-Catholic. In the poems of the non-Catholic John Arany, the valiant Hungarian knights of the Middle Ages take an oath on the Virgin. No one has ever written a warmer book on the Turkish and Kuruc time, poems dealing with the Virgin, than did Paul Gyulai.

In 1905, on the eve of a national upsurge, the assembled politicians of the opposition parties, under the leadership of Francis Kossuth, prayed before the newly completed picture of the Virgin by Julius Benczur. It is no coincidence that our greatest nineteenth century painters, Benczur, Lotz, and Székely, depicted the Patroness of Hungary, her court, and the Hungarian saints.

In 1941 we got back some banners from the East; the flags of the Revolution of 1848–1849 adorned by the picture of the Holy Virgin.

No, I am not happy over the fact that at one time there were bloody clashes between Protestants and Catholics, because in these Hungarian blood was shed, and through these there was brought about a hundred-and-fifty-year occupation of the country by foreign armies. Rather do I wish that Catholics and Protestants emulate one another in peace, in the love of their country.

A religious person, even if he is not a Catholic, sees no dividing force in our love for the Holy Virgin; on the contrary, he sees in it a powerful religious, moral, and national strength.

The non-Catholic blind Bottyán and John Damjanics had the image of the Virgin on their swords. The idea of the Virgin obviously has a magic effect even on those who are not native Hungarians. The palatine of Louis the Great, Prince Ulászló, settled the Paulist Fathers in Poland. They introduced there the cult of *Patrona Poloniae*, which founds its roots in our veneration of *Patrona Hungariae*. The Pole Sobieski, the French Charles of Lorraine, the Italian Marc of Aviano, sent by the Pope Innocent XI, fought the battle of the Patroness of Hungary for the territorial integrity of this nation. Leopold I, inclined toward despotism like most of his contemporaries, became fully aware of his dignity as king of Hungary under the influence of the cult of the Patroness of our people. He even offered this country to the Holy Virgin in his capacity as king of Hungary.

We did not slavishly imitate other nations in this. The cult of the Italian Madonna, the French Notre Dame, the German Schutzfrau differ from the cult of the Holy Virgin of our people, for ours bears the imprint of the national genius.

Thus if someone saw in our veneration for the Holy Virgin nothing but a weak, pious slogan, outdated in these times of misery, he would be highly mistaken.

The cult of the Virgin contained a strong, anti-Turkish element which could not reconcile our ancestors to losing territories and being divided. Thus our Marian cult has always contained a strong, national element.

Because this cult has never preached hate, it has been fully assimilated.

Mary's image adorned the banner under which Hungarians united to rebuild the nation in 1241, after 1686—and after 1946, too.

✠

THE CASTLE OF THE SOULS

*(From the Cardinal's notes: excerpts from remarks at the
dedication of a church rebuilt on the ruins of the war.)*

A church was built over the ruins of the war. This place is sacred
because here we commune with God; here we meet God; here He
is born into our souls. The glory of God and the peace of good men
permeate this place.

Hallowed is this spot. It deserves a profession of faith. This little
sanctuary separates two distinct worlds: the world of the godless
and the world of those who live with God, in God, and avow it
openly in the presence of all.

The house of the Lord's Prayer. The castle of our soul. Just as we
adorn the wall of our house with a blessing, so do I adorn these walls
when I consecrate them with the blessings of the Mother Church:

> Where there is faith, you will find love,
> Where there is love, you will find peace,
> Where there is peace, you will find grace,
> Where there is grace, you will find God.
> Where there is God, there is no need, no want.

✠

THE HUNGARIAN BISHOP

(From a charge delivered at the consecration of the Bishop of Győr, drawing a parallel between the past and the present.)

In the world of revelation the bishop is a father whose vigilant, alert perception is emphasized by the title of his rank in Greek: *episkopos*.

The first pastor and bishop was Jesus Christ. On his ascent into Heaven, his place was taken by the apostles, then by the disciples of the apostles, St. Timothy, St. Titus, and the rest. Then came the martyr bishops, witnesses to Christ clawed to death by lions in the arena.

Among the bishops of the world Church, I desire to make mention of St. Ambrose, Bishop of Milan in times seething with trouble. He came into a world of class and party strife but belonged to no class or party. Though of noble descent, he did not spare the aristocrats, who vaunted the breed of their horses and dogs but forgot the poor. He upbraided the poor also, who, lacking a tunic and bread for the morrow, crowded the taverns and alehouses, seeking to live a shiftless life by lightly appropriating the substance of others. He was everything to everyone but belonged to no one, only to the Truth.

He did not temporize in the struggle between paganism and Christianity. He had no wish to seem a realistic politician in the eyes of the senate.

By that time Milan's churches had forsaken the Christ-denying heresy of Arianism and were all again in Catholic hands. For the sake of the peace, however, the emperor asked that one small church at the edge of the town be relinquished to the Arians. Three times he made his request; three times the bishop refused.

[249]

The emperor proposed that he take part in a public debate with the Arians, following which the emperor would render judgment.

"Where, Gracious Majesty, did you ever hear of worldly powers holding court over bishops?" came the word of St. Ambrose.

The emperor thereupon ordered his expulsion from Milan. This potentate forestalled our own twentieth century by sixteen hundred years. He was so "progressive" that he deemed the shepherd had less right to be with the flock than the wolves. The bishop replied: "It is not my wont to forsake the flock."

Together with his congregation, the bishop took refuge in the church, just as many bishops have done over the course of centuries. Armed soldiers surrounded the building. The faithful, burning with anger, wanted to attack them, but the bishop restrained them, saying, "Tears are my defense." Through the centuries the bishops have wept an invisible ocean of tears.

Long was the night for the faithful of Milan. They grew sleepy and dispirited, like Christ's followers at Gethsemane. Then the bishop prayed with them, and between prayers he had them sing hymns and psalms. That was the origin of the church choir.

Lo, the praying Church goeth forth to battle, and the fighting Church prays, often interceding in Heaven on behalf of the very enemies that seek to destroy her.

In distant Salonica officials of the emperor, guilty of crimes, are killed in an uprising. Evil men rouse the ire of the emperor, securing from him advance approval of vengeance. Under the pretext of a performance, the people are beguiled into the arena, where soldiers set upon them, slaughtering seven thousand men, women, and children in cold blood.

Horror and revolution fill the world, and reach Milan.

The lightheaded ruler and his retinue proceed in full regalia to church, as though nothing had happened; but the bishop bars his way.

"Do you think to clasp in prayer hands dripping with blood, and to partake of the sacrament with those lips?"

The emperor is taken aback; he makes mention of King David, who also sinned.

"David sinned, but repented himself of his sins," spoke the bishop. "If you followed him in sin, then follow him in repentance also." The emperor, deeply shaken, proclaims that henceforth death sentences may not be passed hurriedly, and that such judgments must not be carried out at once but are to be submitted after thirty days for the approval of the emperor.

What, in essence, is the life and work of a bishop? Does it consist in carrying on skirmishes along the fringes of state authority?

By no means! It is the task of the bishop to observe how well the Ten Commandments are being kept in the world: Thou shalt love the Lord, thy God. Thou shalt not have strange gods! Thou shalt not kill! Thou shalt not commit adultery! Thou shalt not steal! Thou shalt not bear false witness! Thou shalt not covet thy neighbor's house: neither shalt thou desire his wife!

It does not suffice to call the past to account on the score of human rights, or to write them into law for future generations. They must be observed here and now, with reference to pagans, Jews, and Christians, too.

And what of Christ's peace in the life of Church and bishop? When Emperor Theodosius the Great died, after repenting his sins and making amends so far as he was able, St. Ambrose rose to deliver a great funeral sermon in his memory, placing the olive branch of peace on the emperor's bier. He was happier making peace than in his role of the angel with a flaming sword, barring the way of a guilty ruler.

St. Ambrose was a dauntless soldier of the faith; but martyrdom, too, characterizes the life of a bishop. The bishops of today hold high the torch of the martyrs of yesterday. Hungarian history is, among other things, a great burial ground.

Into your hands I give the pastoral staff; be vigilant in watching over the orphaned flock. On your finger I place the ring of faith; be a faithful shepherd of your diocese. To your hands I entrust the book of the Gospels that you may spread them before all men, teaching them to heed the words of our Lord Jesus.

And now, set out on the path of the apostles with God as your authority, strength, and shield!

In Him, with Him, and through Him you will achieve what I have asked of you in the ceremony of consecration: never to call light, darkness; or darkness, light; never to call good, bad; or bad, good.

In God you will unite the pastors and their people, through devotion to the ideals of love and truth. And if we are to recover— for which we hope and work and pray—it will be through the Church that our country and her people will be saved. May the Holy Trinity be glorified in the work of the new shepherd! Amen.

✠

THE MIRACLE OF MÁRIAPÓCS

(From an address on patriotism, delivered as Primate of the Roman Catholic Church and metropolitan of the Greek Catholic Church in Hungary.)

I stand, here in Máriapócs, in awe before the miraculous picture of the Virgin Mother to whom both the Greek and Roman Catholics came to pay homage in such imposing numbers.

I came here today in my capacity as your metropolitan, and having observed your religious fervor I am going to report your proven faithfulness, in the tribulations that you are experiencing, to our mutual Father in Rome.

For centuries you and your ancestors have organized these pilgrimages, yet among all of them, this one has special significance. More than two hundred and fifty years have elapsed since your nationally famous miraculous picture of Mary first shed tears. This miracle repeated itself in 1715. This was not merely pious imagining. As the Virgin Mother shed tears, her face turned black and her tearful eyes became red. This was not only seen by one or two pious individuals, but sworn to by a row of witnesses, of which some were educated and some were not; some were from the district and some were not; and by citizens and foreign soldiers, Latins and Greeks, and Catholics and Calvinists.

This picture became so famous that King Leopold I, who was a great admirer of Mary, had it transported to Vienna. It was at this time that the picture became an integral part of Hungarian history. When Francis Rákóczi II began his campaign at the foothills of the Carpathian Mountains, under the banner of the Virgin Mary which bore the inscription "For God and for Freedom," among the hundred grievances mentioned in his manifesto, called the *Recrudescunt*, was the complaint that the miraculous picture of Mary of Pócs had been taken to Vienna and had thus made it impossible for the people of that vicinity to pray before it. All this in spite of the fact that most of his followers were non-Catholics and that the hundred grievances were compiled by the non-Catholic Paul Ráday.

On this anniversary, there would be even more of us here if it were not for artificial barriers and boundaries. The people of the North would be here, regardless of the difference in language, and the faithful people from the East would also be here. Now we are alone in front of this miraculous picture and we are surrounded by the sad event of a second Trianon. Never before have so many irresponsible judges gathered together to forge a judgment over our human destiny.

But we shall not despair, as only heathens are without hope. We know very well that what man hurriedly creates today can disappear by tomorrow. We have seen much human sand flow down the hourglass of history.

We also know that although men have forsaken us we are not alone. We who are in front of the tearful Virgin Mary appeal against the judgment of Paris.

Men proclaim justice in their speech but act otherwise. Men promise and men forget; but in the end the just God weaves the threads of world history. He weaves flowers that human weavers try in vain to eradicate.

We have put our hope in supernatural and natural truths, and in the recognition of these truths.

It is also cheering to see that here, at the threshold of the East, this declaration of faith has been heard by God and will never be forgotten by Him. The church, the parish school, the family house and the cemetery in your village are all encouraging signs and sources of strength to all of us.

Most important of all is the church, where your ancestors have gone to pray and sing for centuries. The church is the strongest bastion of the Hungarian nation. For mutual and peaceful understanding the church is the only meeting place and the only link that binds people together in these times of partisanship and strife.

The spotlight of public attention has been focused on the Catholic school system by those attacking it and even more so by those who have vigorously defended it. The recent opening of the schools has served as a brilliant testimony to the parents' sense of responsibility and has shown in which direction real public opinion lies. We can't recall when there have ever been so many applications for admissions to our high schools and monastic schools. Furthermore, a great many of the parents belonged to parties that professed a different worldly ideology.

Our source of strength is the family home. Blessed be the threshold behind which we grew up. Brentano, the famous writer, in the early morning following his return to the home of his parents, kissed the doorknobs because they bore the imprint of his mother's hands. We are guided by the same feeling. We adhere to the ideal of the father and mother blessed by the sacrament of marriage. We adhere to family prayers said in unison and to everything that makes family life warm and strong.

The cemetery also gives us strength. We cannot live without thinking of the departed ones and without their guidance. The other day I conversed with a Hungarian who came from across the Danube. He declared that if they can chase them away from the soil of their ancestors, they cannot prevent them from digging up their cemeteries and from taking their dead with them. Yes, we have a close connection with our past, from which we gather strength and encouragement.

We do not wish to be anything else but Hungarians! Even the fashions of the day will not make us budge. We will not permit any Hungarian to defame Hungary. No Hungarian should cause another Hungarian to be imprisoned! No Hungarian should betray another Hungarian!

We honor everyone who concurs with us in our patriotism.

✠

THE SWORD WON IT; THE CROSS RETAINED IT

(From an open-air sermon to the youth of Hungary, on Mount St. Gellért.)

The teen-age youths of the Capital, having left their homes at the Pest quay, are looking for something on the rock near the mountain of heathen charm. On the rock there is an inscription, written we know not when, which says, "Atra dies 1046 IX 24." Dark day. In 1046 certain forces rose up in the name of freedom. In their wake arose the old destructive forces of the Plains, and Christian lives fell under the blows of the saber and sacred places of God were reduced to ashes. Those were dark days, indeed, when instead of a blooming Hungary the horrors of destruction became dominant. This was the first dark period in Hungarian history. Christianity received a severe blow, but it was the nation that was stunned and recoiled.

But September 24, 1046, is not regarded by us as Atra dies, Day of Mourning, but as Gloriosa dies, Day of Glory. On this day Bishop St. Gellért, the first Hungarian martyr, was born for Heaven and for Hungarian history. In 1946 we celebrate at the same place his spiritual strength, his heroism, his sacrifice, his zealousness, his disdain of the world, and his exemplary leadership. If there is glory, then all these facts are the foundations on which glory rests.

Each time that we stand before the crossroads of Fate, he points the way for us. In disgrace he was hurled down the mountain in a wheelbarrow; but now his image, chiseled in stone, stands on top of the mountain. He looks down at the Danube, at the Capital, and at the whole country, and steadfastly holds the crucifix in his hand: "With this sign you will be victorious!" This sign taught him forgiveness in his dying agony, and this is what he holds up before a

[256]

world that is drunk with hatred, lovelessness, and the destruction of Hungarians.

But we do not only commemorate nine hundred years. It has been exactly ten and a half centuries that Hungary as a nation has existed on this very soil.

One thousand and fifty years! This is a big wave on the passing waters of Time and a long thread on Time's old spinning wheel. When Árpád and our gallant forefathers looked over what constituted Hungary, and the foreign chronicler of the year 896 wrote, Odo the French King ruled over a territory no larger than one Hungarian county; and one hundred and fifty years later the English princes came to find shelter and a new home at the Court of St. Stephen because the heathen Danes and Normans had taken the soil away from English families, as is happening today to Hungarians all over the world.

Fifty years ago we celebrated our millennium. With this historical thought in mind, we do not celebrate by going to the monument erected to commemorate this occasion; we know why. We celebrate it, rather, at the place of St. Gellért's martyrdom and under his crucifix and in the shadow of his cross. This is as it should be. During the glorious millennium my predecessor, the Primate Kolos Vaszary, said: "The sword has won us our fatherland, but the cross has retained it for us."

The St. Gellért anniversary gives us the theme for these ten and a half centuries. *Anonymous* does not start calling our country Mary's country from the year 1038. He is right! Our first king, St. Stephen, already referred to this country in the year 1028, when the Emperor Conrad II attacked Hungary, as the heritage of Mary. *Anonymous* even stated that it was the Blessed Virgin that led the people of Árpád into the territory between the Danube and the Tisza. It was because of her entreaty that the great St. Gellért was born to us between the years 977–982.

You say: What gaping whirlpools this country has fallen into. You are right! Europe has declared one of its oldest countries, in this year of its ten and a half centuries of existence, to be the sinner of sinners, because among all peoples it has been punished the most mercilessly. It is the unhappiest loser of the World War. What nation has not inherited our country and would not prey on us?

If the prayers of Moses secured the Promised Land for his people, if Joan of Arc saved the French people, so the power of Mary and her condescending motherly mercy is the only key to the understanding of Hungarian history.

In the periods of decline and fall she is our consolation, source of strength, and the motherly hand that lifts us up. The change of periods is marked by our turning toward her. The way out of our present-day crisis can be shown by the power and mercifulness of our Great Lady.

Therefore, under the waves that engulf us, in our bottomless mortification, in the midst of the tempting whirlpool of despair, I solemnly dedicate this country to our Great Lady of Hungary in the same way that she gave it to us and unified it for us in faith.

With this faith we will never become degenerate Hungarians, soulless stumps, nor mediocre epigoni of our ancestors and saints.

We might very well be pitiful unfortunates torn apart, racked with hatred, the victims of great and small lies; but we do not want to be anything else than our forerunners were for a thousand years, the family of the Great Lady.

Eja ergo Advocata nostra: therefore our Advocate, mighty Queen of Heaven, our Lady, look mercifully on us. Show that you are our dear Mother as ever before, that you are the crusher of Satan, the Great Lady of Hungary, our Patron, who shall lift us up and save us. Amen.

✠

RELIGION IS OF PUBLIC CONCERN

(From the Cardinal's papers: from an address dealing with the role of religion in modern society.)

Religion is not an unimportant, Lilliputian fact of life, but its axle and main girder, society's foundation, the compass needle of the ship of life, the lighthouse on the sea of life, and the pilot that guides the ship of life safely to harbor.

It does not only think in terms of continents and thousands of years. The Church also concerns itself with man's endless despair and the misery of man's body and soul. It was the Church that inaugurated care for the sick and needy, places of refuge for the poor, and that lifted up the uneducated, the forsaken ones, the incurables, the lepers, and the degraded ones.

The distance is immeasurable between the tent and the house, and between making one's own living or in living by the efforts of others. The Church has traveled this distance with the civilized peoples of the world. The Church has created agriculture, craftsmanship, and art. The Church has helped to defeat slavery. The Protestant historian Arnold stated that the Church has brought about a new respect for work, which is in direct opposition to the heathen, who considered work to be degrading. It is the Church who informs us in the Scriptures that Christ, from the age of twelve to thirty, worked by the side of St. Joseph as a carpenter. In the Scriptures there is one sentence that says more than all of the Socialist books, movements, or parades have said throughout the centuries: The worker deserves his wages. To withhold a worker's wage is considered to be a great sin by the Church. The Church issued the Rerum Novarum and the Quadragesimo Anno in the name of justice and love to protect the worker. She always stands on the side of the weak.

What we speak about is no small ripple on the sea's surface, but is rather a tremendous wave that has its origin in the very depths of the ocean.

I think it is at least as important for society to decide: Is there a God and an immortal soul? Is there any connection between the two? Is there any such thing as the brotherhood of man, or are we nothing but a pack of wolves?

The notion that religion is a private affair is basically evil and sinful.

There are no two ways about religion. Religion is either true or false. If it is false, it should not be tolerated in the most hidden recesses of one's house and one's soul. It must be done away with as one does away with morphine and marked cards. If religion is true, then, like all truth, it must be publicly recognized and we must let it be effective in every facet of life: in the town hall, in the state legislature, in Parliament, in industry, in the factory, on the railroad and in offices, so that it may provide true leadership both to the private individual and the public official on life's highway.

If we do not wish to give religion its due recognition, then we hang truth itself; but if they wish to do away with it and send it once more into the underground of the catacombs so as to silence it, our suspicions are aroused: they do not want religion to stand in the path of their deeds and to pass judgment on their sinful heads. Those who would like to prevent religion from entering into public life would themselves like to gain recognition and have their own sorry private lives publicly recognized. There must be a reason why one should not be allowed to say outside of the Church: thou shalt not kill; thou shalt not commit adultery; thou shalt not steal; thou shalt not lie or bear false witness!

This theory is in itself impossible: in his home he is religious and Catholic; on the street he becomes a heathen, and at his workbench he is godless.

But in the same way that we are able to recognize a tree by its fruit, so too can we discern the true meaning of this theory. Where religion is merely a private affair, the whole of life becomes corrupted, sinful, and cruel. I have studied a great deal of history and I have been particularly interested in those ages that claimed religion to be a private affair. Napoleon, in summing up certain aspects of the French Revolution, said that in a world without religion people kill one another by the score for a beautiful woman or a luscious pear or a jug of wine. Wherever this theory is propounded, there we find murder, immorality, stealing, robbery, lies and libel. If this flood is let loose, it will be a great menace to the general welfare and mighty difficult for the state to curb and control. Is it wise for a state to allow such a menacing theory to gain a foothold? Let us be clear about it: either society concerns itself with religious morals or with sinful corruption. This is life's relentless logic.

Hitler also made religion a private affair. As a result there was Dachau, Auschwitz, an empire of prisons, gas chambers, the Gestapo, and so forth. Nietzsche was the forerunner of all this. It was he who declared that we have outgrown the old-fashioned concepts of good and bad. "Now that God is dead, you, Man, can resurrect." What a glorious life without God: by order of the state, doctors legally kill the old, the sick, and the crippled; the Jews are thrown into gas chambers, sixty million soldiers go to war; ten million more are in their graves; and twenty million Europeans are homeless. A whole world goes insane in this valley of tears. Then we see a little revolver appear, and with it Hitler kills himself. This is how successful this private affair was. The prophets who proclaimed that religion is a private affair have vanished—but its victims remain. Unhappy humanity is now looking on to see who will take over Hitler's bankrupt ideology and what kind of happiness will result.

It would be a good thing for the new Hitlerite heathen to learn from the old heathen. Aristotle says that the state's main obligation should be religion. Plutarch says that religion is the pillar of society and the foundation of legislation. Valerius Maximus said of heathen Rome that the city always recognized the necessity of placing religion ahead of any worldly considerations.

So much for the heathen; yet this also means a lot to us: the enormous amount of energy that has been expended in words and writings to minimize the importance of religion is ample proof to us that religion is first of all and above all else a matter of public concern.

Christianity's mission is to transform public life. Leo XIII has said that man is compelled to be religious and moral, not only as an individual, but also as a member of a community that is a state.

Serious-minded statesmen have said the same thing, even though they did not belong to the Church. Washington declared before the Congress of 1789: "Of all the dispositions and habits which lead to political prosperity, religion and morality are indispensable supports. In vain would that man claim the tribute of patriotism who should labor to subvert these great pillars of human happiness, these firmest props of the duties of men and citizens."

It has also been our experience that the most important factor in human society is faith in a supernatural God and in a supernatural existence. There is no power that would penetrate human life more forcibly and affect human souls more deeply than religion. Morality can only thrive on a stanch foundation of religion. Great men, heroes, and saints can only be created from those who believe in God and in eternal life, and those who wallow in sin and misery can only be redeemed by religion.

✠

NO NEED FOR REACTION

(From the Cardinal's notes of an address at a convent answering the charge that the church had reactionary tendencies.)

In place of party struggles and internal disputes, people are demanding a united nation capable of treating with the Great Powers to attain a just peace. They desire order and tranquillity, and resent being duped. They say we should help one another and the country with mutual good will.

The attitude of the Church regarding respect for human life and property has never been in doubt. During the time of racial madness, in the face of contrary doctrine and example, she proclaimed, and will ever proclaim, the commandment, "Thou shalt not kill!"

Torture, in whatever form, is likewise a grievous sin in the eyes of the Church, whether it is committed on the eardrums or the soles of the feet.

The strictest laws are unavailing by themselves. We achieve more through uncompromising religious morality. Whoever limits, in any way, the free exercise of religion increases the number of murderers, criminals, and delinquents. For a thousand years we have stood for a united nation, and we have seen that internal disputes and party squabbles bring only turmoil. The peaceable settling of differences, on the other hand, leads to resurrection and reconstruction. Let there be peace and tranquillity. The fever-worn patient needs quiet and rest, instead of domestic brawls and the ever exciting echo of street fights. Unity urgently demands that the God-given oneness that binds together apostles, bishops, priests, and communicants should exist as a matter of course among us all.

We subscribe to the proposition that there is no need for *reaction*, nor for the *action* that provokes it. What the country does

[263]

need is true democracy free from fear, with a guarantee of human rights, religious freedom extending beyond the walls of the Church, freedom of the press, freedom of assembly, and real equality.

Of late the question of Catholic schools, and religious schools in general, has been dragged, alas, from the realm of culture into that of politics. Through the sacrament of baptism, the Church, in the role of God-given father and mother, joins the child's earthly parents, who are linked in the sacrament of marriage. Whoever attacks the rights of the Church in education also attacks the rights of the parents. Whoever attacks the rights of the parents wounds the fatherly and motherly heart of the Church.

The state, too, has its rights in the field of education. It has the right to set standards of education for its citizens, particularly for its officials; and the people have the right to demand that a sufficient number of schools be available. It would be a strange sort of reconstruction that sought to tear down undamaged buildings instead of restoring gutted ones.

We hear a lot of talk about the necessity for eliminating certain sins and planting virtues in their place. If we desire to cultivate virtues such as love of country, mutual understanding, tranquillity, harmony, the termination of party squabbles, and neighborly love instead of hate, then we shall need a firm basis of religious morality rooted in the teaching of the faith. For no one can escape sin or prove capable of self-sacrifice who does not believe in a Heavenly Father, through whom we all are brothers and sisters, and who calls us to account for our actions.

✠

FREEDOM

(From a paper by the Cardinal before the assembly of the Catholic laity, at the annual meeting of St. Stephen's Society.)

It has now been over sixty years since we have been praying, after the Low Mass, for the freedom and glorification of the Church. Pope Leo XIII, in 1884, having the persecuted French Catholics in mind, ordered this prayer.

The freedom of the Church is, all over the world in our era, a very timely matter. It is at least as important as the much discussed freedom of the individual. The freedom of the Church, like the freedom of the individual, is never at its greatest when it is proclaimed and announced most vehemently. The freedom of the Church and the freedom of the individual are usually both simultaneously shackled. This can best be recognized by the history of the first three centuries, the French Revolution, and Hitler's Third Reich.

What is freedom and what is the Church? And what is the connection between the two?

According to Roman law, "Libertas est naturalis facultas eius, quod cuique facere libet, nisi si quid vi, aut iure prohibetur." (Freedom is a natural human faculty which enables us to do as we please unless we are prevented from so doing by force or by law.)

The Church is supernatural in her nature and essence, since she is the Body of Christ, living with the life of Christ Himself, with a supernatural life. Even though, by origin, the Church is not of this world, it has to function among human beings. Therefore, besides being a supernatural entity she is also a perfect society, with rights and privileges. As such, she has the right to freedom, as her proper functioning depends on it and as man's salvation depends on her proper functioning.

Cardinal Gibbons says that freedom is the invigorating air of the Church, without which it could no more exist than could a plant without sunlight.

The Church has a very real and legal claim to freedom for itself and for its members, who are not only souls, but people. Christ does not consider his disciples to be servants, but friends. "If therefore the son shall make you free, you shall be free indeed." And it is also said: "And you shall know the truth, and the truth shall make you free." The Apostle of all nations writes in a letter to the Galatians: "For you, brethren, have been called unto liberty." He shows no differentiation between master and servant. He regards them both as sons of God who are entitled to real equality and the same rights and freedom.

The canon law, according to Christ's instructions, proclaims that the Church has the right to teach freely throughout the world, to christen freely and thereby gain new members, independently from all temporal might.

It has the right to found and sustain schools of all grades; it is free to teach religion and morals in its own and any other schools, and it is free to supervise all schools as regards their teaching of religion and morals.

The Church as a society requires law and freedom. The state says: Salus rei publicae suprema lex esto; and the Church says that because of its interest in the supernatural it must claim: Salus animarum suprema lex esto!

The history of the Church consists not only of a defense and an analysis of its teachings, but of the putting into effect of its rights and laws. The Church has always proclaimed its own freedom and that it is not subject to the authority of the state. The Popes have always refuted the theories (caesaropapism, Gallicanism, Febronianism, Josephinism, states' rights monopoly, statism, and so forth,) according to which the Church is merely a dependent of, and is submissive to, the state. It has always opposed, with protest, all interference by the state, whether in matters of faith or in Church administration.

The Church is a perfect society because it has its own aims; to achieve these aims it has its own methods: by its teachers, by its priests, and by its governing bodies.

In its capacity as a supreme teacher, the Church is entitled to freedom. This is revealed truth.

This authority to teach, possessed by the Church, has its origin in the proclaimed words of Christ: "For it is not you that speak, but the Spirit of your Father that speaketh in you."

The Apostles proclaimed the Gospel and were prepared to suffer persecution and death for it. St. Paul said unequivocally to the powers that tried to restrict him: "The word of God is not bound."

The Church, in the knowledge of its divine mission, relentlessly pursues its right to teach religion. It has always opposed any state control as regards its proclamation of faith and its religious teachings, whether or not these controls were attempted by legislation or by a state monopoly of schoolbooks. It has vigorously fought the secularization of the schools, claiming for itself the right to teach and rear children. It recognizes, however, that the school is the joint responsibility of the family, the Church, and the state, but only in so far as it is the parents' privilege and duty to bring up their children in religious, moral, physical, and civic knowledge.

It has direct authority in the religious teachings of all kinds of grades of schools, in the training of the teachers of religion, in their appointment; also to approve by virtue of its canonical mission all religious schoolbooks and to supervise the religious and moral upbringing of all students.

The state founds its own schools, and it can exercise the prerogative of supervising those schools that are not maintained by the state.

Christ has given the Church the authority and power so that it might, with the grace of the sacraments and with God's intercession, sanctify souls.

It is this sacerdotal power that organizes public services and processions and that is responsible for the administering of the sacraments and the entire liturgy. Like the open and public services of the faithful, according to Romano Guardini, one cannot merely rely on the taste and whims of the individual. We also cannot leave to the individual's taste and whim the decision as to whether or not the procession, which is a two-thousand-year-old ceremony and which is a part of the Catholic ritual and originates in human nature, should or should not take place; and if the decision is in the affirmative, whether it may be held in a garden or in a street, on the main thoroughfare or in an alley.

Christ gave the Church the authority to govern. This is also a revealed truth. "As the Father hath sent me, I also send you." Jesus Christ has made full use of his authority as a lawmaker, judge, and enforcer of the law. With the power of binding and absolving, the power to enact laws and to exclude disobedient heathens, he also handed over the judicial power and the power to punish. He has turned over all of these rights and powers to His Church. The Apostles and the Church have made full use of these rights and powers at all times.

The early Christians never opposed any state and never constituted a revolutionary faction. St. Coloman of Rome and St. Polycarp have handed down to us moving prayers that the Christians used when praying for the civil authorities. These prayers date from the year 96. From the year 210 we have a sermon of St. Hippolytus, which is an excellent example of how the state and the heathen emperors were honored. Justinian, Minucius Felix, and Tertullian refute the accusation that they were politically unreliable; Tertullian even states that the best citizens of the Roman Empire are Christians. They did not and would not subscribe to the state cult which centered around the person of the emperor, as recounted to us in 180 by Theophilus of Antioch, but died, rather, the death of martyrs. By means of a Roman law regulating the burial of the dead, the Christians were legally able to stay in the catacombs until 260, when the Emperor Valerianus prohibited all visiting of cemeteries.

The heathen empire of Rome withered away and became weary of persecuting the Church, but the Church never became weary of its martyrdom.

In the year 313, Constantine the Great stated in his Milan Proclamation that the Christians be given the same rights as the heathens. In the year 380 the Emperor Theodosius the Great and Gratianus made Christianity the religion of the state.

This was the greatest turning point in world history since the birth of Christ. The heathen citizens, the officials and soldiers and even the emperor, became Christians. Nevertheless, the heathen ideology of the emperor cult remained unchanged. The Pontifex Maximus cult made the emperor the supreme religious authority and believed that after his death he would become at least a comet and one who, as time passed, was regarded as God himself, even more than was Jupiter. He had his own religious cult, his own priests, his own holidays and temples, and those who did not pay him homage were looked upon as being atheists and public enemies; but pride and vanity are so much a part of human nature that new emperors looked back on these times with yearning and found it difficult to renounce these customs. These feelings are so deeply rooted in human nature that the heathen emperor Decius said that he would rather suffer another emperor in Rome than a bishop.

When Constantine the Great attended the first council at Nicaea, in 325, he was only there as a crowned disciple and as honorary chairman, and he had less authority in the spiritual hierarchy than the lowliest priest. We cannot say that he was entirely happy about this state of affairs, but we do know that his sons deeply resented it and therefore became the most powerful supporters of the Arian Schism. The decreasing importance of Rome, the influence of Constantinople, the religious fights and schisms all contributed to the revival of the old emperor cult, which was now called caesaropapism.

It would be difficult to determine whether the influential patronage of the emperor's court fanned the various eastern schisms into a sea of flames, or whether the emperor's jealousy of the growing spiritual power of the Church (infringing upon the might of the Byzantine Empire) was responsible for the spread of the heresies—which grew stronger, usurping the Church's sole prerogative to teach and infringing upon its freedom—and channeled these forces into the formation of a state church. We can consider this to be the first appearance of a totalitarian state.

The fact is that the emperors' growing lust for religious power went hand in hand with the growth of the schisms. Arius, although he was an Alexandrian priest, found protection and was rehabilitated in Constantinople; Eutyches was a monk; and Nestorius, Sergius, and Photius, were all patriarchs of Constantinople. It is also true that the emperors found religious authority very much to their liking. They made many liturgical decisions and even ventured into the realm of dogmatics. They promulgated a series of credos (Enciklikon, Henotikon, Ekthesis pisteos, Typos).

They endeavored to settle religious disputes. They considered this function to be as rightfully theirs as the hiring of soldiers or the waging of war, even though the canonical law does not give them this authority. As the Church continuously and determinedly opposed this overreaching of authority, the state, in 1054, took over this schismatic and fettered part of the Church. This state church became stultified, and the Occidental Church disintegrated into various national churches. Three hundred years later the Byzantine Empire that was responsible for these happenings was itself destroyed.

The infiltration of politics into churchly affairs, originating in Constantinople, had a wide sphere of influence and spread as far as the emperors of the German-Roman Empire, the Hohenstaufens, who replaced the Christian-Roman Empire in 476. The gallant Frederick Barbarossa and his grandson, Frederick II, were similarly influenced, in the twelfth century, by the revival of Roman law in the Italian universities that were imbued with the spirit of Constantinople. Barbarossa called for a general council in Pavia, to which he even summoned the Pope. This Ghibelline trend toward *Eigenkirche* brought about the inauguration of bishops by giving them the bishop's ring and staff. This practice created a whole hierarchy of unworthy prelates and sinful practices, like Simony.

The same course was pursued in England, under Henry II, later on by Henry VIII and Elizabeth; in France, under Philip the Fair, Louis XIV, and Napoleon, in Portugal, under Pombal, and in the Habsburg Empire, under Joseph II, this same trend was also followed.

The Church, under Gregory VII, dealt with this situation that flared up in the East, and evaded it in the West, during the Middle Ages, by declaring war against these worldly seizures and everything that pertained to them; thus it was able to shake off these yokes and to regain its full freedom. Therefore one acts against the current of history when one accuses the propertyless Church of feudalism in

1947, when the Church itself fought against and defeated feudalism in the twelfth century.

On the tender, motherly face of the Church we see the marks of her martyrdom and of her fight for freedom, which she has not sought but has accepted whenever challenged.

The catacombs are the great cemeteries where lie buried those who fought for the Church's freedom. From its origin to its liberation in the reign of Constantine the Great, thirty-two Popes have held office, of whom thirty have died the death of martyrs and two have been exiled. They were the successors to the College of Apostles, whose every member died as a martyr. St. John was the only one to survive, after he had been boiled in oil. Blood on the papal throne is not inherited, but swirls around it from century to century.

With the fight for freedom come exile, imprisonment, and violent death. People like St. Athanasius were exiled five times; the golden-tongued St. John was twice exiled, as were Popes Martin and Gregory VII and many more. Forty thousand priests were exiled by the French Revolution; Popes were imprisoned, like Vigilius VI and Pius VII. St. Thomas Becket and St. Thomas More and twenty-one Jesuits were martyrs of the English Schism, as St. Josaphat and Andrew Bobola were martyrs of the Eastern Schism. The faithful ones today face death in the same spirit, for the sake of Jesus and the Church, as was found in the early days of Christianity. Yet those who are the persecutors of today have been brought up in a civilization created by the Church. On the bulwark of decency and humanity for the individual is rising a new world order for the individual, the family, and society.

This is our rock, surrounded by waves. The martyrs of the persecution of the Church in Hungary are: St. Gellért and two of his fellow bishops, Governor Szolnok, and the three martyrs from Kassa. If we search for the names of the primates who have fought for the Church's freedom, we come across the name of Lucas Bánfi, who died in 1178 in the odor of sanctity. When the insatiable mighty ones raided both the properties and rights of the Church, he rallied the Hungarian prelates in 1169 at Esztergom, and together with them appeared at the court of Stephen III, where he revealed the wounds and injustices suffered by the Church. Robert, who died in 1238, excommunicated all the counselors of the crown and the palatine. He also forbade all public religious ceremonies throughout the country. George Pálóczy, who died in 1439, defended the rights of the Church and its unity of faith against Hussitism very energetically. When Leslie Zalka and Matthias died the deaths of heroes at Mohács and at Mohi, they did not only die for their country. The fortunes of John Vitéz (1465) and John Kanizsay (1419) were disappropriated.

They fought not only for their country's constitution, but also for the freedom of the Church. Vitéz was held prisoner in Visegrád and died a prisoner. Martinuzzi, in 1551, in Transylvania, was the last great supporter of the Church. He was disgustingly murdered. Pázmány, an outstanding fighter on the Church's behalf, was exiled. The saintly John Hám was forced to abdicate in 1849. Justin Serédi also fought for the human and ecclesiastical rights of the Church to the very end.

In our age the fight against the freedom of the Church has taken a new direction. Up to now the churches have been taken away from the faithful; but now the faithful are taken away from the churches. This has been carried out in a fiendish way for the past twelve years by Hitler. Cardinal Faulhaber has called it "the move of Satan."

It started with the misleading Concordat. Then the curtains were lowered all around, and contact between the bishops and Rome became increasingly difficult. To inform foreign countries as to what was happening became practically impossible. The slogan for this deliberate campaign was: Keep on tightening the noose. The object was to remove religion from public life; the goal was the complete destruction of independence.

Everybody took part in this barrage: the entire press, the theater, the movies, the radio, exhibitions, posters, party agitators, choir groups; and, at the same time, the Church was denied the use of these instruments of propaganda. The freedom of the press and of speech, and freedom of assembly, were suspended at the very beginning. The privacy of the mail and telephone services and the secrecy of the ballot box ceased. New sects and apostate priests appeared on the side of the party agitators against the Church. The Nazis started a movement designed to induce people to resign from the Church. With a few poor words like Blood, Race, State, and Leader, a wave of propaganda on a dizzy scale was launched to discredit Rome, the German bishops, and the whole German priesthood, and to make all steadfast Catholics lose their faith. The possibility of legal defense was non-existent.

At the beginning the Nazis were careful, but later on their persecution became brutal and bloody, with an animallike cunning. They said they held no grievance against religion, but that they were only attacking the bishops. They attacked the more prominent members of the Church's hierarchy more than they did the ordinary priests. The newspaper *Angriff* published an article attacking the Pope in more than one hundred thousand editions. The bishops were openly called liars, rascals, and traitors at public meetings. The authorities and some of their hotheaded followers broke up public meetings and forcibly made the bishops leave. The Bishop's Palace in Munich was attacked. The homes of the bishops were frequently searched. The famous Morals trials also had a purpose, which was to weaken the economic standing of the Church.

Politics became an issue in their war against the Church polity, by declaring that they considered all bishops and priests to be Communists. In the government the minister of the interior and the minister of justice, the police and the Gestapo, all banded together to put shackles on the words of God, on services (the forbidding of processions), on priestly functions (administration of the sacraments), on the functioning of the Church in the schools and seminaries, and even on its charities, which were destroyed by new taxes. They opposed religious teachers; they were against prayer in schoolrooms, against having the Crucifix placed on the wall; they were also opposed to any religious teachings, and they opposed the pastoral letters of the bishops. They meanwhile published reassuring news. As an example, in 1937, Minister Kerrl proclaimed that no priest had ever been harmed because of his profession, no Mass had ever been prohibited, and no Catholic teaching had ever been forbidden.

The first banned organizations—where "conspiracies in the interest of Moscow" were unearthed—were the so-called "enemies" of the state. If the organization reappeared, it had to appoint a president who was above suspicion. Later on, singing lessons were also forbidden. Bible-reading classes had to apply for permits a month in advance or they were not allowed to meet. The Actio Catholica was considered to be a political organization. Propaganda was mostly centered on factory and white-collar workers and on youth.

The children of government officials, and, at a later date, all children, were forced to leave the religious schools and were made to enroll in public schools, and all religious teachers were dismissed. In 1941, in the archdioceses of Breslau alone, sixty monasteries and church institutions were seized. Twelve hundred Bavarian nuns were rendered homeless, and they were robbed by the authorities while they were being moved out.

Toward the end of their regime, the Nazis desecrated and closed a great many churches and seized large quantities of missals. Priests were sent in a constant stream to Dachau and other concentration camps. On March 15, 1945, 1,493 German and foreign Catholic priests, among them an archbishop, a bishop, 2 suffragans, 2 abbots, 4 prelates, 482 priests, and 342 chaplains, were found half starved and living like animals in the various concentration camps. Between 1940 and 1945, 2,800 priests from various countries passed through these camps. They suffered untold hardships. Hunger and other privations brought about mass destruction. They were subjected to so-called "scientific" experiments, such as breaking their bones in order to observe what sort of wounds would result and to see how these wounds would heal.

Those who were released had to sign papers binding them to complete silence concerning their experiences in the camps. These were the camps where the authorities officially put to death all those persons unable to work, and the old and the sick.

After the groundwork had been laid, all the youth were severed from the Church. All members of the Hitler Youth organizations were prohibited, from the very beginning, from taking part in processions. Hitler demonstrations were scheduled for Sunday morning at the same time that the Sunday Masses were read. The purely religious functions of the Church were hampered. Processions were banned in Munich on the grounds that they obstructed traffic. The secret orders given by Reichsleiter Bormann for the destruction of the Church; and the secret orders of the Gestapo, with the same purpose in mind, but which said that the Church was illegal, as an excuse; and Johann Neuhausler's book *The Cross and the Swastika*, in which these and many other facts were enumerated, revealed to the world that Voltaire's flaming hatred of the Church was naught compared to all this, and that this was just a beginning.

One asks oneself whether this satanical war against the Church will go any further? Will this much condemned campaign of Hitler find followers? I must point out to you, with satisfaction, the gallant fight that the youth of Germany, who were most endangered, and the faithful and the priests and bishops of the German Church waged on behalf of the Church's freedom. They stand side by side with the martyrs of the first three centuries. The marvelous unity displayed by the bishops, the determination of the priests, and the steadfastness of the faithful, and above all, the strength of the youth makes valid the claim of the German Catholics that the cross still stands, and the swastika is a thing of the past.

This fact we must acknowledge as we gaze with horror at the past.

There are ideas and trends born in the name of freedom that use its flag only to have us discover, at a later date, that they are in reality the professional gravediggers of liberty. The persecution of the Church is a two-faced phenomenon; one face resembles glorious freedom, while the other one bears the ugly features of despotism. These despots publicly preach human rights and freedom, but behind closed doors they deprive people of their rights in a most ruthless fashion.

According to Hitler's *Mein Kampf*, those holding political power should leave the people's religious teachings and institutions untouched at all times; any other road would lead Germany to catastrophe. In 1933, according to his official statements, Hitler said that he considered the Catholic religion and Protestantism to be the greatest single factors in maintaining a nation's morale, and at that time Hitler refrained from any interference with these rights. He guaranteed to preserve the Church's influence in the schools and advocated, not religious, but only political changes. The Concordat says in the first chapter, "We guarantee freedom of religion and the free exercise of Catholicism."

In 1937 the Pope declared that the open persecution of the Church by the Nazis was a fact which had first been practiced upon the priests and had reached as far as the most humble believer.

There are those who cover evil with the cloak of freedom.

Today, all over the world, there are charters guaranteeing freedom of religion. This is also the case in our country. The Parliament of January 30, 1946, guaranteed to every citizen "Man's natural and inalienable Rights." Among these rights were: personal freedom, freedom from persecution, freedom from fear, freedom from want, freedom of speech, freedom of religion, freedom of assembly, the right to own private property, personal safety, the right to work and to receive adequate compensation, the right to education, and the right to participate in government.

"No one can be deprived of these rights without trial." In other words, freedom of religion is guaranteed by law.

No political party has been in opposition to the granting of these rights; not even a single deputy has raised his voice in opposition. This law was unanimously approved. Even a Marxist deputy said: "We embrace these principles, and this magnificent and high-minded declaration of human rights, wholeheartedly."

Previously, on September 5, 1945, Prime Minister Miklós stated: "The censorship of the press, instituted by the Provisional Government, has been lifted because its continuance would not be in accord with democratic principles." But he specified what constituted the freedom of the press in the following order:

Every citizen has the right to publish articles and hold public office.

All parties forming the Independence Front have the right to publish newspapers, pamphlets, posters, and leaflets.

All religious publications and pamphlets are not to be censored before publication.

The leaders of all parties and the head of the Church are directly responsible to the Censorship Bureau.

This was all approved by the Parliament.

Since then two pastoral letters, before their publication, have been held up by the authorities.

It is unjust and unfair to confine the Universal Church, in its functions, within the framework of the rights granted to an ordinary organization and to apply to it the same laws and regulations that apply to any ordinary society, as if it were no better than a sporting organization or a hunt club. It has even been denied the rights or the same legal standing granted to a political party. The Church has its own aims which are not simply a part of the state's aims. Services and processions should not be dependent on police permission; religious organizations and pastoral letters should not be passed upon by the ministry of the interior.

Restrictions of this kind are in direct opposition to the constitution of the Church, particularly at a time when the world tolerates, and even aids, the activities of disruptive organizations. It is also unfair, inasmuch as the Church has publicly and openly proclaimed its teachings and has held services for the past two thousand years. The requirement that the Church submit its teachings for approval denies the fact that it is a perfect society, and revives a similar law passed by Emperor Joseph II, which has since become obsolete. Even the cynical Strindberg was shocked by the forbiddance and the breaking up of Catholic processions, especially as street carnivals are celebrated with great displays of dissipation, under the protection of the police and at government expense.

We are of the same opinion as St. Ambrose: "It is not worthy of the Emperor and the authorities to deny freedom of speech, and it is also not worthy of a priest to withhold his opinions. Nothing can enhance the popularity of an Emperor more than his respect for his people's freedom."

The difference between good and bad rulers is that the good ones embrace freedom, whereas the bad ones prefer slavery.

Nothing is as dangerous before God, and as mortifying in the eyes of the people, as when a priest does not dare to proclaim the truth as he sees it.

When St. Ambrose, the Bishop of Milan, was requested to resign his position by the emperor, his answer was:

"I cannot leave my flock. You force me to revolt, but this is not of my choosing. Against your arms and your Gothic mercenaries I have but one weapon, my tears. But I shall not leave and I will not forsake the Church in its time of tribulation. I am ready to accept the bloody sentence of the Emperor. We render unto Caesar the things which are Caesar's and unto God, the things which are God's. Taxes belong to the Emperor and we do not withhold them from him. But the Church belongs to God and so we cannot surrender it to the Emperor. The Emperor has no rights over God's Church. . . . The Emperor's might can create another Emperor, but it cannot make a priest! . . . The Emperor cannot enter the sacred enclosure surrounding the altar."

What is, then, the legal status of the Church and the state, and their relation to one another?

Both are perfect societies, created by God, each having its own, independent goal, and each possessing the means to achieve its ends. Neither is subservient to the other; each is supreme in its own way.

God, who created nature, also created the state; and God, who created supernatural grace, is the creator of the Church; one was created for our worldly welfare, and the other works for our eternal salvation; one is active in the realm of temporal activities, while the other holds sway over men's souls. These two orbits of influence do not differ in substance, but, rather in what they have been ordained for.

As Pope Leo XIII writes: "Anything that is holy in the affairs of Man, and anything that pertains to the salvation of souls, to public services, by its nature or by reason of its ordained purpose, comes under the jurisdiction and the authority of the Church. All other matters we refer to temporal authorities." Considering these ends and ordained purposes, it then becomes apparent that not only do the sacraments, the holidays, and the preaching of the Gospel pertain to the soul, but also the Churches and the Church properties. To safeguard religion, and all matters pertaining to it, comes under the Church's authority.

The Church also defends the rights and freedom of the state. No one can be more cooperative to the state than the Church. According to Origenes, Christians are the salt of the state in that they preserve the bonds that hold society together on this earth.

The first rule of Christian statesmanship is: The best safeguard of a state is the name of God. The second rule is: To follow the Christian moral order is the best safeguard for preserving the state's authority.

The work of the state is advanced and made easier by the Church's development of conscience, character, respect for authority, and the appreciation of spiritual values; but it is quite certain that the Church cannot accomplish these things without complete freedom and independence.

Where the freedom of the Church does not come into its own is found *libertas perditionis* (the freedom of perdition).

This is a sketchy outline of the essence of ecclesiastical freedom, its history, and its direction.

What about the glorification of the Church? From time to time, throughout history, the Church is permitted a glimpse, wherever its cross appears, of this glorification. But the Church's cross is a worldly heritage, and the real and complete Easter will not achieve complete fulfillment on this earth until the thread of world history completely unwinds itself and judgment has been passed on the world. Not until the faithful sons of the Church and its enemies are measured will the cross shine and the gates of Heaven lift up, and the Church Struggling, and the Church Suffering march into the Church Triumphant, its face recognized by all, made a spectacle to the world, and to angels, and to men. Until then we will have to find strength in the Revelations: Have confidence, I have overcome the world.

The gates of hell shall not prevail against the Church.

✠

CATHOLIC PARENTS

(After the nationalization of the Church schools, the Cardinal released the following letter at the opening of the school year 1948–1949, in behalf of the Hungarian episcopate.)

With the opening of the school doors each year, when the youth sing in our churches the *Veni Sancte*, a certain anxiety takes hold of the hearts of responsible, loving fathers and mothers despite their confidence. A thought, a biblical question emerges: "What an one, think ye, shall this child be?" At the threshold of the school year of 1948–1949, this anxiety and the weight of this question increase and lie heavily upon the hearts of millions. This school year differs in every respect from any other preceding one. It is the first year in which those who for a thousand years have stood beside the Hungarian school child are no longer in the schools. The spirit of education which was based on revelation, the spirit which alone was able to quiet anxious parents in troubled times, the spirit which has proved its value in bringing up men and women in the fear of God and in the love of their country: no longer can it be found in our schools.

There are people instigated by others to criticize our priests and monks for not teaching in the secularized schools of Hungary. For this they blame the Church, that is to say, the clergy.

These people forget that the priests and religious orders of Christ can teach only in the spirit of God. This is because they are priests and monks. They could undertake to teach and educate heretofore because by doing so they were practicing their profession. If they cannot teach in conformity with their philosophy of life, they cannot continue their activities lest they come in conflict with themselves. The schools have been taken away primarily in order to eliminate this spirit from the schools. Thus in the schools that have been taken away, this guiding principle cannot prevail, with the exception of classes in religion where the teacher of religion will give instruction in religious truths.

The state did not expel the priest from its schools; on the contrary, in all declarations made to you it supposedly tried to keep them there. Actually, the given circumstances and conditions, however, morally render their remaining impossible.

I want to point out only two things:

1. When, in the seventeenth century, the emperor of Japan demanded that the European missionaries make their first step on Japanese soil by stepping on the crucifix that was put on the soil, the Mikado and his ministers did not forbid Europeans to land in Japan; they merely created a situation which was equivalent to a ban. Some Europeans settled in Japan nevertheless; but the missionaries and priests were unable to step on the cross and did not. Since our schools have been taken away from us, the priests, monks, and prospective priests could enter their threshold only by tramping upon and betraying inviolable eternal principles. These principles are: the divine right of our Church to teach (it has done so in this country for nine and a half centuries); the right of parents to select their children's teachers; and the seventh and tenth commandments. The world nowadays considers all these trivially. We, however, consider them eternally valid.

2. The materialist movement, as proclaimed on May 9th, expects the labor unions and other associations of workers to participate in guiding and controlling education. We have had our experiences last year and can easily see, from the rest of the proclamation, what the future holds in store for us. The party of Hungarian Workers, the Communist party, confesses and follows "the ideology of Marxism-Leninism; applies and develops the teachings of Marx and Engels . . . fights consistently against any divergence from the philosophy of life of Marxism-Leninism in the schools," in the interest of eliminating all remnants of prejudice.

The party of those who made this declaration has the decisive power in Hungarian public life. Thus if, as they say, they want to participate in guiding the education and want to educate in the spirit of Marx and Lenin, they have the power to do so. And what is Marxism? you will want to know. The answer to this question was given by the Marxists; and Lenin himself in his *Marx, Engels, Marxism*, which was published in Moscow in 1947, says:

Marxism is materialism. As such it is the inexorable enemy of religion. Its fundamental principle: we must fight against religion; we must destroy religious faith. Just as materialism is atheistic, so Marxism also is opposed to any religion. The instruction, training and education of today's youth must aim at educating this youth in Communist morals.

This is what the Marxist creed declares. This confession of faith professes no God, no immortal soul, no revelation, no supernatural truth; there are no Ten Commandments, Church sacraments, or prayers. All these are denied by materialism. Moreover, as we just heard, materialism wars against them, and instead of the morals of the gospel, it aims at Communist morals as the goal of education.

We ask: Can priests and nuns participate in this kind of education? Every thinking person can give only one answer: *No!* And if those responsible for the secularization of our schools maintain that they do not expect our priests and our nuns to do so, we ask: In that case what was the purpose of taking our schools away? Why don't they let us have our institutions, and let our priests and members of our teaching orders educate in a spirit whose value has been proven by age-old practices, in a spirit that has been so much praised by the very people who took our schools from us?

Even if they did promise us that our schools will not become antireligious and remain neutral, so that in case our priests stayed on they would not come in conflict with their conscience, we ask: Where is the guarantee that it will be so? The Church has had experience in such matters and is fully aware of the true value of such promises.

We must realize that we have been eliminated from all schools as elements which might mold the children's character. The party units have separated the unity of natural and supernatural, God and man, time and eternity. Concentrating on smaller details, they neglect the immensely bigger one. They do not look upon the individual as being redeemed by Jesus; they rather look upon him as a prospective party man, a party member to be. The teachers, curricula, and books of our present schools all cause us to ask: "What then shall this child be? What is to become of this child?" Whenever new life springs on Hungarian soil, the first sigh of the mother is for a religious upbringing.

Let us dry the tears of parents; let us save the immortal souls of children!

Even though the strong fortress of God, the religious school, has been taken away from us—a wound that shall never heal—our other fortifications, the Catholic family, Church, and parish, are not lost. In these fortifications, by the command of God, you must stand guard, dear parents!

The personal and sacred obligation of Catholic parents, in the field of child education, according to the Church, is: It is the parents' duty to do their utmost in behalf of the religious, moral, physical, and civic education of the offspring.

The bringing up of children in a Christian spirit is not merely the right, but the duty of the parents and their substitutes.

Hear ye, parents, what are your responsibilities!

In the family: The religious school could not function without the sanctity of the family home. If schools teaching religion cease to exist, the importance of the role that the family will have to play will increase. How many parents said in the past when their children did not want to pray: "There is the school, let it teach them!" This attitude has never been justified; as a matter of fact, it has never been so little justified as today. The child cannot find members of teaching orders, nuns, or religious teachers. This is the time for parents, fathers and mothers alike, to assume the responsibility of the former. Teaching children to pray must become a serious task. The teaching of religion in schools will not suffice to fill the child with all that Catholicism means. Let parents spend evenings and Saturday afternoons repeating the catechism and the Bible with their children. This religious instruction within the family will reawaken in the fathers and mothers the sweet memories of their own warm childhood.

The Church: The hearth and symbol of the faithful avoided by the godless. The church spire of the town, village, and hamlet points toward Heaven. The knees of our ancestors wore off the threshold and the steps of our churches, pointing out to us the kind of life we must lead. Our prayers echo their prayers. Let us make our children love the Church. During the recent persecution of the Church in Germany, the best of the youth manifested beautiful examples of their loyalty to the Church.

Community: This is the legal community of the faithful, where youth lives socially on the soil of faith, in the framework of the Church, in the arms of his Mother, with her ideals in his heart. The work of our youth organizations, once so flourishing, is getting more difficult by the hour. Just as the parent keeps our inexperienced youth from association with non-Catholic circles, loud and foreign to the Hungarian soul, our youth organizations set a lofty ideal to our children. There they remain faithful to God, Church, and country.

Don't say, dear parents, that you have never studied theology or pedagogy, or that you have enough earthly worries anyway. In approaching the souls of your children, we urge our priests to guide you through sermons and lectures in educating children, a task more difficult than polishing diamonds. When the time comes, do not fail to be present and take part in the work. Do not forget that God has endowed parents, particularly mothers, with special gifts. God gave you natural forces to procreate children; you are "a chosen generation, a kingly priesthood."

Thus will materialize what Pope Pius XI said: Church and family form the oneness of the temple of Christian education. The foundations of both are fear of God and respect for authority, both so badly needed by our generation.

God has placed parents in charge not only of the body, but of the immortal souls of their children as well. Every parent is responsible before God for the salvation of his children. On Judgment Day this soul will have to be accounted for. "Give an account of thy stewardship."

Children are the temple of God and parent. Be conscious of this and do not let it lapse for one second. By educating them and by the guiding example of your own Catholic life, raise your children within the family to be Christians.

Pray with your children and for your children!

Father! Mother! Be the ever alert and persistent, never dormant, guardians of your children.

Dear parents! The education of youth in the fear of God concerns Church and country alike. We therefore decree that beginning this school year, following each Mass, after the prayer prescribed by Pope Leo XII, we pray the Lord's Prayer and Hail Mary on behalf of the education of our youth in the fear of God.

The very existence of faith is at stake, in the lives of our children, at any rate. We must save Christianity so that it may continue in the lives of coming generations, and this we must do through teaching and example. Thus we shall give to God and country sons and daughters strong in faith, loyal to the Church.

Thus our children "will not be tossed to and fro and carried about with every wind of doctrine by the wickedness of men, by cunning craftiness, by which they lie in wait to deceive."

It is for the faithful parents to solve, with the grace of God and the help of the Church, the great question posed by this year's *Veni Sancte*: "And the child grew, and was strengthened in spirit; and was in the deserts until the day of his manifestation."

"Christ may dwell by faith in your hearts; a faith—rooted and founded in charity."

"To Him be glory in the Church and in Christ Jesus unto all generations, world without end. Amen."

September 1, 1948

JOSEPH MINDSZENTY
Cardinal, Primate, Archbishop of Esztergom

JOSEPH GRÖSZ
Archbishop of Kalocsa and Bács

FRANCIS VIRÁGH
Assistant at the Pontifical Throne
Bishop of Pécs

JULIUS CZAPIK, D.D.
Archbishop of Eger

LOUIS SHVOY
Assistant at the Pontifical Throne
Bishop of Székesfehérvár

NICHOLAS DUDÁS, D.D.
Bishop of Hajdudorog

ANDREW HAMVAS, D.D.
Bishop of Csanád

KOLOMAN PAPP
Bishop of Györ

MICHAEL BARÓT
Protonotary Canon
Capitular Vicar of Szatmár

BARNABAS TOST
Chapter Provost of Kassa and
Apostolic Administrator of
Rozsnyó

JOSEPH PÉTERY, D.D.
Bishop of Vác

ALEXANDER KOVÁCS
Bishop of Szombathely

LESLIE BÁNÁS, D.D.
Bishop of Veszprém

LESLIE PINTÉR
Prelate Canon
Capitular Vicar of Nagyvárad

PAUL SÁRKOZY, D.D.
Abbot of Bakonybél
Deputy of the Archabbot of
Pannonhalma

JOHN FOLBA
Prelate
Administrator of the Military Chaplaincy

✠

THE END

APPENDIX I

✠

THE POLITICAL AND LEGAL ASPECTS

A.

STATEMENT

of Dean Acheson, Secretary of State of the United States of America, made on February 9, 1949 (including a summary of the comments made by Robert A. Lovett, Acting Secretary of State, on December 29, 1948)

The trial of Joseph, Cardinal Mindszenty, upon whom the Hungarian Government has now imposed a sentence of life imprisonment, confirms the Government and people of the United States in the views expressed by the Acting Secretary of State on December 29, 1948. (Asked to comment on the arrest of Cardinal Mindszenty, Robert Lovett, acting Secretary of State of the United States, said that this was a culmination of a long series of oppressive acts taken by the Hungarian Government against personal freedom. He said that this had been going on for some time and now had reached a climax in the arrest of the Cardinal and a number of others. He declared that it was rather a sickening sham to have that action taken on the basis of charges which were patently false, and he said that he thought that it must affect the attitude of other countries to know that this sort of thing could go on. He declared that it had by extension, of course, another significance, in that what was going on in many of the countries of that belief and character was a type of behavior, a type of action which continued to interfere with reaching the goal of peace and made it still an aspiration rather than a reality. He said that he thought that this particular action would be all that was needed to complete the unhappy chain of events in that country and to indicate what the attitude of the Government was toward the liberties to which the rest of the world attaches the greatest importance.) By this conscienceless attack upon religious and personal freedom, as well as by the persecution of Lutheran Bishop Louis Ordass and other respected Church leaders, the Soviet-controlled Hungarian authorities seek to discredit and coerce religious leadership in Hungary in order to remove this source of moral resistance to Communism.

In their conduct of the case of Cardinal Mindszenty, the Hungarian authorities do not appear to have omitted any of the usual methods practiced by a police state. Such proceedings constitute not the administration of justice but wanton persecution. They have evoked universal condemnation, and the Hungarian Government must bear full responsibility for its action.

The cases of Cardinal Mindszenty and other Hungarian Church leaders are not isolated developments. During the past two years, with governmental power entirely in the hands of the minority Communist Party, the people of Hungary have been increasingly denied the exercise of fundamental human rights and freedoms. Parliamentary opposition, an element indispensable to the democratic process, has been ruthlessly eliminated, the totalitarian controls of State and Party have been laid like a deadening hand upon every phase of daily personal existence, and the Hungarian people have been divested of any real independence.

The people of the United States, and, without question, peoples of other freedom-loving nations, are sickened and horrified by these developments and fully comprehend the threat they constitute to free institutions everywhere.

*   *   *

B.

THE LEGAL ASPECTS
OF THE
TRIAL BEFORE THE PEOPLE'S COURT

Comment of Sir David Maxwell Fyfe, K.C., M.P. Prose-
cutor at the Nuremberg trials of the war criminals (ex-
cerpts)

I shall speak of the actual charges on which Cardinal Mindszenty
was tried. There were seven charges. The first may be briefly called
"Sedition"; the second and third were charges of "Disloyalty"
(*Hütlenség*). The remaining four charges were in respect of currency offences. The Cardinal was found guilty on all seven charges
and was sentenced to life imprisonment.

The first charge, that of Sedition, was under Section 1 (1) of Act
No. VII of 1946 which says: "It is a felony to commit an act designed to overthrow the democratic state order or democratic republic set up by Act I of 1946 or to initiate, lead or afford substantial support to a movement or organisation to that end." The
actual charge under this section on which the Cardinal was convicted
was that he acted as leader of an organisation designed to overthrow
the democratic state order and the democratic republic. It will be
noticed at once that the seditious object of the Cardinal's so-called
organisation was alleged to be the "overthrow" of the democratic
state order and the republic. This word "overthrow" is a strong
word and implies something very active to say the least of it, something in the nature of a coup d'état from within or of armed intervention from without. I shall return to this point presently, but first
of all let me just mention another word in the charge, namely, "organisation." It is a matter of doubt whether the word "organisation"
can properly apply to a small group of people of very loose construc-
tion such as Cardinal Mindszenty was alleged to be the leader of.

But let us assume for the sake of argument that Mindszenty's alleged monarchist group was an organisation within the meaning of the Act.

The crucial legal question is, whether that organisation was designed to overthrow the democratic state order and the republic.

In the view of the prosecution—fully endorsed by the Court—any organisation which has the aim of restoring the monarchy is automatically illegal, whether it pursues its aim by illegal means or not.

Even if this view were right, it can be seen at once that it bypasses the requirement of Section 1 (1) of Act No. VII under which the Cardinal was charged, for the charge is that the organisation was designed to *overthrow* the democratic state order.

It does not follow in law that an organisation which wishes to restore the monarchy is designed to overthrow the democratic state order or the republic. It is an historical fact that in every country which has changed from monarchy to republic there have been people who wished for a return of the old days without it ever crossing their mind that they would lift a finger to overthrow the existing regime. To wish for a return of the monarchy (however unpopular such a wish may be) is quite consistent in law with having no intention of restoring the monarchy unless and until the republic has quite independently come to an end. This is the very explanation that Cardinal Mindszenty gave in his defence. As a lawyer it is impossible for me to say that a court must necessarily accept any explanation given. The giving of the explanation, however, underlines the necessity of the prosecution bringing evidence that the organisation was designed actually to overthrow the republic. This they failed to do.

There was evidence that the possibility of another European war was contemplated by the Cardinal and his group (as indeed at that time it was contemplated by millions of other people), and it was only a reasonable deduction from the study of European history that if such a war had happened there might have been an end of the present Hungarian republic, a vacuum which had to be filled with the least possible delay by some form of Government which could save the country from lapsing into chaos. It is hard to say how it could be illegal to prepare for such an emergency. At any rate the mere preparation for such an emergency does not in any way involve the intention of "overthrowing" the republic.

It could only be said that there was an intention to "overthrow" the republic, if the monarchist group could be shown also to have taken steps to bring about the contemplated war. But there was no evidence whatever that Cardinal Mindszenty and his group tried to bring about another European war. He positively denied it, and the probabilities are all against it. The prosecutor put his argument like this: "They tried," he said, "to make certain United States officials and agents believe that there existed a strong Legitimist movement in Hungary, that our people hated the Government of the People's Democracy and that therefore a warlike step would easily be successful, hoping by such arguments that the United States would start a war in the near future against our country."

It is easy to suggest imaginary motives. But in the court of law motives cannot be imputed unless they are substantiated by facts. The facts which the prosecutor appears to have relied on for this purpose were, first, the letter of authority given by Cardinal Mindszenty to Otto Hapsburg enabling him to represent Hungarian Catholics in America, secondly, the Cardinal's request to the Americans to send the Holy Crown to the Vatican, and thirdly, the Cardinal's letter to Minister Chapin suggesting that America should buy various Russian-owned assets in Hungary.

All these things are no more consistent with inciting war than with Cardinal Mindszenty's own explanation. They therefore carry the case no further.

The prosecutor's suggestion is indeed very naïve. Nobody could seriously suppose that the U.S.A. would declare war on Hungary. What many people did at that time suppose was that the U.S.A. might declare war upon, or become involved in war with, Russia. If this had occurred, the inevitable result for Hungary would have been that she would have found herself behind Russia's front line. Far from declaring war on Hungary the U.S.A. would, in the Cardinal's view, have eventually occupied Hungary as a liberator.

Whether this view was right or wrong, popular or unpopular, it is consistent with every piece of evidence produced by the Prosecution on this charge.

The fact that Act I of 1946 declares that Hungary is a Republic does not, as the Court appears to have maintained, mean that it is automatically illegal to form a movement to alter that state of affairs. The law of Hungary itself permits any previous Act of Parliament to be repealed or amended by proper constitutional means. It would not be against the law of Hungary (though it might be foolhardy) to form a monarchist party, and to put forward monarchist candidates at parliamentary elections.

Moreover, the very next section of the Act under which the Cardinal was charged provides as follows:—

"It is a felony *seditiously* to incite to a change of the State order or Republic."

This section shows quite clearly that there is nothing wrong under Hungarian law in inciting people to change the state order or the republic, if the incitement is not seditious, that is to say if it does not propose the use of unconstitutional methods. This lends further strength to what I said before, namely, that the charge of intending to "overthrow" the state order or the republic means intending to do something actively illegal to bring about the downfall of the state order or the republic.

For the reasons I have given, I cannot see how the Cardinal could in law be properly convicted on this first charge.

I have naturally wanted to make my legal analysis as objective as possible, and I have based it upon the broadcast recordings of the trial and upon the official Hungarian publication. I am not able to say what other evidence there was which has not been published in these ways and which is therefore unknown to me, but I must assume that if there had been any more cogent evidence the Hungarian authorities would have taken care to publish it to the world.

The second charge was a charge of Disloyalty under Section 58 of Act III of 1930, which says:—

"There shall be guilty of the felony of Disloyalty and punishable by penal servitude from ten to fifteen years any person who shall

ally himself with or contact any foreign government, or foreign
organisation, for the purpose of bringing about a hostile act against
the Hungarian state; and further any person who shall endeavour
to incite a foreign power to war or enforcing action against the
Hungarian state."

From a legal point of view the Cardinal's conviction under this
section was absurd.

The facts relied upon by the prosecution were exclusively concerned with the Cardinal's letters to the United States ministers in
Budapest and a letter to President Truman. All of these letters were
written before the Peace Treaty came into force on 15th September
1947, that is to say, they were written during a period when legally
speaking a state of war between Hungary and the U.S.A. was still
subsisting. Hungary was an "Occupied Country" throughout the
period, the U.S.A. being, legally speaking, one of the occupying
powers. Therefore, in law, there could be no question of inciting
the U.S.A. to war or hostile action against the Hungarian state.

Moreover, quite apart from these legal considerations it is perfectly clear from the letters upon which the Prosecution relied that
the Cardinal's references to "American intervention" and "American aid" meant purely and simply the use of the influence with the
Hungarian Government which the head of the United States Mission could, if he chose, have exercised by reason of being the representative of one of the three principal Allied Powers forming the
Allied Control Commission in Hungary at that time.

The third charge was another charge of Disloyalty, this time
under Section 60 of Act III of 1930 which says:—

"There shall be guilty of the felony of Disloyalty and punishable
by hard labour up to five years . . .

"(3) a person, who having become possessed or aware of a secret
(otherwise than by espionage, or by virtue of his official position)
publishes this secret or communicates it or makes it otherwise available to a person not entitled to it, provided that the Act endangers
the interests of the state."

This felony is punishable by penal servitude for life if it was
committed for the purpose of communicating a secret to an authority

of a foreign state or a foreign organisation and if it resulted in a serious harm or threat to the interests of the state. Probably both these conditions were considered proved, for the Cardinal was sentenced to imprisonment for life.

Let us see what was really proved against the Cardinal in respect of this very serious charge.

It was proved that in February 1948 he agreed to supply Mr. Chapin with reports on the Hungarian political and economic situation and the democratic parties, based on information from the clergy. It was also proved that such reports were in fact conveyed to Mr. Chapin.

It is a long jump from that to bringing in a verdict of "guilty."

Quite apart from the question whether that information which was given to Mr. Chapin caused or could have caused any serious harm or threat to the interests of Hungary, there was not any proof whatever that the reports sent to Mr. Chapin contained "secrets" within the meaning of the Act under which the Cardinal was charged.

The mere fact that Mr. Chapin may not have known this information before it was communicated to him, or the fact that he chose to get this information privately from the Cardinal rather than from the Hungarian Government, does not mean that it was a secret within the meaning of the Act. It is obviously necessary in a prosecution for such a serious charge to show quite clearly that the information in question is secret in the legal sense of that word, that is to say, that it is information which those who know it are under a duty not to disclose.

It is rather significant that in order to introduce an atmosphere of the betrayal of military secrets it was stated that the Cardinal obtained and communicated to the British and American Missions the draft budget of the Soviet troops in Hungary and information on the situation in the Sub-Carpathian Ukraine. Both these matters are, of course, irrelevant to the charge that I am now speaking of because the law in question does not protect the secrets of a foreign army of occupation nor information relating to a foreign territory.

But even supposing the information communicated to Mr. Chapin could legally be called "secret," it was quite wrong to say, as the indictment said, that Mr. Chapin was not entitled to receive that information. As head of the United States Mission Mr. Chapin was entitled under Article 39 of the Peace Treaty to receive all information relevant to the execution of the Peace Treaty, and particularly of course to receive information calculated to throw light on the way in which the Hungarian Government was carrying out the Human Rights clauses of the Peace Treaty.

Considerable emphasis was also placed in the Yellow Book (and at the trial) on the espionage centre which it was alleged was set up by Monsignor Mihalovics.

It was alleged that Mihalovics left Hungary with the consent of the Cardinal and that when he reached Austria he contacted the American Counter Intelligence Corps. From this it was boldly deduced at the trial, without a shred of evidence, that Mihalovics must have contacted the Counter Intelligence Corps upon the direct instructions of the Cardinal.

The evidence on this third charge was merely political prejudice; it was not capable in law or in logic of proving the crime with which the Cardinal was charged.

The remaining four charges against Cardinal Mindszenty are charges relating to foreign currency.

Every lawyer who has had to do with the foreign currency laws, knows how intricate and complicated, and often technical, they are. It would be quite impossible for me on the scanty information available to form an opinion as to whether the Cardinal's guilt on these charges was properly proved. Let us assume that he did break the currency regulations.

It is not unimportant to point out that his defence was that he did so without intention. His defence counsel pleaded that he had not properly understood the regulations relating to foreign currency. Even the judge seems to have had this point in mind, when he emphasized the Cardinal's "seclusion from practical everyday life." We may fairly conclude that the currency charges were regarded both by the Prosecution and by the Court as a relatively minor part of the indictment. . . .

I shall show that some of the fundamental principles of justice were ignored in the trial of Cardinal Mindszenty, and I shall compare the conduct of this trial with the conduct of trials by the Special Courts (Sondergerichte) and the People's Courts (Volksgerichte) under the Nazi regime in Hitler Germany.

The two fundamental principles of justice which I wish to emphasize particularly are first that the judge must be unbiased and independent, and secondly that the accused must have a fair opportunity of making his defence.

For ten months I conducted the Prosecution on behalf of the British at the trial of the major war criminals at Nüremberg. During that time I investigated the methods used by the Nazis to obtain control of the German state from 1935 onwards, and I learnt in detail, and by admissions out of their own mouths, how human rights and all that civilisation stands for can be destroyed by poisoning the fountain of Justice.

The fountain of Justice can be poisoned even without abandoning the traditional legal forms and the normal rules of procedure in courts of law. All that is necessary is to abuse the forms and the procedure, to use them in an unfair way.

I want to illustrate from the evidence given at the Nuremberg trial how the Nazis set about this abuse of legal procedure, and I want to compare with that the methods which were employed at the trial of Cardinal Mindszenty. I now quote verbatim from the evidence given at Nüremberg by a German judge:

"Until the end of 1933 the Supreme Court (Reichsgericht) was the highest German tribunal with jurisdiction over cases of treason and high treason. For that reason the Reichstag fire trial still came before the Supreme Court. As is well known, it ended with the acquittal of most of the accused, whom the regime had hoped to see convicted as members of the Communist Party. After this trial the Supreme Court was deprived of its jurisdiction in matters of treason and high treason. This jurisdiction was transferred by the law of 28 April 1934 to the newly created People's Court, which consisted of only two professional judges (even those of course were selected primarily because of political considerations) and five higher party functionaries. Thus this court offered a guarantee that the law would be applied exclusively in accordance with the principles of the Nazi party."

A captured German document which was given in evidence at Nüremberg and which was written on 16th October 1942 by or under the orders of the German Minister of Justice, Dr. Thierach, described the official Nazi view of the functions of a judge.

The Nazis declared that a judge was a direct assistant in the administration of the state, and responsible to the leadership of the state (Staatsführung). The Nazis said that if the judge took this as his guiding principle he would find many a decision made easy which at first seemed very difficult to solve. They therefore insisted that every judge must be in direct and close contact with the leadership of the state and must be made familiar with the problems facing the leadership of the state. They thought it absolutely necessary to have leadership in the administration of Justice. Dr. Thierach's description of the Nazi judge continues as follows:

"Leadership in the administration of justice does not bind the judge to precise regulations made by the leadership of the state. The essence of the *so-called independence of the judge—a word that should be eliminated from the vocabulary* for the above reasons—his free though regulated decision (freie, weisungsgebundene) should and will remain, otherwise he would no longer be a judge. *But* the leadership of the state should and ought to give to the judge the general rules to be observed if justice is to fulfil its purpose. This is the object inter alia of the confidential judges' letters (Richterbriefe) edited by me which every German judge and public prosecutor receives."

Thus you see the Nazis wished to eliminate the words "independence of the judge" from their vocabulary. Why? Because they feared and despised unfettered justice. Justice had to be their servant.

The first of these judges' letters written by the Nazi, Dr. Thierach, began as follows:—

"According to the ancient Teutonic conception of justice the leader of the nation was also its supreme judge. If, therefore, the Führer invests the authority of a judge in a third person, it not only implies that this person receives his judge's power from the Führer and is responsible to him, but it also proves the close relationship between leadership and the duties of a judge."

Here we see very clearly the Nazi perversion of the truth as regards the status and duties of a judge. It does not in the least follow from the fact that the head of the state appoints the judges that the judges must do what the leader of the state wishes. Quite the contrary. If the judge is to be truly independent, he must (as indeed the Weimar constitution of Germany itself provided) be subject only to the law. A judge must be free from all considerations of politics or personal obligations or loyalties, and in dispensing justice he must have regard to nothing except the law of the land, the sacred principles of justice and the dictates of humanity.

Let us now turn back to the trial of Cardinal Mindszenty.

Was the judge truly independent? Did he have, or did he not have, an indication before the trial took place as to what his verdict ought to be?

To me there appears to be only one possible answer. He knew that the Hungarian authorities had prejudged the whole case and that if he gave a verdict of acquittal, as was done by the non-Nazi German Supreme Court after the Reichstag fire trial, it would be regarded as a setback for the regime. Let us ignore for the moment the question whether the judge's verdict was really right or wrong. Can it be said to be in conformity with the principles of justice that the trial should have been conducted by a judge who knew what verdict he was expected by the Government to give?

Let us see what indications there are of pressure having been brought upon the judge who tried Cardinal Mindszenty, such as the Nazis brought on their judges in the Special Courts and People's Courts.

In the first place we have the astonishing fact that the Hungarian Government published before the trial began a book which has become known as the Yellow Book. It was entitled "Documents on the Mindszenty Case." It is published in English (and for all I know, in other languages as well). It contains photographs of Mindszenty and other persons associated with him, and photographs of many documents which were later to be used in the trial, including what purports to be the Cardinal's written confession.

Nothing could make it clearer than the Yellow Book itself that the Hungarian Government had prejudged the result of the trial and would have considered it a disaster if the trial had resulted in an acquittal.

The Yellow Book says in its Introduction:

"The unmasking of Mindszenty and his accomplices, and their arrest, caused the greatest confusion among those whom he served, the western imperialists. Their press, their radio propaganda, and, moreover, statements by certain statesmen and bishops tried, by slander and denial, to whitewash Mindszenty, their accomplice.

"The Hungarian Government wishes to publish in this book a few of those many proofs it has at its disposal, the greater part of which are from Mindszenty's secret buried files which will prove tangibly and irrefutably to any unbiased man that Mindszenty and his company were guilty."

At the end of the Yellow Book appears the following paragraph:—

"The above documents convincingly and undeniably justify the charges against Mindszenty, and the trial that is soon to begin will cast light on every aspect of Mindszenty's list of crimes. But even on the basis of the documents, every objective observer must recognise that there is no question of persecuting the church or the priests, or of infringing the freedom of worship, as some have falsely and tendentiously tried to make out, but of bringing a determined enemy of the Hungarian people to account."

After the publication of the Yellow Book to the world in this way, can it be said that there was no pressure on the judge to swerve from the impartial and unbiased course of justice?

The fact that the result of the trial was regarded as a foregone conclusion is further borne out by the manner in which the official radio broadcast of the trial was conducted. The official commentator introduced his own comments from time to time, for the whole of the Hungarian nation, and indeed the world, to hear, while . . . the fate of the accused was still theoretically undecided.

"The traitors are before their judges," he begins with; then he goes on, "Joseph Mindszenty-Pehm, an extreme right-wing high Church dignitary, who became disloyal to the teachings of Christ, who wanted to drag the country into catastrophe by political slogans wrapped up in pious sermons and pastoral letters, who wanted to deprive the Hungarian people of their democratic achievements . . . The vigilance of our State security organs unmasked this dangerous gang of criminals."

Was it conceivable that against this background the judge should feel able to give a verdict of "Not Guilty"?

It must not be forgotten that under the Hungarian law governing the setting up and procedure of the People's Courts the presiding judge is removable and has no security of office, and that his four assessors are direct appointees of the four parties forming the Government coalition. Is not this just how the Nazi People's Courts were constituted? Could such a court be expected to acquit the accused however the trial went?

Look, too, at the reasons given by the judge himself for the verdict. They consist largely of a political speech. The part occupied by the analysis of the evidence and the explanation of how the evidence proved the charges is extremely small, at any rate in the broadcast version and in the version printed in the "Black Book" published after the trial. The conclusion is hard to resist that there were really no other grounds for conviction except political pressure and political instructions to the judge. Turning from the judge to the defence counsel, one is amazed at the failure of the latter to stand up courageously for his client's rights.

A special point was made at the trial by the Cardinal's defence counsel that he was freely chosen by the Cardinal. One cannot help suspecting that he must have been chosen from a panel of counsel specially approved by the court (as was the rule with the People's Court in Nazi Germany), for he argued no points of any substance in Cardinal Mindszenty's favour. This failure to argue is the more surprising because the inadequacy of the evidence, and the fact that the evidence could nowhere substantiate the charges of sedition and disloyalty, are so obvious to anyone who takes the trouble to compare the evidence with the charges.

There is another principle of justice which I have not yet mentioned, which is considered of fundamental importance in English criminal trials, and I do not doubt that it is considered equally important in Hungary also in normal times. That principle is that justice must not only be done, but must manifestly be seen to be done.

The Hungarian Government, and indeed the judge and even the defence counsel, seem to have been aware of this necessity too, for they were so anxious to tell the world that the trial was fair and did not concern religious matters. So anxious, that the Government published a Yellow Book of the evidence in English! But the amazing thing is that they should have failed to see that the conclusion the world would draw from this would be that the verdict was prejudged, and that the judge was virtually, if not actually, instructed to find Cardinal Mindszenty guilty.

. . . I want to say something about the right to form a political opposition in a democratic country.

Act I of 1946 declares that Hungary is a republic.

That does not, however, mean that by the passing of that Act any movement aiming at a change in the republican form of government has become illegal in Hungary.

The Act is an ordinary Act of Parliament which can be repealed or amended by any subsequent Act of Parliament. This means of course that it can be repealed if the will of the Hungarian people is in favour of repealing it. As a matter of constitutional law, any member of the Hungarian Parliament is perfectly free to introduce at any time a Bill for the repeal of Act I of the year 1946. A fortiori, a repeal of the Act can be legitimately included in the programme of any political party.

The preamble to the Act which declares Hungary to be a republic expressly states that the Republic guarantees to its citizens the natural and inalienable rights of the human being, and especially the right of free expression of thought and opinion and the right of association and public meeting.

Furthermore Article 2 of the Peace Treaty which came into force on the 15th September 1947, and which is also part of the law of Hungary, says:

"Hungary shall take all measures necessary to secure to all persons under Hungarian jurisdiction . . . the enjoyment of Human Rights and of the fundamental freedoms including freedom of expression . . . of political opinion and of public meeting."

Any theory that a movement or organisation for the furtherance of a change in the republican form of government is automatically illegal is quite incompatible with the Peace Treaty and also with the law of Hungary. Some seditious, violent or unconstitutional aim must be proved.

This legal position was apparently not recognised either by the Prosecution or by the Court at the Mindszenty Trial. The Prosecution it is true made a great show of proving a seditious attempt to overthrow the republic by inciting America to war, and the court held this proved. But from the prosecutor's speech and the judgment one gets the impression that they did not consider that it mattered in law whether it was proved or not. And, as I showed [earlier], it was not in fact properly proved from a legal point of view.

If the prosecution had really proved that Cardinal Mindszenty and his friends had tried to incite foreign powers to war against Hungary, the case would indeed have been quite different because such incitement might well be said to have been aimed at the unconstitutional overthrow of the republic, and moreover to have been aimed at it in a violent manner.

Thus it seems that this right under Hungarian law to form a movement for a change in the constitution by constitutional means, this right to form a political opposition, only exists theoretically. The Mindszenty Trial demonstrates its futility in practice.

Mindszenty's theoretical lawful opposition to the Government's policy brought down on his head the farce of a trial which was a clear proof to any other person who may wish to form an opposition party, that seditious motives and seditious actions will be imputed to him on purely imaginary grounds, and that he will be eliminated as a focus of reaction.

The right to form a political opposition, which, as I have said, is guaranteed by the law of Hungary, including the Peace Treaty, is altogether a meaningless right unless it is guaranteed and enforced by a truly independent and fearless judiciary.

Ex hypothesi an opposition party, in its early days at least, is a minority. Therefore it is not democratically speaking entitled to dictate or enforce its policy. On the other hand, being a minority it needs protection, and this must be given by the judiciary.

If minority views are not protected they will be stamped out by the majority. Thus democracy becomes tyranny. The essence of true democracy is the protection of minorities and their views.

The Trial of Cardinal Mindszenty was a denial of the fundamentals of democracy, because it shows that in Hungary today justice is a sham and the judiciary is not independent.

As I pointed out . . . the same thing occurred in Nazi Germany, where the courts were incorporated into the Nazi party scheme for removing democratic opposition, in particular of course for removing Communist opposition. This is clearly the prevailing philosophy in Hungarian Government circles today, as is shown by the second paragraph of the final speech of the People's Prosecutor at the trial. He said:

"The interest of the Hungarian people, of the Hungarian working class society, was prompted by the desire that the Government of the Hungarian People's Republic may remove all those obstacles which render the reconstruction of our country difficult. It should remove therefore the focus of reaction—obstructing speedy progress —which was represented lately by certain leaders of the Catholic Clergy and especially Cardinal Joseph Mindszenty."

This philosophy is indeed understandable after a revolution, but those who hold it must face the fact that they cannot call themselves democratic if they do not allow opposition to their policy and their acts to be freely voiced within the scope of the rights laid down by the constitution.

Another small example which seems very extraordinary to a lawyer in a truly democratic community can be seen in the judgment in the Mindszenty Trial in the case of the defendant Dr. Leslie Tóth. In enumerating the relevant aggravating circumstances according to the procedure of the court, the judge included the following circumstance:

"The fact that, as a well-known Right Wing journalist of the past regime and former editor of *Nemzeti Ujság*, he was acquitted by the People's Court and yet he turned against the democratic State order."

Here again, we see clearly demonstrated the philosophy of totalitarianism. The fact that Dr. Tóth was acquitted by the People's Court is represented by the judge as a sort of favour for which he ought to have been grateful. One would have thought that, if the People's Court operated upon ordinary principles of justice, Dr. Tóth had previously been acquitted because he was not guilty. A free judiciary does not dispense justice as a favour but as a right.

The charge against Cardinal Mindszenty of Disloyalty by giving away secrets to persons not entitled to receive them, is an excellent illustration of what happens if citizens are denied their right to form a political opposition.

This charge could never have arisen upon such facts as were alleged against Cardinal Mindszenty in a truly democratic state. It could not have arisen in Hungary if the rights of free speech and free expression of opinion guaranteed by the law of Hungary had really been allowed to be enforced.

The information which the Cardinal was accused of giving away was information which he collected through the clergy about the Hungarian political and economic situation and the political parties. This is precisely the sort of information which it is the recognised right of any political opposition to collect by normal observation and enquiry, and which in a free country is regularly made public in Parliament and in the press. Such information (even though it may be severely critical of the Government) can in England for example be freely collected and discussed and can be disseminated for use both at home and abroad.

The prevailing philosophy in Hungary is evidently that no one must disseminate information or express views which are adversely critical of the Government. The philosophy is illustrated by some of the questions put to Cardinal Mindszenty by the presiding judge.

Asking the Cardinal what information he thought could properly be given away, the judge said, "Information which praises the results, the achievements here, such material should be passed on in order to enable these Americans to see the limit of the Hungarian people's efforts." And then, in dealing with the data which the Cardinal communicated to Minister Chapin, the judge said: "I would be interested to know whether they were positive data. If one meets foreigners one prefers to show proudly one's country's achievements, cultural, scientific and economic and political results. Did you too show such results?" Mindszenty replied, "Rather negative ones." To which the judge answered: "Rather negative results? What was the aim of those negative results? Please state it. To influence the American Government to adopt a hostile attitude against the present regime? Is that not so?"

It is quite plain what was in the judge's mind, and of course any supporter of the Hungarian Government would sympathise with it. The judge thought it wrong for the Cardinal to mention anything but the positive achievements of the republic. This may or may not be a practical or a desirable view to take, but it is certainly not democratic, and it is certainly not in keeping with the freedom of expression of opinion guaranteed by the law of Hungary.

When one sees the judiciary failing to hold the scale of justice evenly between the individual and the state, and assuming instead the role of stamping out opposition views and smothering criticism, that is the quintessence of tyranny.

That is one of the things that Cardinal Mindszenty fought against in Hungary. May his martyrdom not be in vain.

*   *   *

C.

TEXT OF THE NOTE
SENT BY THE
GOVERNMENT OF THE UNITED STATES OF AMERICA
TO THE
GOVERNMENT OF HUNGARY
on April 2, 1949

The Legation of the United States of America presents its compliments to the Ministry of Foreign Affairs of Hungary, and, acting under the instructions of the United States Government, has the honor to refer to Article 2 of the Treaty of Peace with Hungary, and to the Hungarian Government's record with respect to fulfillment of its obligations under that Article to protect human rights and the fundamental freedoms.

Article 2 of the Treaty of Peace reads as follows:

"1. Hungary shall take all measures necessary to secure to all persons under Hungarian jurisdiction, without distinction as to race, sex, language or religion, the enjoyment of human rights and of the fundamental freedoms, including freedom of expression, of press and publication, of religious worship, of political opinion and of public meeting.

"2. Hungary further undertakes that the laws in force in Hungary shall not, either in their content or in their application, discriminate or entail any discrimination between persons of Hungarian nationality on the ground of their race, sex, language or religion, whether in reference to their persons, property, business, professional or financial interests, status, political or civil rights or any other matter."

Since the entry into force on September 15, 1947, of the Treaty of Peace with Hungary, the United States Government, as a signatory of that instrument, has observed closely developments in Hungary with a view to ascertaining whether the Hungarian Government has been fulfilling its obligations under the Treaty. The United States Government attaches particular importance to the obligations, set forth in the aforementioned Article, which require the Hungarian Government to secure to all persons under Hungarian jurisdiction the enjoyment of human rights and of the fundamental freedoms. On the basis of its observations during this period, the United States Government concludes that the Hungarian Government, although it has had ample opportunity to carry out its commitments in good faith, has deliberately and systematically denied to the Hungarian people, by means of privative measures and oppressive acts, the exercise of the very rights and freedoms which it has pledged to secure to them under Article 2 of the Treaty. The disregard shown by the Hungarian Government for the rights and liberties of persons under its jurisdiction, as illustrated below, has indeed become so notorious as to evoke the condemnation of free peoples everywhere.

The abridgment of rights and freedoms begun by the Hungarian Government in the armistice period has continued without abatement since the entry into force of the Treaty of Peace. Through arbitrary exercise of police power and perversion of judicial process, the Hungarian Government and its agencies have violated the rights of citizens as free men to life and liberty. Denial of freedom of political opinion is complete in Hungary. Democratic political parties which held substantial mandates from the people have been through the Government's initiative successively purged, silenced in Parliament, fragmentized and dissolved. To enforce rigid political conformity the Hungarian Government and the Communist Party which controls it have established a vast and insidious network of police and other agents who observe, report on, and seek to control the private opinions, associations, and activities of its citizens.

The Hungarian Government, despite the provisions of the Treaty of Peace, has circumscribed freedom of expression. Freedom of press and publication does not exist. Basic decrees pertaining to the press are restrictive in character and are so interpreted in practice. No substantive criticism of the Government of the Communist Party is permitted. Government control of printing establishments and of the distribution of newsprint has been exercised to deny freedom of expression to individuals or groups whose political opinions are at variance with those of the Government. In the field of reporting, absence of formal censorship has not obscured the record of the Hungarian Government in excluding or expelling foreign correspondents who have written dispatches critical of the regime or in intimidating local correspondents into writing only what is acceptable or favorable to the regime.

Freedom of public meeting on political matters has been regularly denied to all except Communist groups and their collaborators. In the case of religious meetings, on various occasions attendance at such gatherings has been obstructed and the principals subjected to harassment. The Hungarian Government, moreover, has pursued policies detrimental to freedom of religious worship. It has sought by coercive measures to undermine the influence of the churches and of religious leaders and to restrict their legitimate functions. By arbitrary and unjustified proceedings against religious leaders on fabricated grounds, as in the cases of Cardinal Mindszenty and Lutheran Bishop Ordass, the Hungarian Government has attempted to force the submission of independent church leaders and to bring about their replacement with collaborators subservient to the Communist Party and its program. Such measures constitute violations of the freedom of religious worship guaranteed by the Treaty of Peace.

The Hungarian Government bears full responsibility not only for acts committed since the effective date of the Treaty of Peace which are in contravention of Article 2, but also for its failure to redress the consequences of acts committed prior to that date which have continued to prejudice the enjoyment of human rights and of the fundamental freedoms. The United States Government, mindful of its responsibilities under the Treaty of Peace, has drawn attention on appropriate occasions to the flagrant conduct of the Hungarian authorities in this regard. The Hungarian Government, however, has failed to modify its conduct in conformity with the stipulations of the Treaty.

In the circumstances, the United States Government, as a signatory of the Treaty of Peace, finds that the Hungarian Government has repeatedly violated the provisions of Article 2 of that Treaty. Inasmuch as the obligation of the Government of Hungary to secure to all persons under Hungarian jurisdiction the enjoyment of human rights and the fundamental freedoms is expressly stipulated in the Treaty, no specious argument that the matters raised in the present Note are purely of a domestic character can be accepted. The United States Government, accordingly, calls upon the Hungarian Government to adopt prompt remedial measures in respect of the violations referred to above and requests the Hungarian Government to specify the steps which it is prepared to take in implementing fully the terms of Article 2 of the Treaty of Peace. . . .

*   *   *

D.

STATEMENT

of the Honorable Benjamin Cohen, on behalf of the United States of America, at the meeting of the United Nations General Assembly on April 18, 1949

In January 1942 in the first formal declaration of the United Nations, the nations engaged in the struggle with the forces of tyranny expressed their common intention to fight on to victory in defense of liberty, independence, religious freedom, and human rights for all peoples.

In February 1945 at Yalta, the three war leaders of the United Nations—Stalin, Churchill, and Roosevelt—gave a solemn pledge on behalf of their respective countries to the peoples of Europe then on the threshold of liberation that freedom should be restored, not to their former rulers and not to a new set of rulers, but to those peoples themselves. To them we promised the right to create, through free elections, democratic institutions of their own choice. And under the Peace Treaties signed at Paris in February 1947 the states formerly allied with Germany undertook as an international obligation to protect and safeguard the fundamental freedoms and human rights of their peoples.

Under the Charter of the United Nations all the members of the United Nations also solemnly committed themselves to take joint and separate action in cooperation with the Organization to promote universal respect for, and observance of, human rights and fundamental freedoms for all without distinction as to race, sex, language, or religion. In Paris . . . without a dissenting vote, the General Assembly adopted a Declaration of Human Rights and called upon all peoples and organs of society, by teaching and education and by progressive measures, to promote respect for these rights and to secure their effective recognition and observance. . . .

A serious responsibility rests upon the Members of the Assembly to refrain from making recommendations which may not only be ignored but may, in fact, in certain situations create greater intransigence on the part of those criticized and aggravate the position of those most deserving of our sympathy and assistance. The task of the Assembly is to promote respect for and the observance of human rights and fundamental freedoms and not to make recommendations which, in fact, defeat the practical realization of its objectives. Moreover, the General Assembly obviously cannot itself act as a court to review all the individual cases in which it may be alleged that human rights and freedoms have been infringed. But an appreciation of the practical difficulties in promoting respect for and observance of human rights should not and cannot be exploited as an easy excuse for not trying to do anything in any situation.

It will require a great deal of time and concerted effort to establish adequate minimum standards of respect for human rights and freedoms everywhere in the world as envisaged in the Charter. The General Assembly rightly took as its first step the working out of a general Declaration of Human Rights so that we may have some standards with which to start. In all our countries, including my own, much remains to be done, and none of us can afford to assume a self-righteous attitude. But if we are serious in our quest for peace, we cannot fail to do our part and make every effort toward promoting minimum standards of human rights. For as Secretary of State Marshall said at the opening of this Third Session of the Assembly, "Governments which systematically disregard the rights of their own people are not likely to respect the rights of other nations and other peoples."

There are in this changing and diversified world varying concepts of the functions of the state and the status of the individual. We generally agree that within the widest limits the rights of the individual in relation to the state should be determined by the respective states. But there are limits.

I think that we are all in agreement that, in the light of our pledges in the Charter, the functions of the state should be of a character to promote and not to destroy human rights and fundamental freedoms. Let us grant that in the absence of a treaty we must accept the judgment of the respective states as to what functions of the state promote the rights and freedoms of its citizens and what is the exact substantive content of these rights and freedoms; there is nevertheless an obligation on the part of every civilized state to exercise its judgment in honesty and good faith. No state has the sovereign right claimed by Hitler's Third Reich to declare war on freedom and religion. State sovereignty does not mean State tyranny. In fields of thought and religion where men cannot agree, freedom is the only alternative to tyranny.

Unless a state allows freedom for the peaceful expression of ideas, the road toward peaceful change and progress is blocked. Unrestrained political power, no less than unrestrained economic power, has a corroding effect upon those who exercise it. This is particularly true when the wielders of power deny themselves the benefit of any views not meekly submissive and subservient to their will and caprice. Power which is unwilling to combat error with reason is not likely itself to be guided by reason. No state need fear the errors of dissenting opinion and non-conforming thought where reason is free to combat them. It is uneasy privilege, not confident progress, which prefers the arbitrament of force to the test of reason. Suppression of non-conforming opinion has always characterized the police state which fears the freedom of its own citizens. Tolerance of dissent is the most certain sign of a free state which cherishes and does not fear the freedoms of its citizens and uses force only to protect and not to suppress that freedom.

As I have already indicated, the Governments of the ex-enemy states undertook a solemn international obligation to safeguard the civil and religious rights of their people. These governments have formally recognized that the observance of the human rights set forth in the Peace Treaties is not merely a matter of their own domestic concern. Three Allied powers signatories to the Treaties were given specific functions with respect to the execution of these Treaties. Moreover, the Peace Treaties provide definite procedures for the settlement of differences concerning their interpretation and execution. Having in mind these procedures, on April 2 my Government took initial action in this regard in notes addressed to the Governments of Bulgaria, Hungary, and Rumania, formally charging them with violations of the human rights clauses of the respective Treaties. Other signatory states have taken similar steps. The receipt of replies from Hungary rejecting the charges has confirmed the existence of disputes for which the appropriate settlement procedures are laid down in the Peace Treaties. . . .

The issues involved in these charges have come recently into the focus of world opinion as a result of the prosecutions of church leaders in Hungary and Bulgaria. They are of intense concern to the entire international community organized in the United Nations and not only to the states parties to the Treaties of Peace. It seems to us only fitting and proper that the members of the General Assembly who are deeply concerned and anxious about the charges of suppression of civil and religious liberties in these countries should express that concern and anxiety. That should help the Governments of these countries to understand that the resort to the Treaty procedures and to the General Assembly is supported not, as it has been charged, by a few powers for undisclosed imperialistic reasons but by the world community of nations because of principles which are deeply and universally cherished.

There is no intention whatever, on the part of the United States Government, to interfere in the internal affairs of these states or to favor this or that political group. Concern over violations of human rights cannot properly be pictured as a policy of intervention, of encouragement to reaction or of opposition to social reform. On the contrary, it is our belief that sincere observance of the human rights and political liberties of individual citizens makes possible more genuine social reforms which emanate from the people themselves and may be enjoyed by them in an atmosphere free from fear. . . .

It is our intention to outline only the broad pattern of developments in these countries. In each country it is a pattern of a minority group seizing the instrumentalities of government through force and intimidation and maintaining itself in power through suppression of every one of the human rights and fundamental freedoms which these states have solemnly undertaken to observe. It is a pattern disclosing a clear design to suppress first the leaders of political groups and parties and then the leaders of religious groups and organizations, because these leaders had refused to subordinate themselves, or to use their influence to subordinate their followers, to the dictates of the Cominform.

In nearly all countries there are different concepts as to the exact and appropriate scope of civil and religious freedom. But making all due allowances for legitimate differences of opinion, we cannot see that any substantive civil or religious freedom can survive in these ex-enemy countries if the shabbiest sort of excuse suffices to liquidate political and religious leaders who refuse to accept and support the prevailing totalitarianism. These leaders have been driven from office or brought to trial on the pretext that they have violated national laws. Actually there is reason to believe that they are being persecuted and tried not for the offenses with which they have been charged, but because the governments had decided to liquidate them as sources of independent opinion. We cannot accept the proposition that under the guise of dissolving fascist or subversive organizations a state may suppress the expression of views that are odious or even hostile to it. We do not question the right of the state to protect itself from those who endeavor to overthrow the state by force and violence, but that right does not justify the suppression of efforts to seek changes by peaceful means even though those efforts are displeasing to the ruling groups. Has there ever been a tyranny, however ruthless, which did not regard its own authority as beneficently exercised in the interest of the people and its own objectives as a facile excuse for the suppression of freedom?

Let us now consider, more specifically, the situation obtaining in Hungary. . . . (Quotes second article of the Treaty of Peace with Hungary. See page 306.)

It is the view of my Government that freedom of political opinion, one of the fundamental freedoms guaranteed under this provision, has virtually ceased to exist in Hungary. In the national elections of 1945 the Communist Party obtained only 17 per cent of the vote. But this minority party, having arrogated to itself key positions in the Government, embarked upon a campaign of force and intimidation on a nationwide scale in order to eliminate all actual and potential opposition and to nullify the popular mandate.

The majority Small Holders Party, which had polled 57 per cent of the national vote in 1945, had its parliamentary majority greatly reduced through purges and arrests of its leaders; Communist-inspired action against its accepted leaders drove them from positions in the government and in the party, to be replaced by politicians subservient to Communist dictates.

In new elections held in August 1947, the inability of non-Communist parties to campaign freely because of Communist interference and governmental restrictions, the arbitrary disfranchisement of many voters, and practices such as multiple voting, made impossible a fair expression of the popular will, as the United States Government had occasion to inform the Hungarian Government at the time. But not satisfied even with the results of these elections, the Communist-dominated Hungarian Government proceeded to silence and to destroy the non-Communist parties. By the forced dissolution of the Independence Party and the Democratic People's Party, whose leaders had to flee the country, over one and one-half million voters were deprived of their representation in Parliament. The historic Social Democratic Party was forced into a merger with the Communists following the arrest and imprisonment of those leaders who opposed the merger and a purge of party members who voiced their opinions against it. The forced extinction, earlier this year, of the Christian Women's Camp, whose leader had the temerity to introduce into Parliament a motion requesting the United Nations to undertake an investigation of the state of religious freedom in Hungary, marked the disappearance of all organized opposition from the Hungarian legislature.

Safeguards for an independent judiciary have been critically impaired. Under the provisions of Act XXIII of March 19, 1948, the Minister of Justice in the Hungarian Government was given authority to transfer or retire any judge. The exercise of this authority and the establishment of a system of politically controlled People's Courts have together reduced the judiciary to political subservience to the regime.

As for freedom of expression, another right which Hungary had undertaken to respect, the plain fact is that people are afraid to express themselves and a significant silence obtains throughout the land except for those vocal few who speak for the regime.

Under the present Hungarian law the utterance of an untrue or even true statement which is considered by the authorities to be detrimental to the Republic or disturbing to the existing order is an offense punishable by law.

Freedom of press and publication has ceased to exist in Hungary. Governmental authority is used to prevent the publication of any views distasteful to the ruling group, and journalists have been subjected to arrest and imprisonment for independent reporting.

Freedom of public meeting has been denied regularly since the middle of 1947 to all except the controlling minority group and its collaborators. Prior to that time meetings of democratic, non-Communist parties were broken up by organized mobs with the acquiescence of the police.

Another freedom of fundamental importance guaranteed in the Peace Treaty is the freedom of religious worship. Religious worship, of course, means more than mere formal participation in religious ritual. Religious freedom is not assured merely by a constitutional provision to that effect, or by the fact that churches remain open. Religion as a creative force in a free society requires freedom to teach and voice views based on religious tenets, freedom to associate with those of like belief.

The Hungarian Government, however, in pursuing its objectives of bringing all aspects of Hungarian life under a uniform totalitarian system, has sought by coercive measures to restrict the legitimate functions of the churches. A systematic campaign has been conducted to dissolve church organizations or transform them into new organizations under "acceptable" leadership. In carrying out this program the Government has resorted to numerous repressive measures, arbitrary arrests, trials of priests and nuns, interference with religious processions, and restrictions on the opening of religious chapels.

By threats and arbitrary proceedings against church leaders and by perversion of the judicial process, the Government has attempted to force the retirement or submission of independent church leaders and to bring about their replacement by those willing to adopt a subservient attitude. Those who refused, like Lutheran Bishop Ordass and Cardinal Mindszenty, were arrested and imprisoned.

Bishop Ordass was informed by Government representatives that he would be in danger unless he resigned. He replied that he would not desert his flock. Thereupon he was taken into custody by the political police, held for several days, then freed. When he still would not resign he was rearrested on charges of embezzlement and black-marketeering, and sentenced to a prison term by a "People's Court."

Because of his high ecclesiastical office and his criticism of the policies of the Government, Cardinal Mindszenty became the focal point of the attack upon the Catholic Church. Religious meetings at which he was present were disrupted or interfered with; his associates and followers were subjected to threats and sometimes to physical violence on the part of the police. Finally, the decision was taken to silence the Cardinal, whose prestige among the people and whose open disapproval of the repressive methods of the regime marked him for elimination. After the Government had been unable to induce or frighten him into submission, he was arrested and tried on charges that were mere pretexts for the Government's principal objectives of discrediting him and of destroying his influence. This, in our view, is the true significance of the action against Cardinal Mindszenty. . . .

Whatever action might be taken, we should not lose sight of our real purpose in the field of human rights and freedoms. It is not to set neighbor against neighbor or nation against nation but to unite the world on the basis of principles which recognize the freedom and dignity of all men and all nations.

We are all of a common humanity. We have all, under the Charter, expressed our determination to respect the dignity and worth of the human person, to practice tolerance, and to live together in peace with one another as good neighbors. Despite the various ways of life we may pursue and despite the different ideas we may cherish, let us learn to tolerate ways of life we cannot ourselves practice and ideas we cannot ourselves share. Let us strive then to find the strains of common humanity which can bind us together. Let us then, as members of a common humanity, agree to reject all forms of tyranny over the mind and soul of man. Let us approach these problems of human rights with the firm determination to find common standards upon which we can build a world community of free nations and of free men. Enduring peace must rest upon the acceptance of common standards of human rights that can command the willing allegiance of all humanity.

✠

APPENDIX II

✠

CHRONOLOGIES

A.

CHRONOLOGY
OF MAJOR EVENTS IN THE HISTORY OF THE PEOPLE
AND THE CATHOLIC CHURCH IN HUNGARY
Up to the Twentieth Century

400 B.C. to A.D. 100—Formative years of the Hungarian tribe.

100–453 : The Hungarian tribe lives near river Ob.

453 : Death of Attila, King of the Huns.

465 : The Hungarians move to the territory bordering Caucasus and river Don.

558–568 : Domination by the Avars.

568–615 : Domination by the Turks.

615–679 : Domination by the Onogurs.

680–890 : Domination by Khazars.

830–889 : The Hungarians live as nomads between Dnieper and Don.

890 : Move to the region known as Moldavia and Bessarabia.

890–907 : Reign of Árpád, as prince.

892 : Alliance of Árpád with Frankish King Arnulf. The War in Moravia.

894 : Alliance of Árpád with Byzantine Emperor Leo the Wise. War in Pannonia.

895–900 : Settlement of territory of present-day Hungary (895, eastern part—900, Pannonia, the western part).

915 : Arnulf, Duke of Bavaria, takes refuge in Hungary; alliance between Bavarians and Hungarians.

926 : Hungarians at St. Gallen, with first conversion to Christianity by Bishop Prumwart.

940–950 : Greek missionary activity in Southeastern Hungary.

955 : German Emperor Otto defeats the Hungarians at Lech.

969 : Birth of St. Stephen.

970–997 : Reign of Prince Géza, his father.

970 : Géza establishes residence in Esztergom.

973 : Géza sends envoys to Emperor Otto, at Quedlinburg, asking for Christian missionaries.

974–975 : Reigning family converted to Christianity.

992–996 : Defeat of pagans opposing Christianity; establishment of a social order.

995 : St. Adalbert in Hungary.

996 : Catholic Church organized in Hungary; coming of the Order of St. Benedict.

997–1038 : Reign of St. Stephen (997–1000 as prince; 1000–1038 as first king of Hungary).

997 : The Abbey of Pannonhalma is established.

1000 : Pope Sylvester II sends crown to St. Stephen; he is crowned on December 25.

1001 : Archbishopric of Esztergom and bishoprics of Veszprém and Györ established.

1006–1009 : Archbishopric of Kalocsa and bishoprics of Pécs, Vác, and Eger established. Following 1018 bishoprics of Marosvásár, Bihar, and Transylvania, Abbeys of Bakonybél and Zalavár are established; St. Gellért in Hungary.

1038–1041 : Erection of first basilica in Pécs.

1040–1074 : Struggle against German emperor for independence of Hungary.

1046 : Martyrdom of St. Gellért.

1055 : The establishment of the Abbey of Tihany.

1061 : Last uprising of paganism.

1064 : Immigration of the Jews and Ishmaelites to Hungary.

1077–1116 : Reigns of St. Ladislaus (1077–1095) and Coloman (1095–1116); completion of work begun by St. Stephen, in establishing statehood and laws.

1083 : Canonization of St. Stephen and St. Gellért.

1098 : Right hand of St. Stephen is declared a sacred relic and placed in "church of the right hand."

1142 : King Géza II founds first Cistercian monastery in Cikádor; invites French monks from Heiligenkreuz.

1147 : Alliance with Louis VII of France, who passes with his Crusaders through Hungary; Géza II builds church and pilgrim hostel in Jerusalem.

1178 : First Premonstrant monastery established by French monks at Garáb.

1179–1184 : French Cistercian monks begin work at Eger, Pilis, Zirc, Pásztó, and Szentgotthárd.

1185 : French and Hungarian masters begin building basilica and royal palace in Esztergom.

1192 : King Ladislaus is canonized.

1200 : Hungarian missionary expeditions to the Bosnians, Serbs, Bulgars, and Macedonians.

1217 : King Andrew II leads Hungarian army of Crusaders to Holy Land.

1221 : Paul Boldog, jurist of University of Bologna, commissioned by St. Dominick, establishes Dominican monasteries at Székesfehérvár, Veszprém, and Györ.—A few years later the first Franciscan monastery is founded in Esztergom.

1222 : Granting of "Golden Bull" (Magna Charta of Hungary).

1227 : Archbishop Robert converts the Kuns.

1232 : Independent Franciscan Order of Hungary is constituted.

1234 : Elisabeth, daughter of Andrew II, canonized.

1235–1236 : Frater Julian's trip to East, visiting original settlements of Hungarian tribes.

1241 : Battle of Mohi, and overrunning of Hungary by hordes of Genghis Khan.

1250 : Canon Özséb of Esztergom founds only monastic order of Hungarian origin: Paulist monks, named after St. Paul.

1278 : The Hungarians, allied with Rudolf, Count of Habsburg, defeat King Ottokar of Bohemia, in battle of Moravian Fields.

1290 : The National Assembly meeting in Buda establishes rules for constitutional government.

1331 : Bishopric of Nándorfehérvár (Belgrade) established.

1342–1382 : Reign of Louis II, "the Great"; Hungary becomes a major power.

1343 : Pope Clement VI asks Christian kings to protect Christianity against Turks.

1348–1349 : Black Plague.

1352 : Turks establish first foothold in Europe at Gallipoli.

1367 : University of Pécs founded.

1381–1382 : Bishoprics of Havaselv and Szörény established.

1385 : Order of St. Augustine holds canonical synod in Hungary.

1388 : Founding of University of Buda.

1404 : *Placetum Regium* provides that papal decrees may be published in Hungary with royal permission only. King reserves right to appoint Church dignitaries.

1410 : King Sigismund of Hungary elected King of Germany, bringing personal union between the two countries (and later the Empire).

1433 : Sigismund is crowned Holy Roman Emperor by Pope Eugene IV.

1437 : First Hungarian attempt to translate Bible.

1456 : Defeat by Hungarian army under Palatine John Hunyadi of Turks at Nándorfehérvár (Belgrade)—the anniversary decreed by Pope Calixtus III to be observed as Feast of Transfiguration.

1458–1490 : Reign of Matthias Corvinus. Establishment of regular army.

1459–1472 : Janus Pannonius, poet, is Bishop of Pécs.

1463 : Emperor Frederick III of Germany returns Holy Crown of Hungary on payment of 80,000 gold ducats.

1465–1472 : John Vitéz, is Archbishop of Esztergom.

1467 : Founding of University of Pozsony (Bratislava).

1471 : First printing plant in Buda.

1473 : First printed book, *Chronica Hungarorum*.

1475 : First library, the *Corvina*, containing more than 500 volumes.

1480 : Royal palace of Buda completed.

1494 : The Portugals adopt the Hungarian Paulist order. Their monastery in Buda-Szentlörincz becomes a place of pilgrimage.

1497 : The Sodalitas Litteraria Danubiana is founded, uniting humanist trends of Buda and Vienna.

1500–1501 : Holy Year, including a pilgrimage to Rome by more than five hundred Hungarians and establishment of Paulist mission to South America.

1510–1524 : Pilgrimages to Aachen.

1512 : Hungarian Paulists in Rome receive Church of Santa Maria near Lake Bracciano, from Pope Julius II.

1514 : Peasant revolt. Verböczy publishes *Tripartitum*, codifying all laws and regulations.

1518 : Invasion by the Turks.

1526 : At Mohács 100,000 Turks defeat 25,000 Hungarians. Hungary comes under Turkish occupation.

1527 : Parliament moves to Pozsony.

1529 : First siege of Vienna.

1541 : Buda falls to Turks. Pozsony the capital. Hungary divided into three parts.

1547 : Law granting right of succession to Hungarian throne to male issue of Habsburgs.

1553 : Nicholas Oláh, Archbishop of Esztergom, leads counter-reformation.

1567 : Law in Transylvania requires clergy to preach in "language of the villages." First synod of Calvinist Church in Debrecen.

1577 : The first University printing shop for scientific books at Nagyszombat.

1584 : *Corpus Juris Hungarici* published in Nagyszombat.

1591–1606 : Fifteen years' war with Turks.

1597–1598 : Invasion by Tatars.

1615 : Jesuit order settles at Nagyszombat.

1616–1637 : Peter Pázmány, Archbishop of Esztergom.

1623 : *Pazmaneum* is founded in Vienna.

1635 : University founded at Nagyszombat.

1645 : Peace Treaty of Linz guarantees freedom of religion to all.

1678–1680 : The Plague.

1683–1699 : War of liberation from Turks.

1686 : Buda freed from Turks.

1691 : In gratitude for the liberation Prince Paul Eszterházy, palatine of the king, leads a pilgrimage of 8,765 to shrine of Mariazell; Transylvanian princedom acquired by king of Hungary. (Diploma Leopoldinum.)

1697–1700 : Part of the Rumanian clergy joins Church of Rome.

1703–1711 : Francis Rákóczi leads first Hungarian war of liberation from foreign rule.

1705 : First newspaper, Mercurius Hungaricus, printed in Latin, at Kassa, to inform West of conditions in Hungary.

1708–1715 : Black Plague takes 410,000 lives.

1716–1718 : Last Hungarian territory freed from Turks.

1722–1723 : Parliament accepts claim to succession to throne of female issue of Habsburg Dynasty, known as Pragmatica Sanctio.

1738–1744 : Black Plague.

1740–1780 : Reign of Queen Maria Theresa.

1773 : Dissolution of Jesuit Order with 2 universities, 3 academies, 7 conventuals, and 41 gymnasiums—its properties given to University of Buda.

1777 : University moved from Nagyszombat to Buda.

1791 : Hungarian language added to school subjects.

1804 : Bishopric of Eger raised to archbishopric, bishoprics of Szatmár and Kassa organized.

1809 : Battle of Györ lost to Napoleon.

1825 : Count Stephen Széchenyi, a reformer, founds Hungarian Academy of Science.

1831–1832 : Cholera epidemic, with 500,000 deaths.

1832–1836 : Appearance of Francis Deák and Louis Kossuth.

1834 : In Budapest the Jewish Community establishes and maintains a school teaching in the Hungarian language.

1839–1840 : National Assembly adopts Hungarian as official language.

1843–1844 : Parliament opens civil service to all citizens, abolishes feudal fealty.

March 15, 1848 : Bloodless revolution of Budapest.

1848 : National Assembly establishes cabinet responsible to Parliament, full freedom to own property, freedom of press, union with Transylvania, and regulates general suffrage. Accession of Emperor Francis Joseph I, who suspends Hungarian Constitution, bringing on War of Independence.

1849 : Imperial decree annexes Hungary to Austria. Parliament meeting in Debrecen dethrones Habsburgs in Hungary. Louis Kossuth becomes Regent. Parliament meeting in Szeged grants equal rights to Jewish citizens. Francis Joseph, having failed to subdue Hungarian army of Kossuth, requests help of Russian army, which invades Hungary. On August 13 a surrender is effected.

1849–1867 : Austrian absolutism.

1851 : Erection of basilica of St. Stephen in Budapest begins.

1867 : Through mediation of Francis Deák, Dynasty becomes reconciled with Hungary on basis of Austro-Hungarian dualism. The Hungarian Constitution restored.

1896 : Hungary celebrates the Millennium.

B.

CHRONOLOGY
OF
JOSEPH, CARDINAL MINDSZENTY
Archbishop of Esztergom
Prince Primate of Hungary

1663 : Mother's family receives privileges from the Crown.

1732 : Father's family receives privileges from the Crown.

March 29, 1892 : Joseph Pehm (Mindszenty) born. Father, John Pehm; mother, Barbara Pehm, née Kovács.

1902–1911 : Student at Latin School (Gymnasium) of Premonstrants at Szombathely.

1911–1915 : Student at Theological Seminary of Szombathely.

August 23, 1914 : Reports for duty as a nurse, in accordance with army orders, at Auxiliary Military Hospital at Szombathely.

June 12, 1915 : Ordained priest.

August 1, 1915, to January 25, 1917 : Chaplain in village of Felsö-paty.

January 26, 1917, to October 1, 1919 : Teacher of religion at State Latin School (Gymnasium) of Zalaegerszeg.

1917 : His book *Motherhood* published.

1918 : Editor of *County of Zala.*

1918–1919 : Editor of *News of Zala County.*

1919 : Publishes pamphlet *Beware of the Newspapers.*

February 9, 1919 : Imprisoned by revolutionaries and released two weeks later.

March 21 to May 19, 1919 : Imprisoned by Communists.

October 1, 1919, to 1921 : Vicar at Zalaegerszeg.

1921 : Becomes parish priest of Zalaegerszeg.

1921 : Appointed Dean.

1924 : Receives title "Abbot of Pornó."

1927 : Appointed Special Commissioner of the Bishop.

1927 : Publishes pamphlet *Zala Cries Out for Help.*

1934 : His historical work *The Life and Times of Martin Padányi Biró* is published.

1937 : Appointed a Papal Prelate.

March 29, 1944 : Consecrated Bishop of Veszprém.

October 31, 1944 : Demands that Hungarian National Socialist regime end bloodshed and save Transdanubia.

November 21, 1944 : Arrested by regime and imprisoned in penitentiary of Sopron-Köhida.

April, 1945 : Liberated from prison.

April, 1945 : Justin, Cardinal Serédi dies.

October 2, 1945 : Pope appoints him Archbishop of Esztergom; Prince Primate of Hungary.

October 17, 1945 : First presides at Conference of Hungarian Episcopate.

February 21, 1946 : Created Cardinal; attends consistory in Rome.

March, 1946 : Returns to Hungary.

May, 1946 : Conference of Episcopate issues declaration against Communist inroads.

June 29, 1946 : Cardinal, in an address, points to necessity of peaceful relations between Church and State.

July 20, 1946 : Extraordinary Conference of Episcopate protests against dissolution of Catholic Youth Societies order by Soviet.

August 1, 1946 : Cardinal speaks against policy of revenge.

August 25, 1946 : Message of Cardinal to peace negotiators.

October, 1946 : Cardinal offers Hungary to grace of Holy Virgin, "Our Great Lady of Hungary."

December, 1946 : Soviet authorities prevent Cardinal's trip to Prague.

December 6, 1946 : Cardinal writes to United States Minister H. F. Arthur Schoenfeld, asking that the United States raise its voice against transgressions of the law in Hungary.

December 16, 1946 : Second letter to Minister Schoenfeld.

February 10, 1947 : Cardinal sends message to peace emissaries.

June–July, 1947 : Cardinal attends Marian Congress at Ottawa, Canada, and visits New York and London.

August, 1947 : Cardinal sends memorandum to Hungarian Government regarding inhuman methods exercised in the expulsion of population groups in Slovakia and Hungary.

August 15, 1947 : Cardinal opens Marian Year in Hungary.

August 30, 1947 : Cardinal sends a letter to Prime Minister protesting against corruption exercised in performance of the expulsion of population groups.

August 31, 1947 : Cardinal sends a letter to United States Minister Selden Chapin concerning return of Holy Crown of Hungary.

October 1–3, 1947 : Cardinal personally leads a three-day devotional exercise of Marian celebrations.

October 8, 1947 : Conference of Episcopate sends a protest to Prime Minister against anti-Church decrees of Government.

October 24, 1947 : Cardinal protests to Prime Minister against compulsion exercised on masses to join Communist party.

February, 1948 : Visit of Mr. and Mrs. Selden Chapin at residence of Primate in Esztergom.

March 5, 1948 : Conference of Episcopate addresses protest to Prime Minister on behalf of Hungarians in Czechoslovakia.

May 30, 1948 : Celebration of tenth anniversary of Eucharistic Congress in Budapest.

June 16, 1948 : Hungarian Parliament votes "secularization law."

August, 1948 : Cardinal visits United States Minister Selden Chapin.

September 1, 1948 : Cardinal addresses his famous letter to "Catholic Parents."

October 8, 1948 : Government communiqué states that Cardinal "was the rallying nucleus of counterrevolutionary forces" and "the government is ready to prove its strength, no matter how high his position."

October 10, 1948 : Cardinal's address on importance of religious education.

October 22, 1948 : Government communiqué declares: "Government will not tolerate that the Archbishop of Esztergom rudely endanger the foreign policy of Hungary."

November 3, 1948 : Bishops of Hungary make public a declaration of loyalty to Cardinal, assuring him of their "trust and sympathy."

November 18, 1948 : Cardinal's last pastoral letter to Catholics of Hungary.

November 19, 1948 : Cardinal's private secretary, Father Andrew Zakár, arrested by secret political police.

November 22, 1948 : Cardinal's last pastoral letter to clergy.

December 26, 1948 : Cardinal arrested by secret political police.

February 3–8, 1949 : Trial of Cardinal, in Budapest.

✠

CARMELITE MO
Beckle
Barre